PANZERSCHLACHT

ARMOURED OPERATIONS ON THE HUNGARIAN PLAINS SEPTEMBER–NOVEMBER 1944

Perry Moore

Helion & Company

Helion & Company Limited
26 Willow Road
Solihull
West Midlands
B91 1UE
England
Tel. 0121 705 3393
Fax 0121 711 4075
Email: publishing@helion.co.uk
Website: www.helion.co.uk

Published by Helion & Company 2008
Designed and typeset by Helion & Company Limited, Solihull, West Midlands
Cover designed by Bookcraft Limited, Stroud, Gloucestershire
Printed by Cromwell Press Ltd, Trowbridge, Wiltshire

Front cover images: top – Members of the Waffen SS photographed during fighting in Hungary, October 1944
(Ullstein Bilderdienst); bottom – PzKpfw V Panthers, Hungary, autumn 1944 (Ullstein Bilderdienst).
Rear cover image: PzKpfw IV Ausf J tank from the 1st Panzer Regiment, 1st Panzer Division (Wydawnictwo
Militaria)

ISBN 978–1–906033–16–3

British Library Cataloguing-in-Publication Data.
A catalogue record for this book is available from the British Library.

For details of other military history titles published by Helion & Company Limited contact the above address, or visit
our website: http://www.helion.co.uk.

We always welcome receiving book proposals from prospective authors.

Contents

Preface v
Photographic acknowledgements vi
Key to map symbols. vii

Part I: The Red Menace is Knocking at the Door! August 26th–September 25th 1944

Introduction 1
The Battle for Torda 3
Debrecen Offensive – action in the Russian 53rd Army sector 21
The Battle for Nagyvarad, September 20–October 4 36
Prelude to the Battle for Debrecen 38

Part II: Operation Debrecen begins

The 2nd Ukrainian Front Breakthrough (October 6–8) 51
Strike against Debrecen. 64
The German Counter-Attack begins 85
The Berettyóújfalu and Derecské Battles, October 13–17. 93

Part III: The Final Curtain Drops on the Hungarian Plains

The German Counter-Attack continues 99
The Germans gather their strength 109
The Soviets continue their thrust towards Debrecen and the Tisza River battles. . . 118
Attack and Counter-attack 128

Colour AFV profiles showing camouflage and markings . . . . between pages 144 and 145

Appendices

Appendix I: Orders of Battle

I.1   Order of Battle of Axis ground troops 145
I.2   Order of battle of Army Group 'South', October 2 1944 147
I.3   Order of battle of Army Group 'South', October 16 1944 149
I.4   Hungarian 1st Army. 150
I.5   Hungarian 2nd Army 153
I.6   Hungarian 3rd Army 154
I.7   Hungarian troops outside Hungary 156
I.8   Summary of Hungarian OOB. 156
I.9   Order of Battle of the Hungarian 12th Reserve Division September 1944. . . 157
I.10 German Armour Strengths September 25–October 5 1944 157
I.11 German Armour Strengths October 10 1944 158

I.12   Order of Battle of Axis Air Forces, September 5 1944 159

I.13   German 4th Luftwaffe Air Fleet strengths on October 1, 1944 159

I.14   Hungarian 102nd Fighter Unit 159

I.15   Order of Battle of Soviet ground troops, September 1 1944 160

I.16   Order of Battle of Soviet ground troops, October 1 1944 161

I.17   Order of Battle of the Soviet Air Force 163

Appendix II: General Officer listings

II.1   German troops 165

II.2   Hungarian troops 170

II.3   Soviet troops 171

II.4   Romanian troops 176

Appendix III: Hungarian ToEs & AFVs

III.1   TO&E of Hungarian forces in 1944 177

III.2   Hungarian AFV specifications 182

Appendix IV: Losses

IV.1   Soviet & Romanian losses 183

IV.2   German losses 184

        Bibliography 187

Preface

This book's focus is on the key battles, often ignored, that occurred on the Hungarian Plains in autumn 1944. This area is prime tank country but for the numerous rivers crossing it. The two key battles during this time were at Torda in September and Debrecen in October. Both were attempts by the Red Army to seize Hungary. Torda was the Hungarians' finest show of offensive power as they sent the Romanians reeling back and stalled the Russian recovery. Operation Debrecen occurred in October and nearly trapped all of the German 8th Army. It was only due to the Germans' defensive daring and capabilities that the Red Army failed—narrowly.

Small groups of German units frequently held up large Russian units. However, it was always a game of numbers and one the Germans could not win. The Russians could afford to lose large amounts of men and material in reckless pursuits. The Germans could not—they were already in a weakened state. Numbers tell the story and no matter how skilled an opponent is in their use using weakened units, eventually numbers will prevail. One can only stem the tide for so long.

For those interested in wargame simulations, one is available concerning these operations. Contact the author at perrya@jps.net or visit firefight-games.com to purchase.

Throughout the book common abbreviations are used for military unit size, these are:

Co. = Company
Bn. = Battalion
Reg. = Regiment
Div. = Division

Linguistics

The Hungarian language is not simple. The language changes the words depending on the situation being written about, which makes a non-Hungarian native misspell cities and towns, geographic terrain etc. For instance, using the example of a city called Torda, in a book you may see any of the following regarding location:
Tordán (accent on the a) means 'in Torda'
Torda korul = around Torda
Tordából (accent on a and o) = from Torda
Tordá (accent on a) = to Torda
Tordaert = (e.g. fight) for Torda

Common suffixes:
-ba, -be (into)
-ban, -ben (in)
-on, -en, -ön (on something)
-ért (for something)
-tól, -tõl (from)
-ból, -bõl (from)
-nak, -nek (to)
-ig (to)
-val, -vel (with)

I mention this simply because if there are any misspelled city or town names, this is one reason. The other reason is that there are German and Romanian names (which are totally different) for the same city. For the most part, I believe the spellings are correct.

Acknowledgements

The publishers would like to extend their thanks, first and foremost, to Kamen Nevenkin, who gave us enthusiastic advice, provided us with much order of battle information and assisted us in sourcing a large number of the photographs in this book. Thank you!

We would also like to thank Dénes Bernád, who patiently supplied us with a number of rare photographs. Likewise, Péter Illésfalvi in Budapest, Phil Nix (Birmingham, UK), and Stuart Wheeler at the Tank Museum, Bovington, Dorset UK.

Finally, thank you to Janusz Ledwoch, Wydawnictwo Militaria, Warsaw, who assisted us with the colour profiles.

Key to map symbols

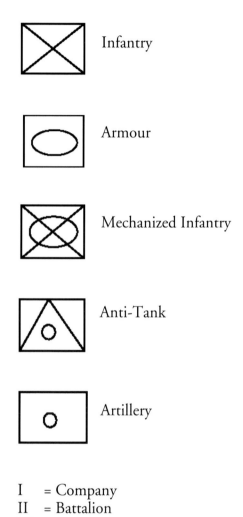

Infantry

Armour

Mechanized Infantry

Anti-Tank

Artillery

I   = Company
II = Battalion
III = Regiment
XX = Division
X = Brigade

PART I

The Red Menace is Knocking at the Door!
August 26th–September 25th 1944

Introduction

The rupture of the German lines weeks earlier along the Romanian border had profound repercussions. Suddenly, within a few days, what was thought by the Germans to be a secure area became a fluid, chaotic region for both opponents. Romania quickly switched sides and the former ally was now a German enemy. Russian troops had burst through as Romania fell quickly. German and Hungarian unit positions had been severely compromised. Many German and Hungarian units simply had no choice but to retreat against the tide of red flood, attempting to grab onto some terrain to hold against this raging, swift, torrent. This was never more great than following the fall of Bucharest. Russian troops literally faced no opposition as far as the Hungarian border. As Russian troops were sent to secure the mountain passes heading north towards Torda, along the Maros towards Arad, they experienced the vast expanses which were now theirs to defend. The Russians carefully had to choose where to send their strong forces – in the last week of August it was mostly northwards or to consolidate the territory they had suddenly won. When Romania jumped ship and switched sides in favor of the Russians, they inherited the Romanian 1st and 4th Armies also. Suddenly, the vastness of the territory was not that vast anymore.

The Germans did act quickly but their efforts were much too weak. On August 23rd they landed 600 men, 17 aircraft, 27 machine guns at Arad airport, just outside the city. Arad was a large city close to the Hungarian border. By the 25th, the Germans had 800 men, 14 AA guns, 10 mortars and 36 aircraft (which included 5 Ju 87 Stuka). Some 700 men were quickly able to seize a narrow railway strip between Gai and Arad. The remaining 100 men remained at the airport. To counter this, the Romanian 'Detachment Arad' was formed from units already in Arad or close by—these former friends now were enemies. The unit was commanded by Col. Plesoianu, who had orders not to allow the city to fall, and to retake the airport, from which the Germans were planning to launch a counterattack. Detachment Arad consisted of:

2nd Battalion, 4th Regiment
11th Regiment
One artillery battery, 88th Regiment
Two platoons of machine guns
Several batteries of 120mm mortars

All together, the unit possessed 1200 men and was part of the Romanian 7th Territorial Corps, 1st Romanian Division. The rest of the 1st Romanian Division defended the Timisoara area with one artillery regiment, two batteries of 75mm AA, and the 5th Regiment. Most of the detachment occupied Arad proper and the small nearby towns.

Detachment Arad attacked early in the morning of August 27th, hitting the German/Hungarian forces near Gai and retaking the airport. The forces near Gai seemed to be mostly Hungarian and the unit, whatever its combat worth might be, steadily fell back after a few hours of fighting to the river for defence. The units in the airport provided the Romanians with stiff resistance and little was accomplished. On the 28th, the Romanians attacked the force near Gai at 0500; this surprised the Hungarians, who surrendered or fled, allowing the Romanians to now encircle the Germans at the airport by 0800. With Romanian artillery shelling the airfield, German aircraft attempted to escape – some made it, others did not. The Luftwaffe personnel put up a good fight but with no escape in sight and no breakout possible, they surrendered. Detachment Arad had secured the city and captured 34 aircraft, nine aircraft motors, 10 trucks and 580 POWs.

By September, the Axis forces had been pushed back and dismembered in Bulgaria and Romania. The weight of the Russian armies simply was too much for the once-vaunted German forces attempting to hold the line. However,

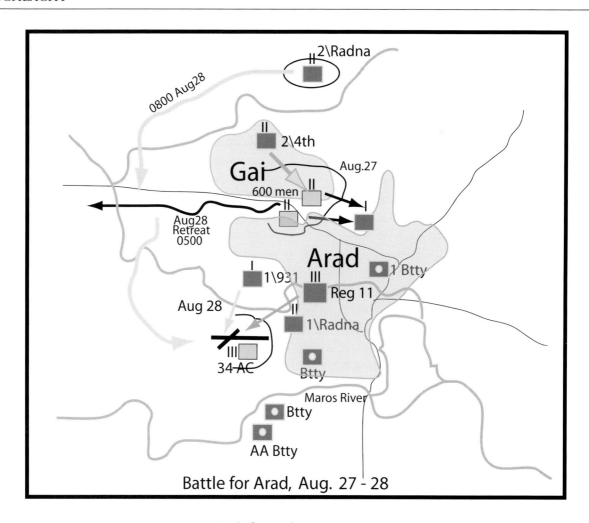

Battle for Arad August 27–28

it was thought that perhaps their saving grace might be in the Carpathian Mountains, which protected Transylvania and Hungary from the northeast and southeast, with many heights reaching 8000 ft. These mountains appeared to be the perfect place to defend with the limited number of Axis troops available, since they were steep and wooded. With the limited number of passes that allowed one to pass through, Hitler felt Hungary could be defended. In addition, the Russian drives towards the Yugoslavia border seemed to indicate to Hitler that the Russians were more interested in reaching the Aegean or towards Turkey. Hungary was important to Germany for its oil, manganese, and bauxite.

Of course, the Russians knew about the few key mountain passes that were a 'must have'. The German 6th Army was all over the map and in pieces, yet, small groups continued to hold the Gymes and Oitoz Passes. The undefended passes lay along the southern Carpathians, namely, Vulcan, Red Tower, Predeal, and Iron Gate. All were for the taking, and at best, lightly defended.

Thus, the race was on. The Russian 27th Army was in and around the Ploesti oilfields in Romania, and the only rapid Russian force, the 6th Tank Army, was mostly in the Bucharest area, with many sub-units moving rapidly into the nearby environs. Defending the southern Carpathians from the Iron Gate Pass (near Turnil Severin) to Brasso (Brasov), a line of over 200 km, was the Hungarian 2nd Army, recently activated and given to General Friessner by Hitler. On September 4th, the Hungarians proposed that their 2nd Army move and occupy Vulcan and Red Tower Passes, which were already occupied by Romanian troops, now on Russia's side. The German 4th Mountain Division sat at Brasso and had repelled all initial enemy attacks. By September 7th, the Russian 18th Tank Corps and elements of the 6th Tank Army had reached Sibiu, meaning Red Tower Pass had fallen. The offensive through the East Carpathians had been intercepted weakly by Axis troops everywhere. Thus, the 23rd Tank Corps conducted a complex march-manoeuvre of about 400 km along curvy mountain roads and into the rear of Axis troops, which defended some of the crossings.

The Hungarian 2nd Army (mainly around Kolozsvár), despite its content, was a welcome sight and needed filler for the shattered German 6th Army. Something is better than nothing. It consisted of the following:

2nd and 9th Corps with the 25th Infantry, 27th Light Infantry, 2nd Armoured, 7th and 9th Reserve Divisions and 9th Brigade. German units consisted of 114th ARKO, 2nd Battalion/818th Artillery (105mm), 1st Battalion/

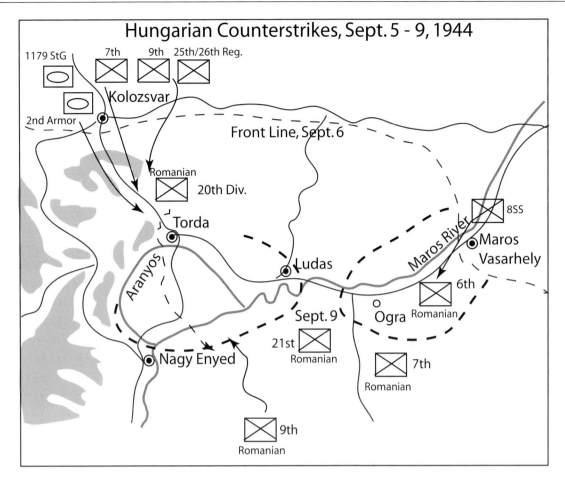

Torda Sept 5th–9th

48th AA and 1179 StuG Battalion (14 Jagdpanzer 38 Hetzers). For full details of 2nd Hungarian Army see Appendix II.

In the Marosvásárhely area, the German Group 'Siebenbürgen' consisted of the 8th SS Cavalry Division and the 76th Infantry Division, but it was the Hungarians that would be used to counterattack the fast-approaching Romanian and Russian troops between Kolozsvár-Marosvásárhely. Undeterred, Army Group South Ukraine devised an attack using all forces available to retake the vital Vulcan and Red Tower passes.

The Battle for Torda (Turda)

By September 5th, the attack group from the Hungarian 2nd Army (consisting of the 25th Infantry, 7th and 9th Replacement Divisions, 2nd Armoured Division) had arrived in the Kolozsvar (Cluj) area. The German 1179th StuG Battalion would also partake in this attack. The German 4th Mountain Division had given way and defended Oitoz Pass.

The Hungarians attacked on the 6th, near Ludas, falling upon the unsuspecting Romanian 21st Training Division of the 4th Romanian Army (the army had 113,759 men in 12 divisions). Spearheaded by the Hungarian 2nd Armoured Division and German 1179th StuG Battalion, it quickly decimated the Romanians and arrived at Torda in good fashion before proceeding towards Nagyenyed. The Hungarian 10th Assault Gun Battalion followed with the 101st and 102nd Armoured Trains. The Hungarian 2nd Armoured Divisions' 40 Turan 40mm tanks, 14 Turan 75mm, one Pzkpfw III, three Pzkpfw VIE, 12 Csaba armoured cars, 21 Nimrod AA, 29 Pzkpfw IV H tanks and five Pzkpfw V Panthers quickly took their toll, as did the 14 German Jagdpanzer 38 tank destroyers from StuG Btn 1179. The Romanians had no tanks and only a few anti-tank weapons. All together, the Hungarian 2nd Armoured Division possessed 140 armoured vehicles (Romanian sources indicate they were attacked with 60 tanks). The Hungarian 7th Division did have an additional 11 Turan 40mm tanks and three Turan 75mm tanks. The attacked continued and despite muddy terrain, pressed towards the Maros River, weakly held by the Romanian 6th and 7th Border Guards. They barely offered any resistance. How could they? It really was a 'classic' from a past time. As a diversion, the 8th SS with its 12 Jagdpanzer 38 tanks conducted an attack between Marosugra-Nagycserged. On the 6th, the Hungarians had quickly routed the Romanian 21st Training Division. However, Romanian artillery was nearby and provided very accurate fire, slowing down the advance.

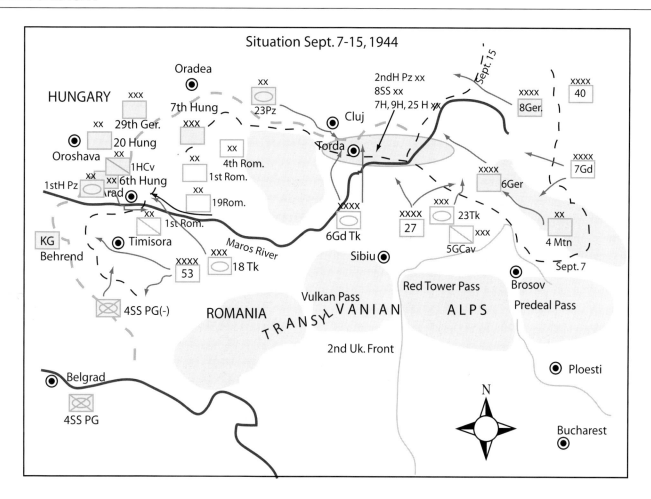

September 7th–15th

By the 7th, the Hungarian 2nd Armoured Division reached Dicsoszentmárt and Somfalva forcing the Romanians to retreat in a coherent state some 20–30 km south of Lechintza and Ogra. The Hungarian troops all performed well and continued to dismantle the Romanians (granted, they did not put up much fight. In more modern times, the Hungarians could be compared to the ARVN in Vietnam as to military value). The Hungarian 2nd Armoured Division then crossed the Maros River, which was also accomplished in good order. Altogether, the Hungarians had advanced around 50 km. Not bad. However, the Hungarians started to run into the lead units of the Russian 2nd Ukrainian Front the further the south their advance went. A Romanian mechanized corps had been summoned and also the 8th Cavalry and 9th Infantry divisions. By the 9th, the Hungarians were stalling and the attack was called off to allow the Hungarian troops to pull back to the Maros and then the Aranyos Rivers near Torda. It was now the 10th. Appearing and halting the Hungarians were the Romanian 8th Cavalry and 9th Infantry Divisions forcing the 2nd Hungarian Armoured Division to pull back into reserve status.

The Russians were also rapidly arriving albeit very scattered. Elements of the 27th Army were at Brasso and Sibiu, both south of the Maros. The 6th Tank Army (upgraded to Guards status on September 13th) was already through the Vulkan Pass, brushing aside whatever had been tossed in the way. It arrived in the Koloszvar area on the 12th, and contained 262 tanks and 82 self-propelled guns. The 53rd Army was moving towards Arad with the 18th Tank Corps. The 6th Guards Tank Army and the 27th Army moved northwards towards Torda, while the 23rd Tank Corps and 5th Guards Cavalry Corps attempted to trap German troops at Szekler.

The six divisions of the Romanian 1st Army (73,844 men) had advanced between Nagyvárad and Temesvár. The independent 4th Corps (56,212 men in four divisions) moved towards the southeast. According to Russian sources, Romanian divisions had between 6–10,000 men. The Romanian 1st Army had over 50% of its men over age 45. It was the 'old man's' army.

On September 13th, 12 tanks from the 5th Guards Tank Corps (6th Guards Tank Army) and about 1,000 infantry secured a bridgehead near Torda against the Hungarian 25th Division, which held the area with only three battalions. Its other seven battalions had to be used elsewhere or were with other units. Its anti-tank unit with 75mm guns quickly destroyed seven of the Russian tanks. On the 14th, the Russians tried again to penetrate and were halted by the Hungarian Mountain Brigade that had just arrived west of Torda. That afternoon, the Russians attacked east of Torda, encountering only weak defences and reached the outskirts of Torda. The remaining units of

Former allies – German and Romanian troops ride aboard a lorry shortly before the latter switched sides, August 1944. (Bundesarchiv 101I–244–2311–03)

Romanian and German troops, as well as civilians, during the withdrawals of summer 1944 before Romania switched sides and joined forces with the Soviet Union. (Bundesarchiv 101I–244–2311–19)

Soviet troops enter Bucharest, 31 August 1944. (Photo archive of the Bulgarian Ministry of Defence)

Soviet troops enter Bucharest, 31 August 1944. (Photo archive of the Bulgarian Ministry of Defence)

Romanian soldiers march German POWs through Bucharest, 1944.
(Photo archive of the Bulgarian Ministry of Defence)

După lupte extrem de violente încercarea perfidă a naziștilor de a pune mâna pe Capitala României a fost înfrântă defini iv

în zona petroliferă și pe Dunăre s'a continuat cu succes acțiunea de dezarmare a trupelor germane

Comunicatul Marelui Sttat Major al Armatei asupra operațiunilor executate în cursul zilei de 28 August 1944

După 5 zile și 5 nopți de lupte foarte îndârjite trupele române ale Capitalei au reușit să înfrângă pe deplin încercarea perfidă a conducerii Germaniei de a pune stăpânire pe Capitala Țării.

Numeroase trupe regulate și formațiuni S. S. au fost nimicite sau capturate.

Peste 8000 de prizonieri, între care 7 generali și sute de ofițeri, precum și o deosebit de importantă pradă de război au căzut în stăpânirea noastră.

Luptele au fost extrem de violente, inamicul utilizând toate mijloacele permise și nepermise.

Bombardarea cartierelor de locuințe și a tuturor instituțiilor de cultu-

ra va sta mărturie a barbariei germane.

În prezent Capitala este complet deblocată și viața normală restabilită.

În zona petroliferă și pe Dunăre s'a continuat — cu succes prin lupte violente — acțiunea de dezarmarea trupelor germane.

Astfel, au fost lichidate rezistențele germane dela Câmpina, Moreni, Gura Ocniței, Pleașa și alte localități.

În aceste operațiuni, au fost capturați peste 3000 de germani, întreaga artilerie antiaeriană din jurul Câmpinei și numeros material de război de tot felul.

Pe Dunăre — în fața o-

rașului Turnu Măgurele — au fost scufundate 2 vase germane.

Alte câteva vase au fost avariate, silite să se refugieze în apele bulgare, sau capturate.

În Ardeal, au avut loc ciocniri între trupele române și germane la Nord Est Brașov, precum și la Arad, unde aeroportul a fost degajat de germani; au fost avariate 18 avioane germane.

La ora 13, stațiunea de radio-difuziune Bod a fost atacată de avioane Stukas.

La Baziaș, Moldova Veche, Orșova și Turnu Severin rezistențele germane au fost înfrânte.

La acțiunea de scufundarea vaselor germane d pe Dunăre, semnalate în comunicatul din ziua de 27 August s'au distins unitățile anticar ale D. 9 I., R. 8 Antiaerian și R. 2 Grăniceri.

A message from the Romanian High Command announcing the elimination of German resistance in the vicinity of Bucharest, 28 August 1944. (Photo archive of the Bulgarian Ministry of Defence)

The Romanian 'Tudor Vladimirescu' Division enters Bucharest, 31 August 1944.
(Photo archive of the Bulgarian Ministry of Defence)

Soviet artillery in the vicinity of Bucharest. The weapon is a 122 mm M 1938 (M–30)
divisional howitzer, towed by a lend-lease truck. (RGAKFD Moscow)

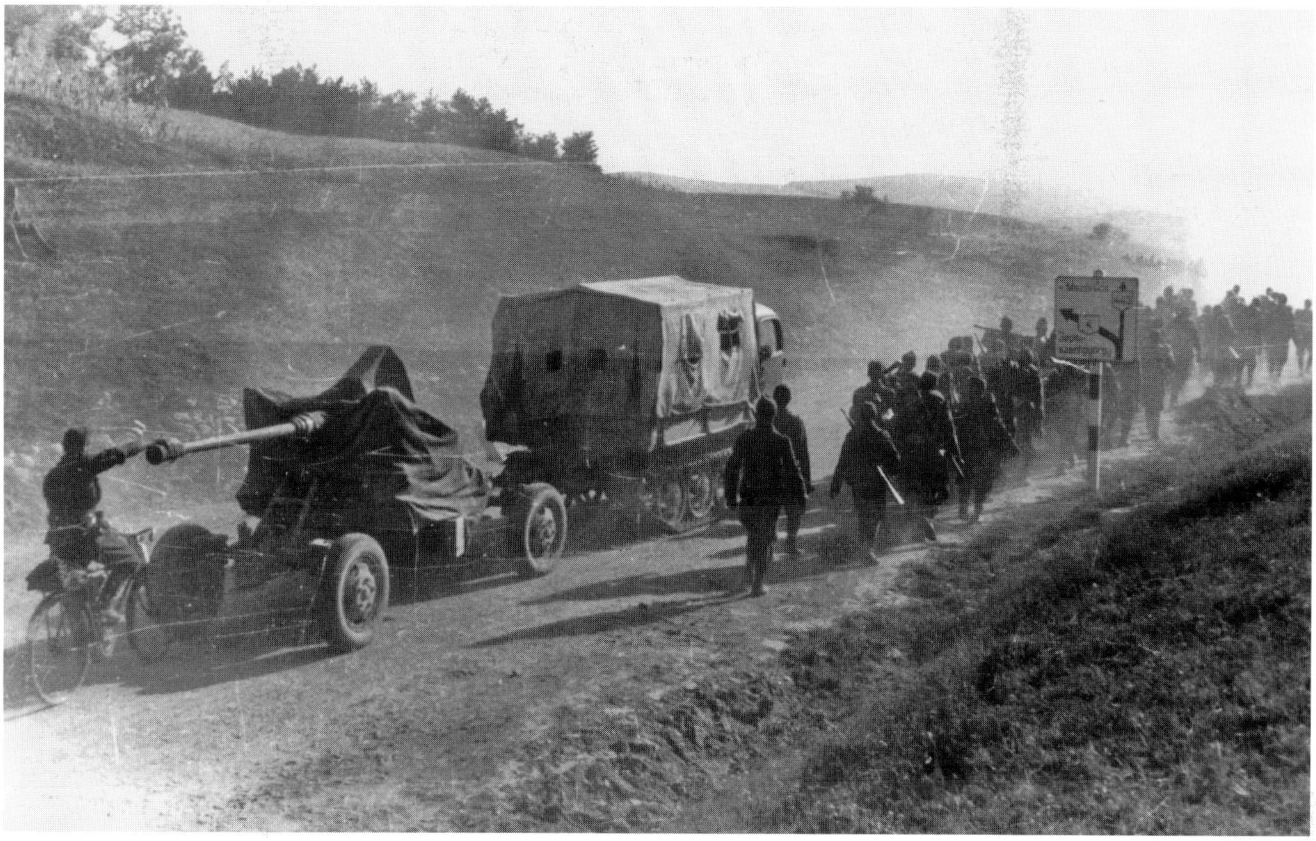

Hungarian troops on the march, southern Transylvania, September 1944. (Kamen Nevenkin)

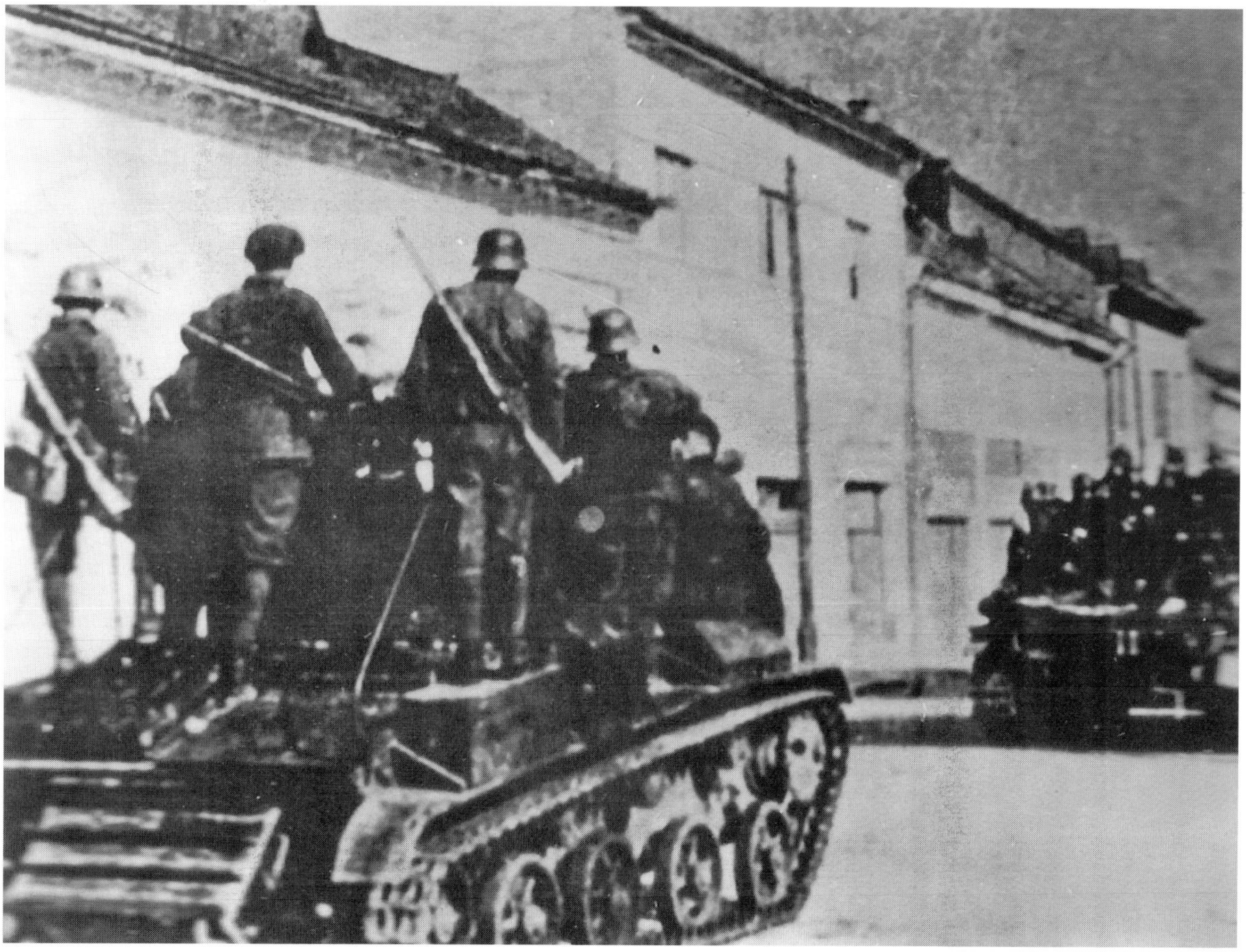

Hungarian Toldi light tanks with infantry riding on them, autumn 1944.
(Photo archive of the Bulgarian Ministry of Defence)

Romanian infantry, North Transylvania, autumn 1944. (RGAKFD Moscow)

Guards engineers under the command of Senior Lieutenant A.H. Lebanin build a bridge across the mountain river, autumn 1944. (RGAKFD Moscow)

Hungarian infantry with a light machine gun deployed in a rather hopeful anti-aircraft role. (Dénes Bernád)

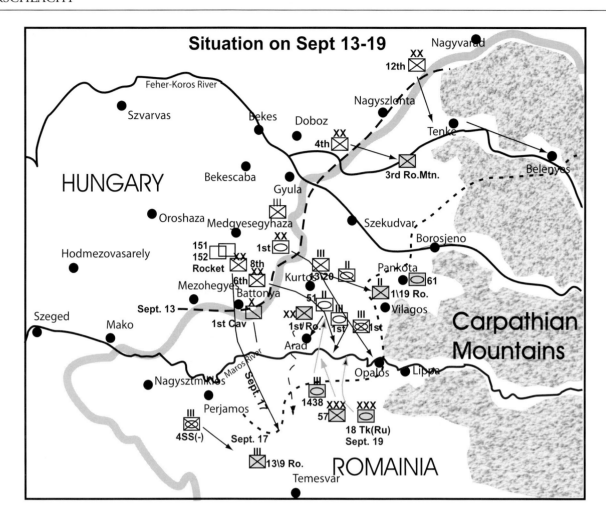

September 13th–19th

the Hungarian 25th Division reorganised and managed to repulse further incursions into Torda. On the 15th, the Russians conducted a major assault with heavy artillery barrages, and this time, it was the Hungarian 2nd Armoured Division that repulsed the attack. While the Russians were knocking at the door, how long could the Hungarians repulse them? Both sides regrouped and the Hungarians prepared for their own counterattack from the 16th to 18th.

Elsewhere, the Hungarian 4th Corps formed defences in the Arad area as reports arrived that the Russian 18th Corps was heading their way. The Corps consisted of the Hungarian 1st Armoured Division, 6th Reserve Division, 8th Reserve Division, 1st Reserve Cavalry Division. The Hungarian 4th, 20th and 23rd Divisions had arrived in the Hódmezóvásárhely district. The 4th Division would come under the Hungarian 7th Corps control on the 12th.

Meantime, in the south, the Soviet units of the 2nd Ukrainian Front occupied the Vulcan Pass and captured Brasov and Sibiu (aka Nagyszeben, Hermannstadt). The Red Army intended to capture Cluj (aka Kolozsvár, Klausenburg) without much effort, while continuing to advance towards the Mures (Maros) River, which the Hungarian 2nd Armoured Division had crossed. The foes collided. Thus, the 2nd Hungarian Army was forced to take a defensive stance on September 10, 1944. The Hungarians quickly fell back towards Torda, along the Aranyos River.

The Russians were more than a little surprised by the unexpected Hungarian offensive, and decided to strengthen their forces in the area to prevent a repeat. They also launched an attack of their own toward Turda (Torda), in concert with the Romanian 4th Army.

Torda was originally defended by the weakened 25th Infantry Division, which had only three battalions immediately available from its 25th Regiment. The other three (26th Regiment) were not expected before September 13.

By September 13th, the lead units of the Russian 5th Guards Tank Corps (6th Guards Tank Army) began their attack upon the 25th Hungarian Infantry Regiment. At 1200 hrs near Bágy, 12 tanks broke into the Torda bridgehead held by Lieutenant Karoly Szentágotai commanding the 25th Anti-Tank Company, which amazingly stopped the Russians with three shots! (destroying three tanks). By the afternoon, the Torda bridgehead was under Russian artillery fire.

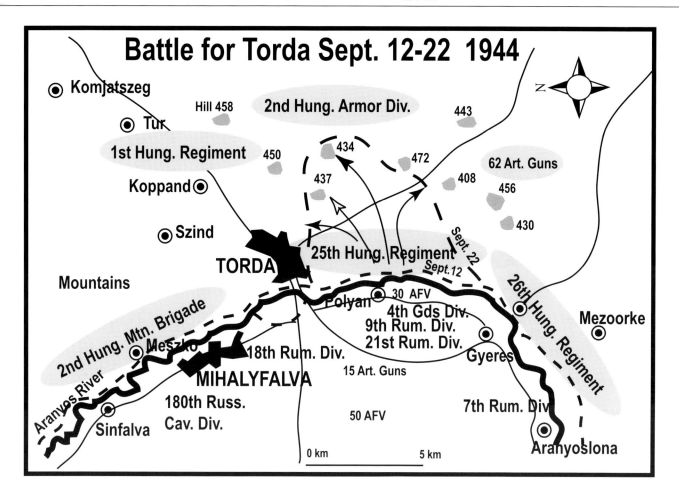

Torda

On the 14th, the remaining nine Russian tanks, with Romanian infantry support, crossed the Aranyos, and attacked along and towards the southeast of Torda. At Egerbegy, the bridgehead was attacked by the Romanian 7th Infantry Division with Russian tanks, which pushed back the Hungarian 3rd Battalion/26th Regiment, but failed to break through. The Romanian 18th Infantry Division, also with Russian tanks, crossed the Aranyos and seized the area along the river. It then penetrated into the main defensive line some 3 km east of Torda. This forced the Hungarian 5th Motorized Rifle Battalion to surrender the Maros-Ludas crossing.

At dawn on the 15th, the Russians had determinedly thrown bridges across at Keresztes, which allowed elements of the 9th Guards Motorized Corps to join the battle. The Soviet-Romanian Mihajlov-Group (with 25 tanks) occupied the Torda-Sósfürdo area, and had reached the southernmost edge of the Szalonnás hills, the northernmost point of Torda. The Romanian 7th Division occupied the Egerbegy bridgehead, forcing the 26th Hungarian Infantry Regiment into the hills along the river to the east. Meanwhile, the Hungarian 2nd Armoured Division's 3rd Motorized Rifle Regiment counterattacked in two directions: towards Szent János and Péterlaka, but failed in reaching the original Hungarian positions. By evening the two Russian bridgeheads had combined.

On the 16th, the Hungarian 25th Infantry Regiment and the 6th Motorized Rifle Battalion attacked to clear the Szent János and Péterlaka area but failed. This was tried once again with the 4th and 6th Motorized Rifle Battalions, but very strong Russian defensive artillery fire stopped it.

On the 17th, the arrival of the Russian 35th Guards Corps and the 104th Corps between the Gyalui Mountains eastern foothills, signalled a new danger to the Hungarians holding Torda. Between the mountains, in the Jara Valley, the Russian spearheads reached the Hungarian 2nd Mountain Replacement Brigade's line at Magyarpeter (the Torda gorge's northern exit).

On the 18th, the German *Sperrverband* Kessel took over the operations in the mountains, and assumed command of the Hungarian 1st and 2nd Hungarian Mountain Replacement Brigades. The German group, commanded by Lieutenant-General Mortimer von Kessel, consisted of: 905th Panzer Battalion, 1015 and 1176 Assault Gun (StuG) battalions, the 721st Anti-Tank Battalion, 3rd Battalion/ Brandenburg Infantry Regiment, II Battalion/241st Luftwaffe AA Battalion, the 92nd Panzer Pioneer Battalion, and the 52nd Pioneer Battalion. The Hungarian 25th Infantry Division, the 2nd Armoured Division, the 7th (13th, 14th, 23rd Regiments), and 9th Field Replacement Divisions remained under the Hungarian 2nd Corps.

On September 19th, the Hungarian 2nd Corps counterattacked in earnest. This attack comprised the 2nd and 3rd Battalions/25th Regiment, the 10th Assault Gun Battalion, German 1179th StuG Battalion, 1st and 2nd Tank Battalions of the 3rd Tank Regiment/2nd Hungarian Armoured Division, the 4th and 6th Motorized Battalions, 52nd AA Battalion, and 2nd Company of Engineers. Reserves consisted of: 1st Battalion/25th Regiment, 25th Reconnaissance Battalion, 5th Motorized Battalion, and remaining units of the 3rd Tank Regiment. These were deployed in the Torda-Sosfurdo and Mezoorke area. Torda, itself was defended by the 1st Hungarian Infantry Regiment.

The western group reached 1 km north of the Aranyos between Sósfürdo and Szent János River, but was stopped near Sósfürdo. The eastern group initially gained ground, although the 5th Motorized Battalion struggled against defiant defence. Soon, the attack stalled before it could get out of the hilly terrain the Péterlaka area. Romanian aircraft also took part in repelling the attack. The Hungarians then attacked the Russian 4th Guards Division using the 25th Regiment and 10th Assault Gun Battalion (equipped with the home-produced Zrinyi) and forced the Russians to pull back by noon. During this fighting, one Russian battalion was wiped out. Despite the success, the Hungarians failed at removing the small bridgehead across the Aranyos River.

On the 20th, the Hungarian 2nd Armoured Division attacked to prevent the further advance of the Russians. It failed. A desperate struggle now occurred for Torda, which remained under Hungarian control.

Far above in the skies, the Hungarians were also being attacked on the 21st from American B–17s escorted by P–51 Mustangs. The air units arrived from the 5th Bomber Wing of 15th US Air Army based in Bari, Italy. The US air raid was minor, consisting of 84 bombers and 22 escorts from the 2nd, 97th, 301st, 483rd, 99th, 463rd bomber groups. Bombing the Békéscsaba area railroads and installations were elements from the 2nd, 97th, 301st and 843rd squadrons. Bombing the Debrecen area railways and installations were the 99th and 463rd groups. American reconnaissance flights had spotted various types of strategic targets back on the 18th. The American aircraft met little resistance flying at 7000 metres.

Attacking the Debrecen area was the 773rd and 774th squadrons who dropped 500 250 kg bombs at 1030 hrs, these were followed by the 775th and 772nd squadrons. Numerous roads, railways and other less significant targets were demolished including homes and churches. These were in error due to navigational miscalculations. The same event was repeated in the Békéscsaba area by a much larger number of B–17 aircraft.

In less than 2–3 minutes, each raid was completed and the Americans returned to their bases in Italy. No damage was reported by Hungarian or German troops.

The 2nd Wing (B–17) consisted of the following:
2nd Group: 20, 49, 46, 429 Squadrons
97th Group: 340, 341, 342, 414 Squadrons.
301st Group: 332, 352, 353, 354, 419 Squadrons.
483rd Group: 815, 816,817,840 Squadrons.
99th Group: 346, 347, 348, 416 Squadrons.
463rd Group: 772, 773, 774, 775 Squadrons.

A lull set in until the 22nd, when the Russians attacked in full strength using three Russian and one Romanian division, and a tank brigade. The Russians were able to penetrate into the defensive lines of the 25th and 2nd Armoured Divisions and the situation became serious. But, then a brief moment of success occurred.

The second battery of Zrinyi assault guns from the 10th Assault Gun Battalion sat in ambush. Together, with 1st Company/1st Battalion in the Sosfurdo area, it conducted a daring counterattack as the Russian 46th Guards Tank Brigade advanced. Eighteen Russian T–34s approached, totally unaware of the Hungarian presence. The six Zrinyi II assault guns opened up and with minutes all T–34s were disabled or destroyed! The Hungarians had lost four vehicles. Russian infantry quickly scattered allowing the Hungarian 25th Reconnaissance Battalion to escape encirclement. The 1st battery from the 10th Assault Gun Battalion with 4 vehicles joined in and pushed the Russians from Sosfurdo, destroying another three T–34s. It was this action that had saved Torda from being encircled. Regardless of this minor success, the day had been costly to the Hungarians, who had suffered over 1,000 men killed. To the west of Torda in the Jara and Hasada valleys, one Russian, two Romanian divisions, and two motorized brigades broke through. The Torda gorge was lost. Further, another Russian and two Romanian divisions supported by the 6th Guards Tank Army elements with Russian aircraft broke out from the bridgehead seized north of the Aranyos near Torda. The dam was breaking. The Hungarian 4th Motorized Battalion held a blocking position in the Péterlaka area, while the 2nd Battalion/3rd Armoured Regiment blocked the Sos area. But, Russian tanks broke into the Sos area and advanced 4 km from the Romanian 18th Infantry Division northwest of Torda at Szind. The eastern attack group had also reached the Fibulae Mountains.

The situation remained critical on the 23rd. The arrival of the German 23rd Panzer Division with 65 AFVs brought needed relief to the Hungarians. The Russian eastern group had reached the Aranyos at Gerbegy, driving back the Hungarians, then turned west towards the bogged-down western group. The Russians then broke out into the completely flat floodplain between Torda and Egerbegy, where it ran into the German 23rd Panzer Division. That advance exposed the German AFVs to the direct fire of the Soviet artillery. The division itself was typically threadbare, possessing 36 PzKpfw V Panther, six PzKpfw IV, two PzKpfw III, 16 StuG IV and StuG III assault guns, as well as four Marder, four Wespe, and three Hummel. Attached to the division was the Hungarian 3rd Company/2nd Armoured Battalion with 7 Turan I tanks. Its timely arrival had prevented another Russian breakthrough.

On September 23rd, General Zhukov issued what amounted to a new order. He was growing more impatient with the Torda situation:

> Taking into account the nature of the locality and the enemy forces before Malinovsky and Petrov, I consider that it is more advantageous for the army of Kravchenko without delay to redeploy and concentrate north Oradea with the task of seizing Debrecen, i.e., move into the rear to the entire enemy group. With the seizure of the Debrecen region, the entire operational defence system of the enemy collapses, forcing them to move rapidly away from the Cluj region and from the Carpathians. The current attack by Malinovsky's frontal offensive leads to protracted combat and gives to the enemy the possibility to quickly arrange its defences.

Soon afterwards, the main Russian forces attempting to batter a breakthrough at Torda withdrew and redeployed.

On the 24th, part of the German 23rd Panzer Division carried out a counterattack to clear the Kolozsvár-Torda highway through the Turi area, afterwhich, it then redeployed to the Nagyvárad area.

By now, one Russian rifle division and two Romanian infantry divisions, with a mechanized brigade, had advanced to within 10 kilometres of Kolosvar. On the 25th, it was clear the Russians had had enough, as they suddenly pulled out the 6th Guards Tank Army elements that had been employed in the Torda area, and in the southeast flatlands. They were replaced with the 2nd Cavalry Group of the 5th Guards Cavalry Corps. The battle for Torda had ended. It was a near thing for both sides. During this fight, the German division had lost up to 40% of its infantry.

Events elsewhere now caught the eye the Russians, who had enjoyed great success against the Hungarian 3rd Army in the Arad area. Because of this, the attacks were called off for more lucrative and cheaper targets. Likewise, the Germans dispatched the 23rd Panzer and 76th Division towards Nagyvarad. The storm had shifted.

The Battle of Torda was a shining moment in Hungarian military lore. They struck, advanced, withdrew and held without much help from the Germans, proving they were a worthy opponent. However, they had paid a heavy price to prove their worth. The 25th Hungarian Division had lost 750 men killed and 1,500 wounded. By September 24th the 2nd Armoured Division had only two PzKpfw V, six PzKpfw IV and nine Turan tanks in the 3rd Tank Regiment's reserve at Nagyordong.

As noted before, the Russian 18th Tank Corps had been instructed to move towards Arad. The only force blocking the Russians was the 4th Hungarian Corps. Some of its units had also deployed at Bekescaba and Gyula. The Corps' mission was to advance past Arad to Lippa. The striking force of the Hungarian Corps' lay with the 1st Armoured Division and 7th Assault Gun Battalion. The 1st Armoured Division had one tank regiment with two tank battalions and one motorized regiment. The 7th Assault Gun Battalion had 30 StuG III. Its 1st Motorized Regiment was hauled in various buses and trucks and contained nine Nimrods and eight AT guns; their infantry were all issued *Panzerfäuste*. Each battalion contained three infantry companies and one heavy weapons company equipped with MG and mortars. Its artillery had three batteries each with four 105mm howitzers. By the 13th, the 1st Armoured Division grew to 61 40mm Turan, 63 75mm Turan, 77 light Toldi tanks, 42 Nimrod AA and 5 Csaba armoured cars. For artillery, it possessed 12 105mm guns. Although sounding impressive, the reality was that the only worthy tanks were the Turan 75mm. The Toldi light tanks were worthless. The Turan 40mm were only marginally useful at best (of the 61, only 30 had 40mm guns). Other sources indicate that in September 1944, it had shrunk considerably to three companies, each with eight Turan 75mm, five Toldi and three Nimrod. This amounted to an armoured force of 24 Turan 75mm, 15 Toldi light tanks and nine Nimrod AA. Total armoured vehicle strength was not more than 60. Its reconnaissance battalion contained four companies: one motorized, one on BMW–750 motorcycles, one Csaba armoured car and one on bicycles! Its 51st Tank Hunter Battalion had 18 40mm Nimrods in three companies. In total, 201 tanks and 8,000 men. According to records, the morale of this division (unlike many other Hungarian units) was high. The troops were ready to strike back at their former allies, the Romanians. As to the other Hungarian reserve units, quality varied. For instance, one battalion contained 500 men with six HMGs, nine LMGs and 450 small arms. The quality of men varied, from teenagers to men over 45. As for anti-tank strengths, many units possessed only six 75mm guns or less.

The 1st Reserve Cavalry Regiment contained three battalions, three light AT guns, three 75mm guns, each company with six LMGs, two HMGs. For artillery, six guns. There was also a heavy weapons company containing four light AT guns and four rocket launchers. A1s of September 1st the 1st Reserve Cavalry Regiment was in the Mezokovácsházára area, with its 15th Bicycle Company (6 LMG, 2 MG), and three (1/II, 1/III, 1/IV) cavalry units. The cavalry unit contained two companies armed with 11 LMG, 2 MG, 2 shotguns and one heavy weapons company with four light AT guns and four mortars.

The 12th Reserve Division on Sept. 8th contained a total of 5,941 men. Its anti-tank unit contained 18 75mm guns.

The Hungarians had originally planned to attack towards Lippa on September 4th and link up with the attacking Hungarian 2nd Army attacking towards the Maros River. However, shortages of fuel and problems in gathering together the troops meant that it was postponed until the 13th. By then, the following Hungarian forces were ready in the Mako area (4th Corps) and at Nagyvarad (7th Corps):

4th Corps
Company 2nd/IV Independent Towed Medium Howitzer Battery
Company 1st Independent Towed Medium Howitzer Battery
151st Towed Rocket Artillery Battery
152nd Towed Rocket Artillery Battery
1st Armoured Division
6th Reserve Division (10th 11th and 19th Regiments)
1st Reserve Cavalry Regiment
8th Reserve Division (12th, 21st and 24th Regiments)
20th, 31st, and 61st direct fire battalions and six tractor companies

7th Corps
One towed medium artillery battery
1st Assault Gun Battalion (3 Zrínyi assault gun batteries)
4th Reserve Division (6th, 8th, 10th and 18th Regiments)
12th Reserve Division (36th, 38th and 48th Regiments)

The general operational plan had the 1st Armoured and 6th Reserve divisions attacking towards Arad from Battonya-Kevermes-Ketegyhaza; once Arad was taken, they were to proceed to Lippa. The 6th Reserve Division, south of Dombegyhaz, would take the most direct route to Arad. The 1st Armoured Division would smash the Romanians between Kevermes-Elek. The cavalry regiment would attack through Battonya towards Opecska and secure a bridgehead across the Maros River, then conduct reconnaissance towards Lippa. Joining in on the attack, the 20th and 31st Direct Fire Battalions would join between the Feher-Koros and Maros River. The 8th Reserve Division along with the 20th and 31st Regiments (20th Division) would also advance on Kisjeno.

The 7th Corps' 12th Reserve Division would attack south from Nagyvarad towards Fekete-Koros River and to Belenyes, while the 4th Reserve Division attacked from the Gyula-Nagyszalonta area to Tenke-Menyhaza and Borossebes. The left flank would remain uncovered from Barakat to Bánfyyhunyadig. In the Bánfyyhunyad area, the Hungarian 2nd Army stood with the 2nd Reserve Mountain Brigade and the 60th Direct Fire group. The Hungarians hoped to delay the arriving Russian units that began to trickle in and prevent them from linking up allowing for stronger units.

At 0600, on the 13th, the attack began with the 6th Hungarian Reserve Division attacking in the Nagyvarjas area containing the Romanian 7th Corps of the 1st Army. The line was held by the 1st Romanian Cavalry Training Division with 3,359 men. By 0900, the Romanians were cut off by the elements of the 1st Armoured Division. The Romanian 1st Air Corps attempted to nullify the Hungarian success. Romanian artillery proved to be effective. Romanian troops, lacking anti-tank weapons, were helpless even against thin Hungarian armour. Resistance was weak and sporadic. Elements of the 1st Armoured Division had encircled a large group of Romanians by 0900. By noon, most of the Hungarian initial objectives had been taken, beating off the weak attacks by the Romanian 1st Training Cavalry Division near Kürtös-Pankota.

Between Kurtos and Masca, the Hungarians, supported by their armour, easily penetrated through the defending cavalry unit by noon. The Hungarian rocket units caused losses and chaos among the enemy. The Romanians retreated towards Pankote and Vilagos. Once at Kurtos, some of the Hungarians turned south towards Nagyvarjas, forcing the Romanians to fall back. The Hungarians were chasing the fleeing Romanians and easily retook Arad! There was no attempt on the part of the Romanians to hold Arad. Hungarian combat groups had also penetrated into Ószentanna, while other groups advanced towards Világos. All this happened by 1300 hrs.

Holding the Kisjeno area was the Romanian 1st Training Division (6,000 men), which also retreated when attacked by the Hungarian 10th Division, but continued to resist and by 1500 hrs was attempting to hold the line Újpálos-Világos-Pankota, using the mountains to their east as a cornerstone of their defence. The Romanian 9th Cavalry Division was sent to defend the Temesvar (Timisoara) area as two SS battalions from the 4th SS Panzergrenadier Division plus 30 StuGs were approaching. Located 30 km to the east sat the Romanian 61st Artillery Regiment. The 1st Romanian Division held the Ineu area. Holding south of the Maros River were elements of the Romanian 19th and 14th Training Divisions near Lipova.

Elements of the Romanian cavalry also held Ópécskát, others fell back towards Temesvár. The Hungarian 1st Cavalry Division had encircled the Romanians in the Pankota area and seized Opecska and then secured a crossing over the Maros River. By 2100, the 6th Reserve Division was a few miles from a defenceless Arad. The 1st Armoured Division entered the city at 1945 hrs, seizing the key bridges and railways and Maros River crossings. However, in the western portion of the city, Romanian resistance with light weapons in a city environment was a different issue. Fighting would continue well into the night by determined Romanian troops.

By 2000 hrs, the Hungarian 1st Armoured Division declared that Arad was secure, as were the bridges and thus a bridgehead over the Maros River. Other Hungarian combat groups had reached Újpanád and Othalom. Part of the 1st Armoured Division moved towards Öthalom, while another part diverted towards Ujpanád. In Arad, as resistance died out, the city became chaotic with looters and crime; trying to maintain civilian control was the order of the day. Hungarian troops set up roadblocks and MG nests as a show of force. Some 40,000 residents remained in the city. A battle raged near the Arad airport with Romanian troops armed with a German 88mm gun. This gun ripped apart the Hungarian Armour for about 20 minutes until German aircraft silenced it.

On the 14th, the 1st Reserve Cavalry Division continued to deal with Romanian resistance west of Arad, the 11th Regiment (6th Division) garrisoned much of Arad while other units secured crossings over the Maros River. By now, the population in Arad welcomed the Hungarians with flowers and general celebration. Martial law was imposed on the population for control and military troops were prohibited from celebrating. Anyone found on the streets between 2000 – 0600 hrs. would be arrested.

The 1st Armoured Division continued to move towards Ópálos, while its 51st Battalion suffered losses near Ujpálos.

Opposing the Hungarian 7th Corps units was the Romanian 3rd Mountain Division, which provided token resistance. The Hungarians were able to advance 15 km to Magyarcseke – Erdodámos.

It was at this time that the Romanian 7th Corps created Detachment Paulis. At the time, little did anyone know that this force- a motley collection of units – would play a decisive role in preventing the Hungarian forces' continued advance along the narrow Maros River valley toward Lippa (Lipova). Detachment Paulis (1700 men) was commanded by Col. Petrescu and contained:

1st Battalion/96th Regiment
2nd Battalion/96th Regiment
1 platoon /93rd Regiment
1 platoon/38th Regiment
Two 122mm batteries (8 guns) from 61st Artillery Regiment

82 LMGs, 16 HMGs, 4 anti-tank guns, 2 AA guns, 21 60mm mortars, 8 81mm mortars, 4 120mm mortars. The unit was well supplied with ammunition: 670 anti-tank rounds, 2,211 60mm rounds, 1,000 81mm rounds, 285 120mm rounds, 2,500 grenades, 3,000 122mm rounds.

Its 1st Battalion contained companies 1 and 2, its 2nd Battalion contained companies 5, 6, 7. A 3rd Battalion was also created from volunteers. The unit was created after the collapse and capture of Arad that same day. Detachment Paulis was the rearguard unit blocking the way. It occupied the key entrance into the Maros River Valley, the towns of Paulis (Opalos), Minis, Gyorok, Curvin and Radna. More importantly, they occupied the high ground behind the towns, such as Hills 372 and 471 (called Bordu). The Romanians had just formed and deployed when the Hungarian 1st Armoured Division began to arrive. At this stage, Romanian forces were near Oradea, Lugoj, Timisoara, Giamata, Radna, Ineu and Tinca. Directly south of Paulis, across the Maros (Muresul) River, the Romanian 1st Cavalry Training Division was deployed. Its 85th Regiment held the area from Pankota to Vilagos.

The first Hungarian attacks from the 1st Armoured Division were rather small, 30 tanks with one infantry battalion assaulted Companies 6 and 7 at Radna, and were repelled, with several AFVs knocked out. Another two infantry companies with AFVs also attacked Company 1 at Gyorok with the same results. Another two infantry companies attacked Company 2 at Cuvin. None of the attacks proved successful.

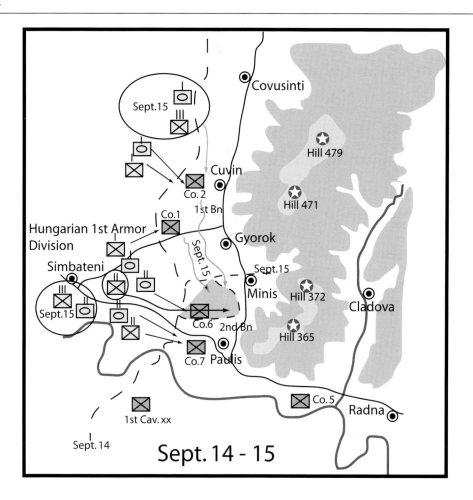

Paulis, September 14th–15th

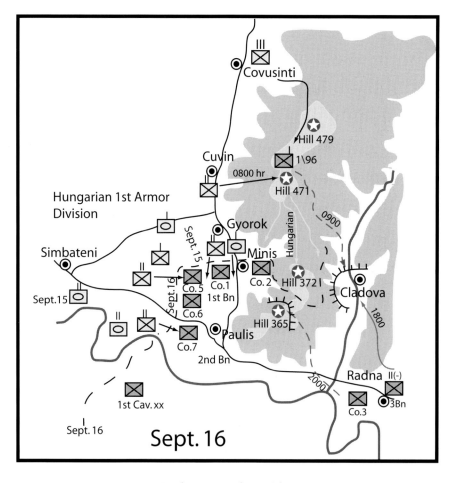

Paulis, September 16th

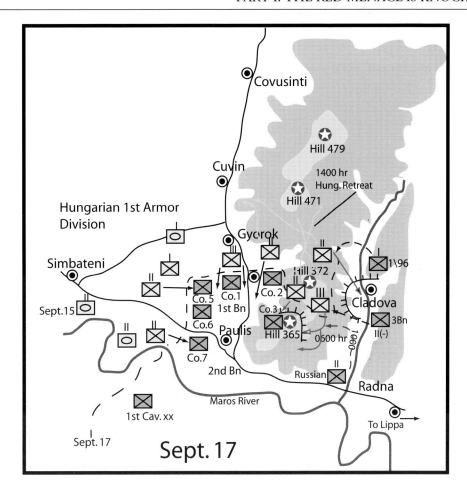

Paulis, September 17th

On the 15th, much of the same occurred; the Romanians pulled back and consolidated the Opalos-Vilagos line. The reconnaissance battalion of the Hungarian 1st Armoured Division advanced to Opalos (Paulis), which was close to Lippa (Lipova). It was there the Romanian 1st Battalion/96th Regiment of the 19th Infantry Division and the 61st Heavy Artillery Battalion stood and fought. The 61st was armed with Russian 122mm guns and 76mm AT guns, which were behind an anti-tank ditch. The Hungarian unit reported this to the 1st Armoured Division HQ; despite this, orders were sent to attack there on the 16th using the Hungarian 1st Motorized Regiment, two tank companies and the 1st Company/51st Armoured Gun Battalion. Some three infantry battalions attacked Company 2 at 0600 hrs, as 20 AFVs ran over a platoon covering the north edge of Cuvin. As this occurred, another two companies assaulted Company 1 near Gyorok. The combined action sent both companies reeling back and by 1600, the Romanians were struggling to hold Minis, just north of Paulis. Another two battalions and a tank regiment conducted assaults on Companies 6 at Paulis. A single Russian anti-tank battery kept the Hungarian tanks (thinly armoured) at bay. However, the infantry penetrated deeply, reaching the outskirts of Paulis. The only thing that saved the situation was its 5th Company, which had been held in reserve. The Hungarians had lost 367 men KIA and 242 POWs plus 17 tanks.

On the 16th, the Hungarians stopped their direct attacks on the towns (oddly, the Hungarians outnumbered the Romanians 7 to 1) and instead tried to reach Paulis and Radna via across the hills behind the towns. A Hungarian infantry regiment successfully advanced from Covasinti and seized the highest point, Hill 479 (Magura) and by 0900, had also taken Hill 471 (Bordu) from the Romanian 1st Battalion/96th Regiment. In conjunction, another Hungarian regiment with tanks attacked from the town of Minis defended by Companies 1 and 2. The Hungarians coming from Bordu seemed like an overwhelming force. The unit went unchallenged, seizing Hills 347 and 372 (Varvuf), which was only a few miles from Radna! The newly created and trained Romanian 3rd Battalion was now sent into action at 1600 and stalled any further Hungarian attacks. They were very close. The attempt to take the town had failed, due to the Romanian artillery and anti-tank guns. Romanian bombers from Group 6/3 made numerous attacks with nine aircraft. The same Hungarian units that attacked towards Lippa succeeded in taking Pankota, north of Vilagos and advanced towards Borosjeno. The attacks towards Opalos continued and by 1600 hrs, Hungarian infantry occupied the high ground above the town, but the attack had been costly: the 1st

Armoured Division had lost (according Romanian sources) 23 tanks. The 1st Hungarian Cavalry Division had arrived at Temesújfalu—Savanyúkútfürdo.

The 17th was the high water mark for the Hungarian offensive. It would be a very bloody day as four Hungarian battalions fought for Minis once again defended by the Romanian 1st and 2nd Companies – a 'mini Stalingrad' as house-to-house fighting all day long gained nothing. Further east, five infantry battalions fought hard for the hills. Four of them assaulted Hill 365 (Paulis), which overlooked the town. The battle was fierce from 1000–1200. It threatened the Romanian 2nd Company, which itself was under attack. Holding the hill was the Romanian 3rd Company. Elements of the Hungarian force had almost reached Cladova, which was very close Radna (a few miles east of Paulis). The Romanian 1st Battalion/96th Regiment was not defeated but had to give ground in the Cladova area. Then, the pendulum swung. At 1000, a Russian infantry battalion from the 32nd Motorized Regiment (18th Tank Corps) finally arrived. It did save the Romanians as the Russian hit the Hungarians on their flank near Hill 365. Chaos amongst the Hungarian troops set in slowly until it affected all of them. The Hungarian retreat impacted the other battalion near Cladova. Soon, a Hungarian retreat back to Hill 471 (Bordu) ensued.

On the 18th, The Russian 5th Air Army appeared overhead in great numbers. They focused on the Hungarian troops, causing chaos and panic among them. Many of the Hungarian troops broke and ran from the 6th Reserve Division, but the 1st Armoured Division maintained their positions. Not all of the 6th Reserve fled, other units continued to fight in the Opalos area until the 19th. The Hungarian 8th Reserve Division attacked on the 17th, some 20 km northwest of Temesvar. By this time, Russian forces continued to arrive into the area firming up the defences to the point where little was to be gained. This part of the Hungarian offensive had failed but they had held their own and had succeeded.

The Hungarian forces taking part in this attack were: 1st Armoured Division, 8th, 10th, 11th, 12th, 13th, 19th and 21st Infantry Regiments amounting to 20,000 men. The Romanians lost 380 men. Hungarian losses came to 919, and 387 POWs, other sources suggest 3,100 men were lost.

The Romanians had captured 40 MGs, 40 mortars, 6 anti-tank guns, 19 *Panzerfäuste*, 6 rocket launchers, and had destroyed 21–25 AFVs and 6 armoured cars. Detachment Paulis had expended 935,700 rounds of rifle and MG, 669 anti-tank rounds, 2,211 60mm rounds, 1071 81mm rounds, 285 120mm rounds, 3000 122mm rounds, and 2538 grenades by the 18th. And this was just a single small-scale battle in the Second World War!

Meanwhile, the 38th Regiment/12th Division had taken Belenyes and Kisszedres and by the 19th, Biharlonka, together with elements of the 10th Assault Gun Battalion. This advance took the Hungarians into the mountain passes. Obviously, there had been little real resistance.

The Germans quickly sent the recently formed 4th SS Panzer Grenadier Division from Serbia towards the Iron Gate Pass area. The division had a total manpower of 16,538 men. It consisted of:

7th SS Panzer Grenadier Regiment of three battalions, 13th SS Company, 14th SS Company, 16th SS (Engineer) company;
8th SS Panzer Grenadier Regiment of three battalions
4th SS Panzer Regiment (three StuG companies, Ausf III and IV), three battalions of self-propelled artillery, a reconnaissance battalion, and one Panzerjäger battalion with two companies of Panzerjäger IV. The anti-aircraft battalion had three 88mm and one 37mm batteries.

The German division arrived in the Belgrade area on the 10th and immediately was ordered to take part in the attack on the 13th towards Arad. The 4th SS was directed to strike towards Temesvar. For this, part of the division was diverted with StuG IVs, its reconnaissance battalion and a regiment; these units would advance towards Temesvar and Lugos. The other part of the division would remain the Belgrade area. Due to delays, this attack could not begin until the 17th. By then, Russian troops were already in the much of the area and the attack only succeeded in taking Birda-Gadja-Szentandras. Securing this left flank of the 1st Romanian Army was the 9th Cavalry Division with 2,700 men. Its 13th Cavalry regiment was ripped apart by the SS. But the Romanians had deployed anti-tank guns and two Russian self-propelled guns, which stalled the 11 German StuG IV assault guns with numerous losses. Temesvar had been entered by the Russian 53rd Army on the 15th.

The SS advance was halted and they quickly went into defensive mode until the rest of the division could arrive on the 18th. The Hungarian 8th Reserve Division had linked up with the SS troops west of Temesvar.

Finally, on the 19th, Hungarian forces occupied Lippa, the target of the offensive. Thus far, the Hungarian 7th Assault Gun Battalion had destroyed 67 T-34 tanks while losing 8 of their own vehicles, and another 22 damaged. This Assault Gun unit was then renamed the 25th Assault Gun Battalion and consisted of 14 StuG III.

The Russian 18th Tank Corps attacked the Hungarians along the Maros, which ripped apart the Hungarian 6th Division near Ópálos killing 919 men and capturing 387. Russian armour approached Arad, encircling the city by

1700 hours and reaching Zimándköz. Other Hungarian units now went into retreat and offered sporadic resistance. The 8th Hungarian Division retreated in haste and chaos when Russian tanks appeared. Luckily, six German Stuka bombers appeared and attacked, forcing the Russian to pause. But, Hungarian armour was no match for the Russians. Only the Turan 75mm was a threat to them and there were too few.

Numerous other Russian units had gathered from Temesvar to Nagybeckskerek: the 46th Army, 7th Mechanized Corps, 4th and 6th Guards Cavalry Corps. The length of the 2nd Ukrainian Front ran some 180 km.

The Russian objectives for the upcoming Debrecen offensive were as follows:

1. 40th Army from Maramarossziget – Szatmarnemeti- Nagykaroly
2. 7th Guards Army from Nagykaroly- Nagyvarad
3. Gorskov Tank/Cavalry Corps Group from Beszterce-Csap
4. 6th Guards Tank Army from Koloszvar-Nagykaroly-Nyiregyhaza
5. 27th Army from Nagyvarad – Nagyszlonta-Nagyzerend
6. 53rd Army and 18th Tank Corps from Deva-Arad-Karansebes-Temesvar-Arad-Kisbecs

The upside was that the Russians greatly outnumbered the Hungarians and Germans. The downside was that all of the Russians were fatigued, had advanced hundreds of kilometres south and through the Carpathians, their tanks needed maintenance and had hundreds of hours on their engines.

Debrecen Offensive – action in the Russian 53rd Army sector

On the 20th, the 18th Tank Corps attacked the Hungarian 6th Reserve Division in the Opalos-Szabadhely area from along the Maros River. The Hungarian division was unprepared for such an onslaught at dawn. Combat was frantic and chaotic, and resulted in some 919 Hungarian KIA, and 387 POWs. Romanian losses came to 377. It was no wonder the Hungarians lost so severely, as 109 Russian tanks had struck towards the city of Arad and by afternoon had advanced to its north and northwest. Some 40 Russian tanks had also met German troops in the area of Simand.

A day earlier, the Hungarian 8th Reserve Division had withdrawn from the bridgehead near Arad. One battalion from the 12th Regiment held Ujarad, while the 21st and 24th Regiments stood in reserve north of Arad. These Hungarian units were ordered to counterattack with the two regiments from Mikelaka and Orthalom. This counterattack was briefly successful before they were forced onto the defensive, with the 12th Regiment repelling the Russian attacks initially.

It was at this time that the Germans demanded that the 4th and 7th Hungarian Corps be placed under their own command to control the damage. This was done and the Germans appointed new commanders to ensure loyalty.

The Hungarian 1st Armoured Division became embroiled in the combat around the Simand and Zimandujfalu areas, north of Arad, early that afternoon. Its 1st Tank Regiment/1st Motorized Regiment with artillery were engaged at Oszentanna and Zimandujfalu. Most of the 13th Regiment/20th Hungarian Division held at Zimandujfalu. When the Russian 1438th Assault Gun Regiment (armed with SU–85s) attempted to enter the village, Hungarian infantry managed to destroy three before the Russians dispersed. The Germans then ordered a Hungarian reconnaissance battalion, one tank company and others towards the wooded area south of Ujpanad to take on the Russian tanks. Another Hungarian group consisting of one tank battalion, one motorized battalion and the 51st Artillery Battalion were directed to the southwest of Zimándújfalu. This attack failed. Meanwhile, German air units supported yet another Hungarian group consisting of a tank battalion and two motorized battalions. They were ordered to move from the Kurtos-Vilagos area to Erdokerék. However, the group mistakenly ran into 25 Russian T–34s!

Overhead, suddenly appeared the famed German tank hunter pilot, Hans-Ulrich Rudel, leading his 2nd Group of tank-busting Stukas. They approached from the Hungarian side to the cheers of Hungarian troops. The Hungarians, now emboldened by this sight, used three tank companies and two motorized companies from the 1st Armoured Division to renew their counterattacks towards Erdokerék. The Stukas swarmed onto the tanks of the Russian 18th Corps' using their antitank guns to great effect in relays of two. Soon, 25 Russian tanks were in flames. The Russian tanks reacted wildly and in disarray, trying to escape, but the coupled effect from the Stukas and Hungarian fire proved deadly. This only proved to be a respite in what otherwise was a Hungarian retreat. By 1700, the Russians kept coming and another 23 T34 tanks approached, losing another seven to Hungarian tanks. The Stukas continued to dive, hover, and strike and by the time they left they had destroyed 30 tanks and 120 trucks, cars and tractors of the 18th Russian Tank Corps. Only one Hungarian tank was mistakenly destroyed.

On the 21st, the Russian 53rd Army moved closer to Arad. The Hungarian 8th Regiment from the 8th Reserve Division penetrated into their flank in the area of Othalom. In the area around Ujarad, the 12th Regiment with

Romanian and Soviet soldiers share a cigarette, Transylvania. (Photo archive of the Bulgarian Ministry of Defence)

Waffen SS troops dug in, Hungary, autumn 1944. (Bundesarchiv 146–1982–090–21)

Lieutenant-General Ivan Managarov, commander of the Soviet 53rd Army, accompanied by Corps-General Nicolae Macici, commander of Romanian 1st Army. (Photo archive of the Bulgarian Ministry of Defence)

Soldiers from a Rifle unit commanded by Lieutenant Gremenkov during urban combat, North Transylvania, 1944. The weapon in the foreground is a 7.62 mm SG–43 Goryunov medium machine gun. (RGAKFD Moscow)

Guards Cossack unit on the march, western Romania, September 1944. (RGAKFD Moscow)

A train with captured German aircraft, Romania, September 1944. (RGAKFD Moscow)

Soviet T–34/85 tanks and Romanian infantry move towards the front, 25 September 1944. (RGAKFD Moscow)

A Soviet T–34/85 tank on the march, 25 September 1944. (RGAKFD Moscow)

A Waffen SS soldier armed with a MG 42 machine gun, Hungary, autumn 1944. (Ullstein Bilderdienst)

German Stuka ace Hans-Ulrich Rudel examines damage to a Soviet tank in Hungary in the company of some Hungarian officers, late autumn 1944. (Dénes Bernád)

Superb study of ethnic Germans (Volksdeutsche) serving within one of the Waffen SS cavalry divisions in Hungary, October 1944. (Ullstein Bilderdienst)

artillery support repulsed Russian attacks and then retreated into the town, which then came under attack with fierce street fighting. The bridge over the Maros River was then blown at 1800 hrs. This retreat soon turned into a rout as the Hungarians came under heavy Russian fire. Russian rockets pounded the Hungarians in the area. As the Hungarians withdrew, the 12th Regiment held the Maros River line. Romanian partisans in Arad also began to cause havoc, making it nearly impossible for the Hungarians to hold it. The two pursuing Russian divisions, the 243rd and 228th from the 57th Corps, followed cautiously. It wasn't until 2000 hrs that they arrived at the Arad Bridge and moved across it.

Legend has it that the Hungarians simply routed from Arad, which is untrue. The Russians did not occupy it until the next day, the 22nd. The 18th Tank Corps had headed towards Nagyvarad. The Hungarian 1st Armoured Division continued to joust with the advancing Russians in and around Zimand. Also in the area, the Hungarian 20th Division and various artillery formations regrouped. Together, the Hungarians conducted a counterattack against the Russian forces in and around Zimand, which penetrated into the town. The Russians counterattacked but failed in retaking it. The Hungarian 1st Armoured Division units aggressively operated and did not fall back until late that night.

In the area of Elek, the Hungarian 1st Anti-Aircraft Brigade and the 7th Regiment (2 battalions)/5th Territorial force, armed with 24 88mm guns and four 40mm guns waited. A very potent force stood idle! Taking control of the Hungarian 4th and 7th Corps, the German 4th SS PG Division and *Kampfgruppe* Ameiser from the 22nd SS Cavalry Division, together with the German 57th Panzer Corps, created a badly needed unified command.

The Russians continued to exploit and push forward their units north of Arad forcing much of the Hungarian 20th Reserve Division to panic and rout. Its 23rd Regiment was located at Nagyvarjas. Most of the division simply fled in the direction of Kurtos-Nadab-Zerend. The Hungarian 4th Corps primarily occupied an area consisting of Tornya, south of Nagyvarjas, and a few miles of Kurtos, Within this same area, German aircraft had spotted over 60 Russian tanks. The Hungarian 3rd Army HQ was further back at Medgyesegyházá. By now, the remains of the Hungarian 1st Armoured Division regrouped in the Békéscsaba area. Its commander had had a nervous breakdown and was replaced.

During the day, two companies from *Kampfgruppe* Ameiser marched towards Orosházá. Elements of the 52nd SS Cavalry Regiment arrived near Nagyvarad. The group had only been formed in early September and was still being equipped as late as the 14th. It was commanded by Anton Ameiser. The unit had 1,000 men in four cavalry companies and one heavy weapons unit.

Although the Hungarian 4th and 7th Corps finally made a tenuous connection with each other, it did not last long. Russian units easily burst through, creating a huge 15–20 km gap in the Gyula area. Defending a key bridge over the Fekete-Körös River was one Hungarian engineer company. The German 57th Panzer Corps situation had become quite critical.

On the 23rd, German intelligence had decided that the direction of the Russian attack was turning northwards towards the Hungarian plains. The following directives were issued: the Hungarian 3rd Army was ordered to attempt to retake Arad, and the 4th and 7th Hungarian Corps along with *Kampfgruppe* Ameiser should repel further Russian attacks. Both the Hungarian 8th and 23rd Reserve Divisions, now a shadow of their former selves, defended west of Dombegyház-south of Battonya- Németpereg-Kispereg. Once again, some of the Hungarians had the jitters and panic set in when they were attacked by the Russians. This time it was some of the Hungarian 23rd Division that fled when the Russian 170th Tank Brigade from the 18th Tank Corps attacked it at noon. It was followed by the 3rd Self-Propelled Artillery Regiment of Russian 53rd Army. The attack did encounter resistance from the German 9th Ground Attack Squadron containing HS 129 B2 aircraft. Likewise, the Hungarian 2nd Corps retreated into the same area that its 8th Division had held.

Russian armour streaked towards Szeged, Kiszombor and Apatfalva, all south of Arad.

Hungarian units attempted to regroup under attack from a large number of Russian units. The Hungarian 8th Reserve Division, 24th Reconnaissance Battalion, and the light Toldi tanks of the 1st Armoured Division held Ferencszállás. The Hungarian 23rd Divisions' advance to Mako had failed. In the Gyula area, elements of the Hungarian 1st Armoured Division and 2nd Reserve Corps also gathered anyone willing to join them. Some Hungarian units did manage to link up with the 22nd SS Cavalry Division combat group (*Kampfgruppe* Ameiser) near Doboz. Another Hungarian unit pushed a reconnaissance in the Ottlaka direction, however, they soon found it was in Russian hands.

While the Russians had lost 60 tanks in the past two days, they possessed far greater numbers, which continued to roll past and over many of the Hungarian units attempting to plug the numerous holes created by September 24th.

The Russian 799th Regiment from the 228th Division of the 57th Corps penetrated into Csanádpalotá but the Hungarians (50 men and various AA troops) resisted and forced the Russians out of the town when the latter's tank support failed to arrive. Meanwhile, elements of the Hungarian 3rd Battalion continued to hold Ópécskár until the afternoon when the Russian 767th Regiment from the 228th Division appeared and forced the Hungarians to fall back to Nagylak and Mako environs.

The Hungarian 8th Reserve Division remnants together with 2nd Battery from the 7th Assault Gun Battalion with 10 StuG IIIG defended the area around Mezokovácsházá. All together, the unit possessed 30 StuG IIIG. It was considered one of the more potent forces available to the Axis forces in the area! The Hungarian 1st Army and 2nd Reserve Corps between Nagyszollos and Oroshaza had only a few artillery guns between them. On the 25th, the Hungarians managed to cut-off the Russian supply route briefly, by deploying its 7th Assault Gun Battalion elements including infantry from the 8th Reserve Division near Mezohegyes. This represented a minor victory of sorts in an ocean of crushing loss. Another brief respite came at Kevermes, where the Hungarians were attacked from several directions by Russian tanks, all of which were repelled. However, the Russian 203rd Division had taken Elek. Arriving at Nagyvarad in the afternoon was the 2nd Motorized Battalion/1st Armoured Division and elements of the 5th Artillery Battalion.

The Hungarian 2nd Reserve Corps remained responsible for the areas Kisperg-Battonya-Dombegyhaz-Kevermes- Ketegyhaza-Nagypel-Zerend. The German SS Ameiser *Kampfgruppe* held the area around Gyulavarsand, while a few battalions from the Hungarian 12th Reserve Division occupied the area around Zerend. The 4th SS Panzer Grenadier Division was now in the Mako-Hodmezovasarhely area. The Russian 110th Guards Division had seized Temesvar.

Thus, the Hungarians did maintain some combat order during the Russian offensive that fell upon them. Most accounts gloss over this fact and simply state the Russians met little resistance. While this was true in some cases and gaps did appear, it is clear that as of the 25th, the Russians had only penetrated into Hungary proper in some areas. The front line hovered along the border between Hungary and Romania.

According to German sources, the Russian 2nd Ukrainian Front had lost 1,100 men, 134 tanks, 112 anti-tank and artillery guns, and 157 aircraft. The 1st Air Corps from the 4th *Luftflotte* had alone destroyed 91 tanks. Impressive, but in reality, a mere drop in the ocean when compared to the massive Russian armies fast approaching.

Attacking on the 26th at Ketegyhaza (defended by the Hungarian 51st Armoured Gun Battalion (Nimrod)) the Russian 610th Regiment of the 203rd Division supported by the 1037 SP Regiment found itself in a desperate battle, to their surprise. However, like most of the battles, the Hungarians were forced to retreat. In the Mako and Hodmezovasarhely area, the Russian 57th Corps, 228th Division, 18th Tank Corps (40 tanks) and the 23rd and 24th Self-Propelled Gun Battalions all fought a series of battles pushing the Hungarians back further and further. The Hungarian 7th Assault Gun Battalion continued to display amazing audacity and skill, not only in the use of their vehicles, but their commander, who proved to be daring. It was obvious he was German-trained as his small batteries of 2–3 vehicles took on Russian armour four or five times their number at close range (100–200 yards). In one such battle at Csandpalota, the 2nd Company (8 vehicles) fought elements of the Russian 1438th SP Regiment. Elements of the Hungarian 8th Reserve Division also participated. The unit managed to destroy 12 T–34s and took 30 POWs. Of course, the Hungarians were forced to pull back, as usual, but damage was done. The 18 vehicles of the 7th Battalion fell back to Oroshaza, *Kampfgruppe* Ameiser held Gyulavarasand, the 2nd Hungarian Corps held a line form Gyula to Nagyszalonta, some 30 km.

On the 27th, the remains of the Hungarian 1st Armoured Division were located near Doboz (near Bekes) while *Kampfgruppe* Ameiser moved to Mehkerek. The Hungarian 8th Reserve Division was in the Mezohegyes and Pitvaros area, the 7th Assault Gun Battalion and 23rd Hungarian Division remained in the Hodmezovasarhely area. Between the 13th and 27th, the 1st Armoured Division had lost 91 men KIA, 260 WIA, 165 deserters. It literally was becoming a 'ghost' unit.

The arrival of the German 4th SS Panzergrenadier Division did have a chilling impact on the Russian Juggernaut slowly rolling forward in the Temesvar area. Two SS Panzer Grenadier battalions, its reconnaissance battalion, one artillery battalion and its Panzerjäger battalion (22 StuG III/IV vehicles) all had arrived on the flank of the Russian 110th, 375th, and 1st Guards Parachute Division belonging to the 49th Corps of 53rd Army. The SS troops, mostly from 8th SS Panzer Grenadier Regiment, were deployed as follows: 2 companies at Nemetszentpeter, a company at Kisbecskerek, three infantry companies and one of StuGs at Billed, two further infantry companies, the reconnaissance battalion and a company of StuGs between Sandra-Perjamos, with a further company of Panzergrenadiers and 3rd Company4th Artillery Regiment arriving. The SS troops were in battle with the Russians constantly from the 21st onwards. It was a like a pit bull's jaw securely fastened onto the Russian leg.

The SS captured one 88mm, 15 76.2mm AT guns, three 37mm and 18 other types of anti-tank guns, 28 MGs, 26 LMGs, 139 rifles. The Russians lost 2,840 men, 195 POWs. The SS had lost 141 men KIA and 582 WIA.

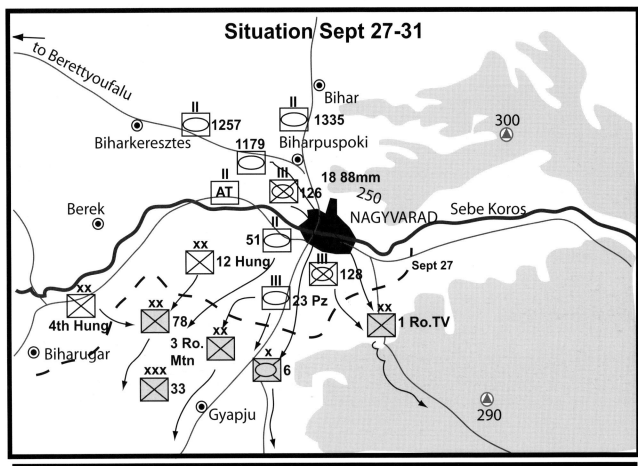

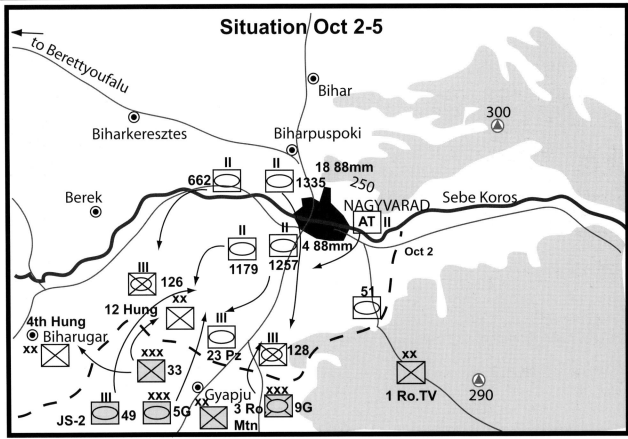

The Battle for Nagyvarad

A SdKfz 251/7 engineer half-track, Hungary, autumn 1944. (Bundesarchiv 101I–715–0212A–27A)

Jagdpanzer 38t Hetzer, a vehicle which equipped a number of the Sturmgeschütz units operating in Hungary Autumn 1944. This particular vehicle belonged to 8th SS Cavalry Division 'Florian Geyer'. (Bundesarchiv 101I–715–0213A–25)

A Romanian mountain troop machine gun team in action, Transylvania, September 1944. The weapon is a Czech ZB vz/30 7.92mm. (Photo archive of the Bulgarian Ministry of Defence)

A mortar unit commanded by N.I. Kovalenko moves through the foothills of the Carpathians, autumn 1944. (RGAKFD Moscow)

A mortar unit commanded by N.I. Kovalenko moves through the foothills
of the Carpathians. (RGAKFD Moscow)

Soldiers from a Rifle unit commanded by Lieutenant Gremenkov during combat, 18 September 1944. (RGAKFD Moscow)

View looking down into the fighting compartment of a Hungarian Nimrod self-propelled anti-aircraft gun.
(The Tank Museum)

A German Marder III self-propelled gun passes Hungarian infantry, 1944. (Ullstein Bilderdienst)

A Hungarian artillery column on the march, autumn 1944. (Ullstein Bilderdienst)

Hungarian infantry line a trench, autumn 1944. (Dénes Bernád)

The Battle for Nagyvarad, September 20–October 4

Arriving south of Nagyvarad at around noon was the Russian 33rd Corps, opposed by the Hungarian 7th Corps containing the 4th and 12th Reserve Divisions. During the confusing battle on the 18th, Axis aircraft mistakenly attacked much of the 4th Division causing it to panic and halt its counter-attack; the 12th Division continued to attack towards Belényest, some 15 km southeast of Nagyvarad.

On the 21st, the 12th Division's two regiments stood between the Hungarian 4th and 7th Corps in the area of Belenyes opposite the Romanian 3rd Mountain and Russian 337th Divisions. The Hungarians, for the time being, were holding the line. The Corps' commander noticing a large undefended area along the line Fekete-Koros, and ordered the Hungarian 4th Reserve Division into the area. By the 23rd, much remained the same except the 12th Division had become embroiled in very heavy combat near Belenyes. Elements of the 4th Division were shifted to the right flank. On the 24th, the Hungarians created a small combat group for an attack consisting of the 8th Reserve Regiment, 48th Regiment/12th Division and artillery. But this proposed group found it increasingly difficult to prepare and deploy in the Pusztahollód area. Some elements were able to attack and retake a small village and the 38th and 48th Regiments of 12th Division encircled some Romanian troops. But on the 25th, enemy attacks became more intense against the 4th Hungarian Division, causing them to collapse. The 12th Hungarian Division soon followed, routing in streams of soldiers towards Nagyvarad, despite attempts to halt them. The 4th Division fled towards Mezobikácsig. Russian units were eight to nine kilometres southeast of Nagyvarad and had taken Püspökfürdo. Little remained of the Hungarian 4th Division as a fighting force. Few Hungarian soldiers were willing to stand and fight.

At this stage, had the Russians known, the road to Nagyvarad was wide open! Luckily, they did not know this and officers of the 12th Hungarian Division quickly regrouped themselves, saw the need and created small Hungarian defensive units. One such unit contained 152 men, 18 LMG, 3 mortars. Another company arrived in the city, the 1/102. The 53rd Battalion with 30 trucks also arrived. The German command was not notified until 1800 hrs regarding the situation at Nagyvarad. Once notified and since no German troops were nearby, at 18.30 hours the German Command issued orders for a Panzer Grenadier battalion from the 23rd Panzer Division to immediately advance to Nagyvarad. On the 26th, the Hungarian 2nd Motorized Battalion also had arrived at noon. Throughout the day, numerous groups of wandering soldiers filtered into the area, each time, officers ordered them to create defensive groups along the Pecze River and the eastern portion of the city. Discipline was strict and even officers were hanged if they did not cooperate. More Hungarian troops arrived including the 53rd Battalion with three gun companies, one machine gun company, one rocket company and bicycle company. The 10th Hungarian Assault Gun Battalion, with three Zrinyi II, had also arrived on the eastern side. During the day, the Hungarian units created defences, that although weak, were better than nothing. The 48th Regiment of the 12th Division and the 53rd Battalion deployed between the Pecze and Sebe-Koros River, while the 36th and 38th Regiments continued to Nagyürögdre. Between Nagyvarad and Nagyzalonta was the 2nd Motorized Battalion. The 4th Division units continued to retreat. Arriving much later in the day were elements of the 3rd Panzer Corps' 23rd Panzer Division. Departing for Nagyvarad was also the German 661st and 662nd Heavy Panzerjäger Battalion with 21 88mm guns! Already enroute were the German 1179th, 1257th, and 1335th Assault Gun Battalions. The 3rd Panzer Corps would assume control over the Nagyvarad area.

The first Russian units to reach the city outskirts from the southeast were small, company-sized elements or smaller. They succeeded in capturing small portions of the city and were met by the first German troops at 1430 hrs. By 1830 hrs, most of the 3rd Panzer Corps was 26 km northeast of the city.

The Hungarian commanders decided to use the Pecze River as a defence line and the following units held along it: the 36th, 38th, and 48th Infantry Regiments. Artillery guns were positioned further back. This artillery consisted of the six 105mm guns. For reserves, the Hungarians used the 2nd Motorized and 53rd Battalions. The defending units were ordered to retreat, when necessary, towards Biharszentjáno. However, upon hearing this, the German commander strongly objected and it was clear from this exchange that the 3rd Panzer Corps was the commanding unit over all Axis forces in the area. The Hungarian 7th Corps could do little but acquiesce. By the 27th, the Hungarian Corps units held a line from Cseffa-Nagyvarad-Fugyi. The Russians were near Nagyvarad and moving towards Koloszvar rapidly. Elements of the 23rd Panzer Division were there, specifically, their reconnaissance battalion led by Rudolf Koppe.

By the end of September, like most German divisions, the 23rd Panzer was really a shell of its former self. Its 23rd Panzer Regiment consisted of 1st Battalion (PzKpfw IV, PzKpfw V, StuG III, StuG IV), and 2nd Battalion (all PzKpfw V) commanded by Ernst Rebentisch. In total, it contained two PzKpfw III, five PzKpfw IV, 51 PzKpfw V (of which only 17 were operational), 19 StuG (9 were operational), 12 105mm Wespe (six operational), five 150mm Hummels, four Marder (75mm) and another 18 75mm AT guns.

The 126th PG (Panzer Grenadier) Regiment contained two PG battalions in APCs (amoured personnel carriers) – its infantry gun support company, AA Battalion and Engineer Company were in trucks. The 128th PG Regiment had only one PG Battalion in APCs. Its 23rd Reconnaissance Battalion had five companies with armoured cars, the 128th SP Artillery Regiment had three battalions. Its 278th AA Company contained three AA guns. The unit had just arrived in Hungary only a week or two earlier. It arrived from Budapest by rail, unloading in Debrecen and Kolosvar. The unit had just saved the situation on September 23–24 at Torda, against fierce Russian attacks.

The Russians attacked Nagyvarad on the 27th with the 33rd Corps and Romanian 1st Tudor Vladimirescu Division (9,014 men), at 1300 hrs. The Russian 337th Division and the Romanians were able to penetrate into parts of the city's suburbs. Gaps had appeared in the defences and the 23rd Panzer units arrived to seal them. Arriving was the 23rd Panzer Reconnaissance Battalion, 51st Panzer Pioneer Battalion, and the 128th PG Regiment, which had unloaded at Biharra. These units had to fight their way to within 4km of the city. Elements of the Hungarian 7th Corps had also left Nagyvarad! The Hungarian 57th Battalion conducted its own counterattack, which proved successful and ended at nightfall. By the end of the day, the city was free of Russian troops.

In the morning of the 28th, the Panzer Regiment from the 23rd Panzer Division with 20 tanks attacked Russian positions on the east and west sides of the city. Attacking Váradszentmárt was the 2nd Panzer Company, 126th PG Regiment, and 51st Panzer Pioneer Battalion. Russian defences resisted. The 128th PG Regiment moved through Alkér taking back lost territory towards the southeast. Meanwhile, the 126th PG Regiment overcame the Russians at Váradszentmárt and continued down the railway line at 1800 hrs. The 2nd Panzer Company joined in the attack with only four operational PzKpfw V tanks. Together, with the other German units, this cleared the village of Hájót. The German attacked continued towards Váradcsehi and Bany – it had succeeded in destroying numerous Russian tanks and SP guns, 31 anti-tank guns, five rocket launchers, 14 bazookas, and the Russian 337th Division had suffered heavily.

During the 28th, the Germans, had in the meantime, sent numerous artillery and armoured units to Nagyvarad via Kolozsvar. Overall, the 23rd Panzer Division was refurbished to some degree and now consisted of 42 tanks, 15 StuGs, 24 75mm AT guns, 15 light and 12 heavy artillery guns in the city. More tanks were *en-route*. Arriving later was the 844th Artillery Battalion with 10 heavy guns, the 809th Mortar Battalion with seven 210mm mortars, the 800th Artillery Battalion, with two 170mm guns and the 43rd Artillery Battalion. These reinforcements were in addition to the 662nd Panzerjäger Battalion with 19 88mm, plus, five Nashorns (88mm). As if this was not enough, the 12th AA Regiment was sent with 24 88mm guns, nine 37mm, and 33 20mm! The StuG units already there were: 1179th (seven Jagdpanzer 38), 1257th (nine Jagdpanzer 38), and 1335th (three Jagdpanzer 38).

It is no wonder that the city would not fall until much later, and would prove to be the Achilles heel for the Russian 6th Guards Tank Army. Meanwhile, the Hungarian 4th Reserve Division pulled back to the north bank of the Sebe-Koros River. The Germans had created a wall of steel with the dreaded 88mm guns.

During the day, the Hungarian 57th Battalion of the 48th Regiment managed to repel numerous small Russian attempts across the Pecze and Sebe-Koros Rivers. These units had only three 75mm AT guns. Thus, many of the battles for the city were small scale.

By the 29th, the 23rd Panzer Regiment reported a total of 15 operational tanks. Its Panzer Reconnaissance Battalion had advanced in a western direction to Nagyszalonta along the route to Nagyvarad. It was able to cut off the retreating Russian units to some degree, which was supported by the arrival of the 128th SP Regiment. The Russian 33rd Corps and the 6th Motorized Brigade came under attack and a vicious battle ensured for the small town. Southwest of Váradcsehitol, elements of the 23rd Panzer Division also collided with the Romanian 1st Tudor Vladimirescu Division and after a brief furious battle, the Romanians fell back, leaving over 200 dead. By noon, the Germans had taken Nagyürögdöt and Nagyszalonta, weak resistance to Nagyvarad continued. Attacking southwards was the 126th PG Regiment, which pursued the retreating Russian and Romanian troops. By nightfall, the German Hungarian lines were from Oláhapáti to Kisürögd. At this stage, the Germans regrouped, refuelled and replenished supplies, except for the 3rd Battalion/128th PG Regiment, which began a new attack upon a Russian ambush site. Troops from both sides were less than 10m apart during the firefight. Once the resupply was completed, the 23rd Panzer continued its attack, taking Gyapjút. The Romanians did not put up a great fight and fell back. They had lost 24 anti-tank guns, six infantry guns, six 122mm guns, 20 rockets, 32 machine guns.

New orders were received from the German 6th Army and indicated that the 23rd Panzer Division should continue its attack south of Nagyvarad in the face of Russian and Romanian units for a short time but not to endanger their position with further losses.

At Komadi, the Hungarian 7th Corps deployed along the right flank west towards Újiráz to where the Russians had created a small bridgehead over the Sebe-Koros River. It was from this bridgehead the Russians would attack the Hungarians from.

Arriving into the area was the German 76th Division of 72nd Corps. This division had already been in several heavy battles and was under reorganization. It contained the 203rd, 230th and 178th Regiments, none up to strength. Its 176th Artillery Regiment had 12 105mm guns, one company with 50mm anti-tank guns, one company with 20mm AA guns, nine trucks. In all, some 10,000 men, with only 3,000 of these being combat soldiers, some armed with the latest MP44 assault rifle. Each regiment had a company armed with *Panzerschrecks*. Its anti-tank unit contained 12 75mm anti-tank guns and eight Jagdpanzer 38 Hetzers.

Prelude to the Battle for Debrecen

It was on September 29th that General Malinovsky ordered the 2nd Ukrainian Front Armies to prepare for an offensive directed at Debrecen. For this, the right flank, consisting of the 7th Guards and 40th Armies were to take Beszterce-Máramarossziget-Nagybánya by October 1. The 27th Army and 4th Romanian Army would strike towards Kolozsvar, Zihlah, Margita, and Szilágysomlyó by October 7.

In the Torda area, the Cavalry-Armour group under Lt. Gen. Gorskov, would join the attack and exploit towards Nagykaroly when permitted. This group contained the 23rd Tank Corps (Lt. Gen Ahmanov) and the 5th Guards Cavalry Corps (Gorskov). The group contained 146 AFVs.

The 6th Guards Tank Army remained with the task of taking Nagyvarad. It was at this time, a new cavalry-tank group was created, the Pliyev Cavalry-Tank Group, using the Stavka reserves consisting of the 4th and 6th Guards Cavalry Corps and the 7th Mechanized Corps taken from the 3rd Ukrainian Front. These units assembled in the Arad area behind the 53rd Army. It had orders to take Bekescsbaba and Püspökladány and move towards Debrecen. The 4th Guards Cavalry Corps was under the direct command of Pliyev. It consisted of the 9th Guards, 10th Guards, and 30th Cavalry Divisions, plus the 1815th Assault/SP Gun Regiment. It concentrated in the Szentmárton, Lökösháza and Mácsa environs. The 6th Guards Cavalry Corps consisted 8th, 8th Guards, and 13th Guards Cavalry Divisions and the 1813th Assault/SP Gun Regiment. It concentrated in the Kisjeno area.

The 8th Cavalry Division contained T–34s and British Valentine IX tanks, 10 SU–76 (154th Tank Regiment); the 8th Guards Cavalry Division had 24 T–34, eight T–70, 40 American M3 APC, plus SU–76 and SU–85. The 13th Guards Cavalry Division contained the 250th Tank Regiment with 27 T–34, eight Valentine IX, several T–70, plus SU–76, SU–85.

The 7th Mechanized Corps also joining the group contained the 16th, 63rd, 64th Mechanized Brigades, 41st Guards Tank Brigade, 1821st and 1440th Assault Gun/SP Regiments and the 78th Guards Heavy Tank (IS–2) Regiment.

The Pliyev Group had completed its concentration on deployment by October 5th and contained 389 tanks and assault/SP guns plus 1,100 various artillery and rockets. This was a steamroller to be reckoned with!

The 53rd Army was to attack along a 170km-wide front with Oroshaza, Szarvas, Bekescsaba as objectives by the 7th. Afterwards, the army was to take Mezotur and reach the Tisza River by the 10th; Kenderes and a bridgehead over the Tisza was to be accomplished by the 12th. It is apparent the Russians, euphoric with their success, thought little of the opposing side's forces. The 53rd Army contained the 27th Corps with three divisions, the 57th Corps with two divisions, and 49th Corps with three divisions. Supporting the army to some extent was the 18th Tank Corps with 72 tanks. The 18th Tank Corps was to advance in the Orosháza-Szentes-Kunszentmárton direction and then onto Szolnok to establish and hold a bridgehead over the Tisza.

On September 30th, one German battle group of the 23rd Panzer Division contained:

One PzKpfw III, eight PzKpfw V, six StuGs
The 23rd Panzer Reconnaissance Battalion
3rd Battalion/128th SP Artillery Regiment

Commanded by Rebentisch, it attacked at 0700 hours towards the Nagyszalonta area defended by troops of the Romanian 4th Mountain and Russian 79th Divisions, which gave way and then withdrew or routed from their positions. The advance stalled when the units reached a blown bridge some 10 km from Nagyszalonta. Luckily, another bridge was found near Püspökradványnál and the 126th PG Regiment quickly took advantage of it upon its arrival. All of the German units crossed the channel and continued onwards towards Madarász. It was here the Russians and Romanians put up a stout defence with 11 anti-tank guns, a collection of artillery and rockets. The intensity continued for some time until, like so many times before, they collapsed and the 126th PG Regiment quickly cleared the town. With its capture, the small armoured force continued and reached Nagyszalonta area around 1800 hrs.

A captured Italian AB41 armoured car passes German troops on the march, Hungary, 1944.
(Bundesarchiv 101I–730–0105–20)

A German anti-tank gun towed by a RSO prime mover passes through a Hungarian town, September 1944. (Kamen Nevenkin)

Romanian trucks from the 'Patriotic Front' filled with presents for the front line troops head for the front, autumn 1944. (Photo archive of the Bulgarian Ministry of Defence)

Romanian volunteers, autumn 1944. (Photo archive of the Bulgarian Ministry of Defence)

The local population in a Transylvanian village celebrate the arrival of Romanian troops, autumn 1944.
(Photo archive of the Bulgarian Ministry of Defence)

Soviet artillery pass along a road in Romania, 7 October 1944. These are ZiS–3 76 mm
divisional guns, towed by lend-lease trucks. (RGAKFD Moscow)

Anti-aircraft gunners under the command of Guards Lieutenant Belousov provide cover to a military route, Hungary, October 1944. They are equipped with 12.7 mm DShK 1938 heavy anti-aircraft machine guns. (RGAKFD Moscow)

Cossack unit moves along a Hungarian Road, September 1944, Transylvania. (RGAKFD Moscow)

Soviet T–34/85 tank in the mountains of Transylvania, Hungary, September 1944. (RGAKFD Moscow)

Wrecked German equipment, including a half-track prime mover in the foreground,
Western Transylvania, autumn 1944. (Dénes Bernád)

The Hungarian 1st Armoured Division, with 32 AFVs and infantry, had already taken the town and the Romanians were fleeing. Further east, elements of the Romanian 1st Tudor Vladimirescu Division fought and were defeated. As evening fell, the Russians and Romanians withdrew and the Germans reached Cséffára around 2200 hrs. Ironically, the battle group continued with its reconnaissance and ran into elements of the Russian 6th Guards Tank Army preparing for their own offensive near Nagyvarad! Confusion and chaos reigned but the Russians were set back and disrupted. Between September 27–29, the 23rd Panzer Division battle group had caused the Romanians a loss of 800 men, 203 POWs, 72 anti-tank guns, 39 rockets, 22 MG, and 78 LMG. Amazing for such a small force.

The German 325th StuG Brigade arrived northwest of Nagyvarad. It was subordinated to the 3rd Panzer Corps. The 228th StuG Brigade contained 17 StuGs and 17 SP Artillery and had arrived at Karcag. The Hungarian 12th Reserve Division moved towards the Nagyvarad area.

Attacking again – at a time when some Russian units were preparing for the Debrecen offensive – on October 1, the 23rd Panzer struck this time with 15 tanks and StuGs, the 2nd and 3rd Companies from the Armoured Reconnaissance Battalion with 30 APCs and armoured cars, 10th Company/126 PZG Regiment and three heavy artillery guns, 1st and 3rd Battalions/128th SP Regiment. The attack began at 1000 hrs towards Mezobikács, defended by seven Russian 76.2mm anti-tank guns. The Germans swept through it and continued on seizing Janosd, defended by five T–34/85, which were destroyed. The German force had now cut the 33rd Corps supply path upon reaching Nyárszeg. The lead Panther tanks ran into a Russian mine field and several were damaged beyond repair. The Russians defended with 10 heavy tanks, forcing the German attack force to fall back by nightfall to Cséffára to refuel and regroup.

On October 2nd the 23rd Panzer Division had lost seven PzKpfw V tanks and two StuGs. Its Panzer Regiment contained two command tanks, one PzKpfw V and one PzKpfw IV. The 1st Battalion contained two PzKpfw III and one PzKpfw IV commander's tank. Its 1st Company contained 13 StuG, the 2nd Company contained seven PzKpfw IV, the 3rd Company had 4 PzKpfw IV, while the 4th Company had 10 PzKpfw V. The 2nd Panzer Battalion contained seven PzKpfw V, 6th Company had 10 PzKpfw V, 7th Company had 11 PzKpfw V and 8th Company had 10 PzKpfw V. Its Panzer Grenadier Regiment contained 96 APCs.

Due to severe combat, the 128th PG Regiment was forced to disband and combine two of its companies. When combined with its Reconnaissance Battalion, the divisional combatants numbered no more than 1,300 men, with an additional 400 non-combatants. The 23rd Armoured Reconnaissance Battalion contained four companies, each with 12 light (Kfz 250) and five heavy (Kfz 251) armored scout cars. The 128th Panzerjäger unit contained two companies with Panzerjäger IV. The third company contained 12 75mm anti-tank guns, five Marder, five captured Russian SU–85 assault guns and two T–34.

The 23rd Panzer Division contained the following assorted weapons:

7908 rifles, 836 MP40 SMGs, four MP 44 assault rifles, 45 sniper rifles, 331 *Panzerfäuste*, 15 Italian MGs, seven Russian MGs, 21 anti-tank Guns.

The 128th SP Artillery Regiment contained 15 light and 12 heavy guns, plus five 150mm Hummel and 12 105mm Wespe.

By October 3rd, the German 8th Army assumed the positions formerly held by the Hungarian 2nd Army. The German 6th Army comprised of the 3rd Panzer Corps and the 72nd Corps and combined contained the 1st, 13th and 23rd Panzer Divisions and the 76th Infantry Division. Also available were the 24th Panzer Division and the Feldherrnhalle (FHH) Panzer Grenadier Divisions. One of these would eventually be assigned to the corps, but not both. The Germans themselves had planned for an offensive southwards, which was to have begun on the 10th. It would join an attack from the Hungarian 3rd Army combining with a general offensive eastward.

However, the Russians would strike first with the 6th Guards Tank Army in the Nagyvarad area. This action was a premature move on the part of the Russians, which diverted the attention from the Pliyev Corps. The 6th Guards Tank Army consisted of the 5th Guards Tank Corps, the 9th Guards Mechanized Corps, the 33rd Motorized Corps, 11th AA Division, 6th SP Artillery Brigade, 202nd Light Artillery Brigade, 24th AA Brigade, 364th Lt. SP Artillery Brigade, and 49th Heavy Tank Brigade (IS–2), 301st Anti-Tank Brigade.

The 5th Guards Tank Corps contained the 20th, 21st and 22nd Guards Tank Brigades, and the 6th Guards Mechanized Brigade. The 9th Guards Mechanized Corps contained the 18th, 30th, and 31st Guards Brigades, and the 46th Guards Tank Brigade (armed with mostly American M4A2 Sherman tanks). The total combined manpower came to 34,494 men and 188 tanks. Supporting were 982 various artillery guns and rocket launchers plus 1,832 vehicles.

The Germans had not been surprised at all. Their reconnaissance units had detected the large Russian forces gathering east of Nagyszalontá and determined that the Russians were going to attack. Thus, the 23rd Panzer Division units pulled back in the morning of October 2 just north of Váradlestő and were placed on alert. As dawn turned into morning, the Russians attacked with 20 tanks, taking the Mezobikács area and continuing towards

Nagyvarad. The Luftwaffe appeared and reduced a potentially strong attack into a weak one after destroying eight tanks and 40 trucks. The Hungarian 12th Reserve Division combined with the German 128th PG Regiment in their attack which was met with heavy Russian fire. This attack failed. Arriving in the Debrecen area was the German 1st Panzer Division. It had been instructed to occupy the following areas: Sáránd, Hosszúpályi, Nagyléta, Álmosd, Bagamér and Újléta. The division had 9,400 men and consisted of:

The Panzer Regiment's (Lt. Col. Streith) 1st Panzer Battalion with – 1st Company containing 17 PzKpfw V, 2nd Company with 12 PzKpfw V, 3rd Company with 13 PzKpfw V. The 2nd Panzer Battalion contained 7th Company with six PzKpfw IV, and 8th Company with 15 PzKpfw IV.

The 1st PG Regiment contained only one armoured infantry battalion. The battalion had three companies each with 60 men. The regiment also contained an engineer and infantry company, which together formed the 1st Battalion. Each company had nine APCs, the remaining infantry were carried in trucks. The 113th PG Regiment (Col. Bradel) contained 1st and 2nd PG Battalions. The 1st PG Battalion contained two SdKfz 250 and 39 SdKfz 251 APCs, with each company having 50 men. The 2nd PG Battalion also had 50 men per company but most were transported in trucks, the heavy weapons company contained 11 rocket launchers and anti-tank guns. The divisional 73rd SP Regiment contained 1st Company with 150mm Hummel's and 2nd Company with 105mm. Its Armoured Reconnaissance Battalion contained one armoured car company with four light and four heavy scout cars, plus 15 SdKfz 250 and 18 SdKfz 251. The 37th Panzerjäger Battalion contained two companies. 1st Company had seven Marders and two 75mm anti-tank guns, while 2nd Company contained five Marders and seven StuGs. For AA protection, the 299th AA Battery was equipped with 3 guns.

On October 1, the actual number of operational tanks the division possessed was 11 PzKpfw V, 8 PzKpfw IV, 1 StuG, 10 Marder and 59 APCs. It had seven operational anti-tank guns. The division also had the following: 679 MP40 SMGs and MP 44 assault rifles, 5929 rifles, 71 *Panzerfäuste*, 2,529 pistols.

At 0730 on October 3, the Russian and Romanian forces attacked east of Váradlesto and were opposed by the German 126th PG Regiment and the 3rd Company/128th PGR. These attacks were repulsed, with the Russians losing eight tanks. The 51st Panzer Pioneer Battalion and 9th Company/128th PGR successfully defended and held Nagyürögdöt. Arriving nearby was the Russian 33rd Corps. It was approaching from the western side of Nagyvarad. German and Hungarian forces met the Russians at Váradcsehito, a small village, which saw bitter fighting, changing ownership three times.

The Russian 6th Guards Tank Army and its 166 tanks tossed 30–40 of them against the left flank being held by the Hungarian 4th Reserve Division. As expected, the Hungarian lines broke and the Russian tanks moved towards the northwest and Nagyvarad. The German 23rd Panzer, now with 16 operational tanks, counterattacked and ambushed the Russians southwest along the railroad. Both side's armour blasted one another, the Germans faced twice their number, managing to destroy five tanks without any loss. Meanwhile, 4th Company of the 23rd Panzer Regiment seized another village called Pankotapusztá.

The 23rd Panzer Regiment had been very successful, destroying 19 T–34, three IS–2 tanks and six anti-tank guns. According to some divisional histories, the tally came to 16 T–34/76 and five T–34/85 tanks. Regardless, the weak German Panzer division had caused significant damage. Its 3rd Company/23rd Panzer Regiment had only one tank and one anti-tank gun remaining! The Hungarian 7th Corps had also come under attack from 23 Russian tanks.

Between September 30th and October 3rd the Russian 6th Guards Tank Army had suffered the following losses: 43 tanks, 34 anti-tank guns, 23 rockets, 66 LMG, eight MG, 20 SMG, 340 POWs, 745 KIA, seven Trucks, and 41 rifles.

Thus, the Russian attempt to seize Nagyvarad had been a failure, and a costly one. It was now decided to implement Operation Debrecen. The Russian 33rd Corps deployed south of Nagyvarad. It was hoped that when the attack began the Russian units would advance along the Zsadány-Komádi—Körösszakált axis and that Berettyóújfalu could be easily taken by around the 10th, and the advance would continue towards Biharpüspöki before focusing on Csatár. Later, the area in the Nagyváradot region would also be seized.

As the Russians prepared for Operation Debrecen, the Luftwaffe continued to fly and it was during this time it destroyed another 15 AFVs. But, despite the losses, these were replaced and by the time the operation would begin, the 6th Guards Tank Army would have 130 tanks and SPs to toss against the Axis forces in and around Nagyvarad!

On the 3rd, the Hungarian 3rd Battalion/48th Regiment near Váradszollósrol was ordered to strike towards Csere, as was the 2nd Battalion/36th Regiment, which was near Oláhapátitól. In addition, the 2nd Motorized Infantry Battalion was ordered to move from Váradszentmárton to Váradcsehi. Other units were also involved in an effort to extradite isolate Hungarian units. By 1700, those units had reached safety through a 1000m wide gap in the front lines.

Ironically, the German 6th Army, like their counterparts, were also preparing their own offensive called, 'Zigeunerbaron' ['Gypsy Baron'], whose objectives were to the south of Arad and near Lippa. Basically, the avenues of this planned advance were Zsadány-Gyula-Zimánd-Arad-Temesvár and from Nagyvárad-Nagyszalonta-Zerénd-Nadab-Zarand-Lippa. However, the Germans had only a few weak corps, so the plan was week. Fretter-Pico, the 6th Army commander, was quite leery of what the Russians would do next and had planned for two possible avenues they might attack towards. He positioned the 23rd Panzer Division near Nagyvarad and the Hungarian 4th Reserve Division defended along the Sebes-Koros River.

On October 4th, the Russians conducted another raid, piercing the Hungarian lines held by the 3rd Battalion/48th Regiment and the 2nd Battalion/36th Regiment, which routed. Coming to the rescue was the 2nd Battalion/128th PG Regiment, which mixed with the 30–40 Russian vehicles, attempting to seal the breaches. Other German alarm units were also called in from the nearby areas. The Hungarian 2nd Motorized Battalion joined but only under pressure from the divisional commander. In the afternoon, the Russians penetrated Püspökfürdore. Having no additional reserves in this area, the commander of the 128th PG Regiment ordered the Hungarian 53rd Battalion to counterattack with a bicycle company near Kethelyi. During the day, two battalions from the German 178th Regiment (76th Division) arrived southeast of Nagyvarad and prepared their defences. The Hungarian 8th Regiment (4th Reserve Division) fought well but was forced to give up Nagyszalont. The Hungarian 1st Armoured Division provide some support in a weak counterattack to retake the town at 1600 hrs. Russian units also approached and were repulsed near Cséffától by the Hungarian 4th Reserve and elements of the 23th Panzer Divisions.

Meanwhile, despite the Russian incursions, the Germans finalized their own operation with Army and Luftwaffe units. The plan was to have Group A (consisting of the 3rd Panzer Corps with the 24th Panzer Division and Feldherrnhalle Panzergrenadier Division) to advance along the following route: Vészto-Okány-Sebes Körös-Sarkad-Gyula-Arad.

Group B (1st and 13th Panzer Divisions) would advance along Zsadány-Atyás-Körösnagyharsány – Nagyszalonta-Kisjeno-Csigérszollos-Lippa, as well as a bridgehead over the Maros river.

The German 72nd Corps was Group C (23rd Panzer Division, 76th Infantry, 4th Reserve Hungarian Divisions) would advance along: Oláhszentmiklós-Cséffa through Nagyszalontán. The 76th Division towards the Fekete-Körös, the 23rd Panzer would follow.

The Hungarian 3rd Army had two groups. Group E (1st Cavalry Division, *Kampfrguppe* Ameiser would strike east, Group D (4th SS Panzer Grenadier Division, 1st Hungarian Armoured Division, 23rd Reserve Hungarian, 20th Reserve Hungarian Divisions) would strike for Arad and occupy it.

The grandiose plan was really just that. The condition of the units was such that any hope of real success was a dream. Group A units were not even close by, and the strength of all the other units was just too weak.

On the 5th, the Russians continued their attacks in and around Nagyvarad. They broke through the right flank of the Hungarian 7th Corps near Nagyszalont, with over 20 tanks breaching the 4th Hungarian Reserve Division defences near Cséffától, and advanced towards Geszt. Another 15 Russian tanks also had arrived in the area and Atyas was taken. Because of these breaches, the Germans committed the 325th StuG Brigade and supporting AA units. This unit contained 19 new StuG III assault guns and their appearance was well received by the Hungarian soldiers, which seemed to stiffen their own resolve. Overhead, the Luftwaffe flew over 90 missions in tank-busting roles and destroyed six Russian tanks in the Cséffá area.

The Feldherrnhalle Panzer Grenadier Division (FHH) was a veteran unit from the East Front and had barely escaped the destruction of Army Group Centre. On October 4, the unit was at Miskolc-Mezokovesed area. Being the 'freshest' of the divisions arriving in Hungary, it contained 6,420 men. Its Panzer regiment had two battalions, plus a Panzer Grenadier Regiment, a Panzer Reconnaissance Battalion (one company of Panzergrenadiers, one armoured car company), an Artillery regiment (one SP artillery battalion with Hummel and Wespe, one heavy artillery battalion, one medium artillery battalion) and one weak AA unit. The unit had the following armaments:

9 SdKfz 250, three 150mm Hummel guns, one 100mm and one 105mm Wespe, six 150mm infantry support guns, 13 75mm anti-tank guns, 31 StuG III assault guns with L/48 barrels.

While the officers were veterans, many of the troops were not. Its logistical support contained numerous Russian POWs. Also in Hungary were two Panzer brigades, the 109th and 110th. The 110th was organized in August near Budapest. At that time, it consisted of:

2110th Tank Battalion of three companies, each with 11 tanks, an AA and supply company. The 2110th Panzer Grenadier Battalion contained five companies of armoured infantry and one heavy weapons company; altogether the unit had 85 APCs. The 2110th Armoured Pioneer Company contained 35 APCs.

The 109th Panzer Brigade was organized in July and led by Lt. Col Wolff. In September, its composition was identical to the 110th Brigade. Each brigade contained one Panzer battalion consisting of three companies, each with 11 PzKpfw V and one company with 11 Pz IV L/70 (the latter were never delivered), a company of four Flakpanzer 37mm IV and one Panzer Grenadier battalion with five companies. Each brigade had 65 officers, 568 NCOs, 1,449 soldiers and 78 Hiwis (Soviet auxiliaries) for a total of 2,089 men. Additional armaments included, per brigade: 157

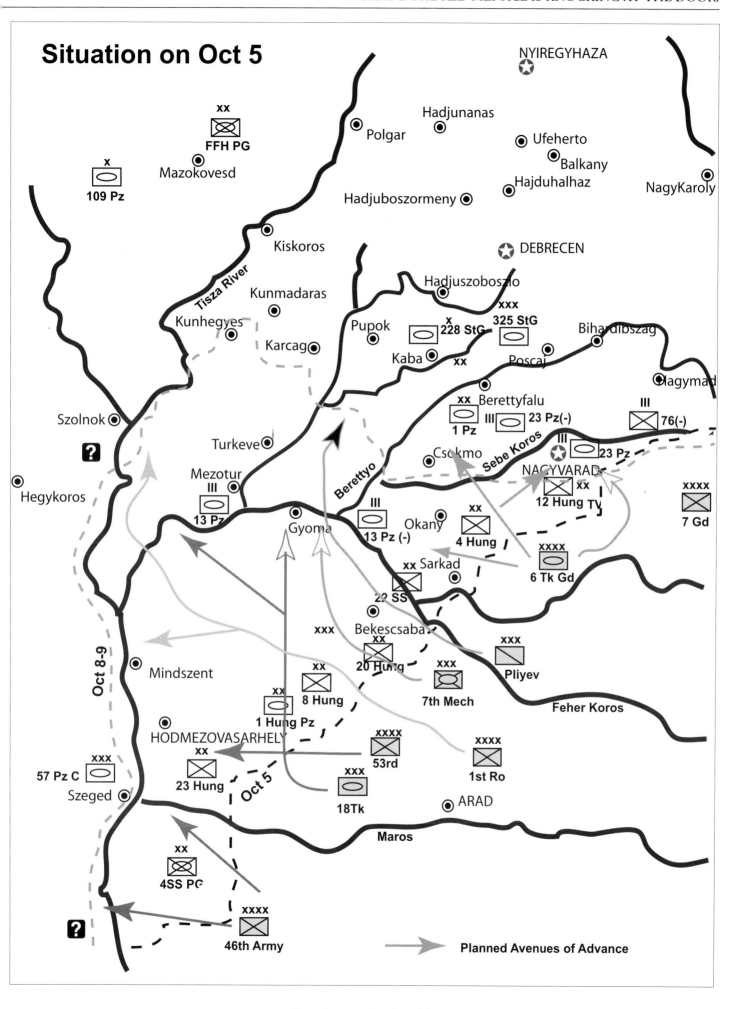

Situation on October 5th

SdKfz 251 APCs, 1,042 rifles, 593 pistols, 342 MP 38/40 SMGs, 112 MP 44s, 236 MG 34, 42 LMG, four 8mm and 12mm rocket launchers, 10 75mm AT guns, 47 Kwk42 L/70 guns in armoured carriers, 45 HMG.

Because of the political unrest within the Hungarian government in September, the brigades were stationed near Budapest. Some 25 PzKpfw V tanks also had arrived in the second week of September in addition to 135 more APCs. All would arrive by the end of October.

The 13th Panzer Division was really a battle group and on September 22nd comprised 127 officers, 1385 NCOs, 4,606 soldiers and 396 Hiwis, for a grand total of 6,524 men. It had only 11 operational PzKpfw IV tanks and two PzKpfw III. It also had nine StuG assault guns. Its Panzer Reconnaissance Battalion contained five heavy armoured cars and only eight 75mm AT guns. For artillery, the 'division' had three 105mm guns, two Wespe and one Hummel SP guns.

Thus, the 109th Panzer Brigade and the new FHH PG Division created a new combat group.

Unlike the 109th Panzer Brigade, which acted as an independent unit, the 110th Panzer Brigade units were used in part to strengthen the 13th Panzer Division. Any units left over would remain as the 110th Panzer Brigade. The brigade's 36 PzKpfw V tanks were used to reorganized the 2nd and 3rd Panzer Battalions of the 4th Panzer Regiment/13th Panzer Division. The 66th PG Regiment was also replenished by the 2110th PG Battalion.

Between October 3rd and 5th, the main attacks conducted by Russian forces rested with the 6th Guards Tank Army attempting to break through German positions at Nagyvarad. The battle revealed how a much weaker force can take on and defeat a much larger force through tactical use of terrain and men. Terrain played a major role here and allowed the German forces to defeat a force much stronger opponent.

On the eve of this great armour battle, which has been overlooked in military history, the 2nd Ukrainian Front prepared for its assault. It had recently acquired the 46th Army and the 7th Breakthrough Artillery Division. The 5th Air Army was reinforced with another air division. Some 500 tanks had been made available to bring all tank units up to full strength. In total, the Front had 698,200 Russian soldiers, 153,572 Romanians for a grand total of 851,772 men. Within it, there were three tank corps, two mechanized corps, one independent tank brigade, nine cavalry divisions, 40 Russian infantry divisions and 17 Romanian divisions (most divisions began with 6–7,500 men). Total gun strength came to 10,238 tubes (with the bulk being 75mm). In AFVs, the Russians had 602 tanks and 223 SP/Assault Guns for a total of 825 AFVs. The 5th Air Army had 1,216 aircraft. It also had the 1st Romanian Air Corps (18 Bf 109G, 35 Ju 87, 15 Hs 129, 8 He 111, 15 Ju 88, 30 misc.) The bulk of the 5th Air Army contained the new Yak–9 in its fighter corps.

Opposing this were the German 6th and 8th Armies, Hungarian 2nd and 3rd Armies. Some estimates state the total for all came to 430,000 men, of which 260,000 were German. These figures are deceptive since they include all men, whether they were rear area troops or front line troops.

The actual number of combat troops the Axis had was between 45,000 to 70,186 men. On October 2nd, Friessner noted he had around 30,000 actual combatants.

On paper, the Germans fielded 10 German divisions and three Panzer divisions, two Panzer brigades and 14 Hungarian divisions. In all, 27 weak divisions. The 24th Panzer Division would not arrive until October 9. The only full-strength unit was the 503rd Tiger Tank Battalion, which was in Budapest, hundreds of kilometres away. Russian intelligence estimated that the strength of the German divisions ranged from 4,000–6,000 men, while Hungarian units were between 3,500–5,500 total men. This was fairly accurate.

Both the Germans and the Russian knew where their own 'Achilles' heel lay, being with their allies. Thus, the centre of gravity for the upcoming Russian operations fell upon the Hungarian Army, which held a 220 km line from Nagyszalonta to Nagykikindaig. Holding this area were six depleted Hungarian divisions, one Hungarian Cavalry Regiment, a SS battle group from the 22nd SS Cavalry Division, and the 4th SS PG Division. Each division was required to defend a 25 km line. For armour, the army had only 20–25 operational tanks. The Hungarian 1st Armoured Division was held in reserve at Orosháza-Tótkomlós. As expected, there were numerous gaps not defended.

According some sources, the Germans had 400–450 AFVs, tanks and assault guns/SP Artillery. But numbers are deceptive. Reality skews everything, and does so here. For instance, the 1st Hungarian Armoured Division had only six tanks and seven StuG III that were operational. The Hungarian 2nd Armoured Division (2nd Hungarian Army) was much stronger with 64 Turan and Toldi tanks, 17 PzKpfw IV, four PzKpfw V, three loaned Tiger II, 15 other AFVs, and four Zrinyi assault guns.

Still, even these numbers of the Hungarian 2nd Armour Division are deceptive, for the 64 Hungarian AFVs were really not much of a match for Russian tanks. Regardless, the Hungarian AFV strength was estimated as around 120.

For artillery, the Axis had a total around 300 guns. In the air, the 4th *Luftflotte* contained the 1st Corps and the Hungarian 102nd. The German airforce contained 73–79 Bf 109, 31 Bf 109 nightfighters, 146 FW 190 fighters, 28

Ju 87 D5 dive-bombers, 17 HS 129, 58 Ju 52 transports, 6 Ju 188, 74 H–16/H–20 biplanes. The Luftwaffe also deployed the dual use 88mm AA gun. It possessed 52 of them, plus 10 37mm, and 23 20mm.

The Hungarian 102 unit contained 27 Me 210, 24 Bf 109, 7 Ju 88, 4 FW 189.

Finally, on the eve of Operation Debrecen, the ratio of forces between each side was as follows (all in favour of the Russian):

Infantry: 2 to 1
Armour: 1.5 to 1
Aircraft: 1.6 to 1
Guns and Mortars: 3 to 1

When the numbers are factored into ratios what is quite apparent is that the odds ratios do not favor the Russian. The ratios are to low for a guaranteed victory and history shows this. The odds were not overwhelming. When one takes into account the numerous intangible factors, such as, training, morale, tactical skill and improvisation on the battlefield and communications, these odds were too low when fighting the German soldier.

This battle and the many before showed how ten German tanks in the right hands could easily take on and demolish a Russian tank brigade three times its size. The Russians were keenly aware of this and were daring only until they ran into such a German unit. Once this happened, the Russian entered into a sort of twilight zone—a zone where every soldier and leader was cautious. While in this zone, the Germans routinely acted quickly and decisively much like a Cobra snake. When the Cobra struck, regardless of actual damage, the cautious zone deepened and a sort of paralysis set in.

Debrecen was going to be such a battle. The Russians would hit the weak links, the Hungarians, then had to slug it out with the small yet deadly German battle groups defending the key bridges. The terrain was the great equalizer and favoured an already deadly adversary. The numerous canals and rivers would force the battle into avenues of attack or advance. Despite the numerous breakthroughs made by the Russians, their follow-up was made slow by weather and terrain. Many times, a small German group with a few AT guns or tanks in a key location stopped a Russian division or larger.

However, numbers would eventually prevail. This was the great 'ace card' the Russians had. One the Germans could not win. German losses would remain lost, while Russian losses would be regained within a week. This month-long battle ground down the German units, already in a weakened state, into threadbare units. That was the name of this game: numbers.

PART II

Operation Debrecen Begins

The 2nd Ukrainian Front Breakthrough (October 6–8)

October 6th began like many mornings this time of year. There was the usual morning mist rising from the ground creating a fog. This would diminish early on. During the previous night the Hungarian 3rd Army had repulsed numerous small Russian reconnaissance attacks all across its front lines. The Hungarian 8th Corps at Mezokovac and Kunagotanal seemed to bear the brunt of most of these attacks. Everyone was waiting. Something was in the air.

At 0430, it began. Thunderous, massive Russian artillery fire saturated the area. Russian units crashed through Ketegyhaza and Gyula supported by tanks. At Gyula, *Kampfgruppe* Ameiser from the 22nd SS Cavalry Division repulsed many of the initial attacks. However, Russian infantry and armour quickly burst through the thinly defended lines in a western direction near Nagyszalonta. Close by at Biharugrara, the German 6th Army's right flank was pierced by the Russians.

First to attack was the 4th Guards Cavalry Corps of Pliyev's massive cavalry-armour group comprising the 4th and 6th Guards Cavalry Corps, and 7th Mechanized Corps. The 7th Mechanized Corps and the 4th Guards Cavalry Corps struck towards the Vasar area. These forces sliced through the Axis front lines from Lökösháza – Breda-Elek- Kétegyhaza – Békéscsaba- Mezoberény, Körösladány advancing towards Püspökladány. The 6th Guards Cavalry Corps moved as quickly towards Siklo-Simand-Gyulavári-Doboz-Veszto-Darvas and Foldes. The Russian 53rd Army attacked around 0500, as did the 18th Tank Corps, which had been subordinated to it. These forces advanced towards Orosháza, as one tank brigade and motorized infantry units struck further south from Kunágota—Magyarbánhegy. A category five hurricane was blowing towards the Hungarian front lines!

By 0600 Russian units had hacked through many of the Hungarian positions stretching from Arad-Békéscsaba. The 20th Hungarian Division offered little effective resistance and soon a 40 km gap opened up. The Russian offensive continued to rapidly develop in the area Békéscsaba-Bekes. The 8th Hungarian Division, defending a 20 km front, followed suit, the 23rd Hungarian Division, covering a front of 20 km failed as well. Everything fell before the Red tsunami.

Lt. Gen Heszlenyi, commander of the Hungarian 3rd Army, issued orders to fall back at 0700, but already Russian spearheads had encircled some Hungarian units. The Hungarian 23rd Division, 1st Hungarian Armoured Division defended and counterattacked Red forces in the Szolnok area, but the soon sought refuge on the other side of the wide Tisza River.

The communications between the Germans and Hungarians had been totally ripped apart. The German 57th and 3rd Panzer Corps did not learn of the Hungarian retreat until noon! The 8th Hungarian Division in the Orosházá area dispersed into many splinter groups as it fell back to the city; by noon, the Russian 18th Tank Corps had arrived. The Division was surrounded by 2200. The bulk of the Russian divisions continued toward Orosházá while Hungarian units sporadically attacked any gaps. Some of the gaps were sealed by scattered and brave Hungarian forces, but this did not last long.

Russian armour and mechanized infantry with cavalry fell upon numerous Hungarian groups and quickly devoured them. By the afternoon, one tank brigade (30–40 tanks) had already reached and taken Orosházát. The 7th Mechanized Corps had reached Kondoros by Noon, turning northwards. The German 57th Panzer Corps barely escaped. By 1700, the Russian advance had slowed and the Hungarian 3rd Army was able to gather whatever remnants and form a weak defensive line along the Sebes-Koros River.

The 9th Guards Cavalry Division (4th Guards Cavalry Corps) with tanks attacked in the Gyula area against modest resistance that gradually collapsed. By 0900, it had seized Békéscsaba. The 30th Cavalry Division took Újkígyós. The 10th Guards Cavalry Division had yet to enter the battle!

The 8th Guards Cavalry Division (6th Guards Cavalry Corps) penetrated and took Gyula. On the Hungarian 3rd Army's left flank *Kampfgruppe* Ameiser fiercely fought the Red tide and their armour near Sarkadkeresztúr. The lead elements of the 8th Guards Cavalry Division with their 136th Tank Brigade met token resistance. German SS

Hungarian soldiers perch atop a Turan medium tank towing a field car, autumn 1944. (Bundesarchiv 101I–244–2306–16)

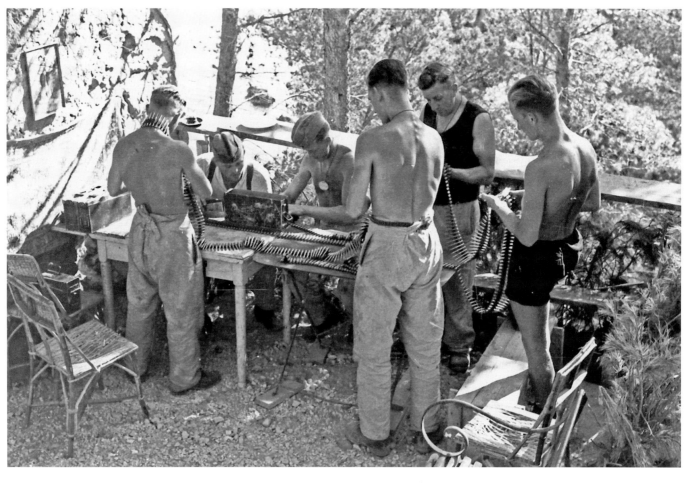

German soldiers loading ammunition belts, autumn 1944. (Bundesarchiv 101I–681–0001–04)

Members of the Hungarian 1st Cavalry Division captured by the Romanian army, Békés, Hungary, October 1944. (Dénes Bernád via Kamen Nevenkin)

Romanian mountain troops move towards the front, Transylvania, autumn 1944. (Photo archive of the Bulgarian Ministry of Defence)

Romanian and Soviet officers confer, Transylvania, autumn 1944. (Photo archive of the Bulgarian Ministry of Defence)

Romanian troops moving along roads in North Transylvania, Hungary, autumn 1944. (RGAKFD Moscow)

Hungarian Toldi I light tanks pass through the streets of a town. (The Tank Museum)

A Hungarian and a German officer examine a Hungarian Turan medium tank. (The Tank Museum)

Members of a Waffen SS Cavalry Division artillery crew, Hungary, October 1944. (Ullstein Bilderdienst)

The Hungarian-produced 44M Zrinyi I assault gun. This version was equipped with a long 75 mm gun, of which only prototypes were produced. The standard version was armed with a 105mm howitzer. (Dénes Bernád)

A destroyed Soviet SU–76M self-propelled gun, autumn 1944. (Dénes Bernád)

troops hung onto their defensive positions along the Sebes-Koros River, but breaches did occur. Despite the Pliyev Group's composition of three Corps-sized units with over 100 tanks, the group had only managed to advance up to 25 km.

On the 3rd Hungarian Army's right flank was the German 4th SS Panzer Grenadier Division in the Nagykikinda district. The line held became unsupportable and the unit was forced to fall back with the Russians on their heels near Zenta-Valcani. The SS fought a tenacious regard action. The Russian 7th Mechanized Corps at Kunágota and Nagykamarás continued to breach the Hungarian defences south of the Oroshaza-Békéscsaba railway line. Its 63rd Mechanized Brigade made rapid advances covering 70 km by 1530! It had made deep penetrations and had reached Endrod.

The German 57th Panzer Corps in the Condors area temporarily halted the Russian advance with the German 1/25 composite anti-aircraft unit comprising five 88mm guns, the Hungarian 11/206 and 9/202, each with four 4 cm guns. The German 3/10 (130 men) at Goya repulsed many attacks. This *ad-hoc* force had the task of holding the Harmas-Koros Bridge and Gyoma, Körösladány.

The T–34/85s rolled on. Cavalry dismounted and fought as infantry reaching west of Gyoma by 1600. The Germans, with their three 88mm guns and six 2 cm guns of 3rd Company/25 destroyed three tanks, but the Russian tsunami was barely affected. German troops armed with *Panzerfäuste* managed to halt the Russian advance, making the Russian advance appear unorganized. POWs were forced to fight against the Red advance near Endrod.

This operation was a minor success, as the Germans were able to reach the middle of the city and forced the Russian tanks to retreat behind infantry lines. Many small isolated Russian pockets were destroyed due to their disorderly advance. Several more Russian tanks were also lost. German StuG assault guns did take a small toll, enough to 'pause' the advance in this area.

At 2030, the Germans conducted a counter-attack with two divisions consisting of a variety of units to retake Endrőd. One division struck and encircled from the west, forcing its way into the southeast sector of the city, the other division ran into a well-defended line; retaking the bridge was deemed impossible by 2300. Both divisions had returned to their starting positions by 0700 the next morning.

The 1st Hungarian Armoured Division also conducted a counterattack using 3rd Company/7th Assault Gun Battalion with four assault guns. As small as it seems, it demonstrates the fluidity of the battle area. The advance with a mechanized infantry unit made good progress until 1400. The attack, made in a northeasterly direction towards Oroshaza and Békéscsaba ended when three of the four StuG IIIs were destroyed. The Hungarian force then became dispersed as the Russians simply overwhelmed them.

The Russian offensive towards Kaszaperpuszta continued and by 1445 this was taken. The Hungarian 1st Armoured Division in the area provided token resistance and was to the Russians, a tempting bait to take. During the night, the Russians continued their advance, encircling some of the division in face of the Hungarian rearguard actions. Luckily, muddy conditions did slow the Russian advance from Hódmezovásárhely to Orosháza. However, the 1st Hungarian Armoured Division retreated in some disorder, many pockets were encircled and its main divisional group (including the HQ) was not aware of what was happening until it was almost too late.

On the western flank of the German 6th Army there was battle activity and chaos. The Russian offensive rolled onto the Hungarian 4th Reserve Division, which held a line behind the Sebes-Koros River. It also embroiled the German 1st Panzer Division, in part, the 2nd Battalion/113th Panzer Grenadier (PG) Regiment led by Captain Stengl. This retook a small bridgehead across the river near Újiráz. However, the Russians also secured their own bridgehead across the Sebe-Koros River at Komadi.

The commander of the 1st Panzer Division issued orders for the 2nd Battalion/1st Panzer Regiment and the 37th Panzerjäger Battalion to support the 2nd Battalion/113th Panzer Grenadier Regimen at the Sebes-Koros River. The 1st PG Regiment was at Csökmon, while the 113th PG Regiment remained near Újiráz to defend the bridgehead.

The 113th PG Regiment deployed overnight. It was hoped that the Germans would be able to breakthrough in their counterattack, with the goal being Szeghalom.

The 23rd Panzer Division battle group comprising Panthers from 2nd Battalion/23rd Panzer Regiment and the 2nd Battalion/23rd PG Regiment found itself on the fringes of the lines in the south-west. It attempted to make its way to Komadi, but Russian armour and mechanized infantry were encountered. The Germans battled their way through the Red morass losing only one PzKpfw V. The advance towards Komadi began at 1730. The march was finally completed at 0600 on the 7th. At Nagyvarad, the Hungarian 12th Reserve Division was embroiled in numerous battles. Its 2nd Battalion/38th Regiment broke and fled when the Russians attacked, creating a huge gap endangering the Hungarian 7th Corps HQ.

The Russian 6th Guards Tank Army's offensive had arrived on the Nagytoti plains area by 1800. This was an area perfect for tanks. However, few of its units had yet to cross the Sebes-Koros River, causing the attack to stall. Various German units began to gather. These were splinter groups trying to sort themselves out of the chaos – 1st Battalion/178th Regiment of the 76th Division, a battalion of Panzer Grenadiers from the 23rd Panzer Division, the 53rd Infantry Battalion and a tank hunter group (100 men) on bicycles armed with *Panzerfäuste* and heavy machine guns. These were in the area of Réthelyi.

The Hungarian front lines between Békéscsaba and Gyula were decimated, as was the Hungarian 1st Cavalry Division in that area. A few thousand cavalrymen sought the safety of the Tisza River, which was six kilometres away from Szentes. The unit held a line of 27 km and as the day went on, the important bridge over the Tisza became increasingly the objective of both sides. The 1st Battalion/2nd Regiment of the Hungarian division had secured a small bridgehead, which was being compressed by Russian attacks. The Hungarian division had been pushed around and scattered. Regaining divisional control proved impossible. Later, 2nd Battalion/2nd Regiment was able to assist those Hungarian units holding the battered bridgehead. Eventually, the 2nd Regiment of the Hungarian division fell back into safety. The German 13th Panzer division, meanwhile, had managed to regroup and the FHH Panzer Grenadier Division was alerted and to be ready to deploy southwards from the north towards Tiszafured.

In the air, the Russian 5th Air Army conducted 460 sorties, while Hungarian fighter-bombers flew 260 missions in groups of 8–10 aircraft upon ground troops. Most of these missions were directed at Gyula.

The Hungarian 3rd Army continued its own retreat, attempting to stay one step of the Russian tsunami; their losses had been extremely heavy as the retreat or rout moved towards Arad. Meanwhile, at 1055, the German High Commanders met and conferred, attempting to salvage what they could. Many connections with the German 6th Army had been severed by 1700, many of the Hungarian troops were ordered to become subordinate to German Army and Corps HQs.

For much of the day, the German High Command had been in the dark regarding the fast-moving Russian offensive. At 2230, additional information had arrived indicating the Russians were moving northwest from Gyula towards numerous key crossing points along the Tisza River. What was left of the Hungarian 3rd Army immediately came under the 6th Army command. The 3rd Panzer Corps, General Breith, grappled with the fluidity of the battle, attempting to keep his 1st, 13th and 23rd Panzer Divisions intact and from being swept away. Breith had hoped to attack the Russian eastern flank, through Békéscsabá towards the north-west to reach Fehér-Körösön.

The German 72nd Corps continued to resist stoutly near Nagyvarad, while the Hungarian 3rd Army attempted to prevent the Russians from breaking through the Szentes-Mezotúr line. The German 4th SS PG Division secured a bridgehead over the Tisza River. The Hungarian 1st Cavalry Division gathered at Kecskemét. The newly formed Fretter-Pico Group, containing the 228th StuG Brigade, at Debrecen, some 35 km away; *Kampfgruppe* Ameiser, and elements of the 76th Division (178th Regiment, 1st Battalion/76th Artillery Regiment, 176th Tank Hunter Battalion and the 3rd AA Battalion).

The second phase of the Russian offensive was also launched, this codenamed, 'Debrecen'. The Pliyev Group was ordered to seize the city. The Russian 53rd Army and the 18th Tank Corps had burst the German-Hungarian front wide open –over 40 km! The attack front alone was 100 km. During the first day, over 100 Hungarian villages and towns had been taken. There was a 150 km gap between the Hungarian 3rd Army and the German 6th Army. One of the main objectives for the Russians was Sznolnok on the Tisza River. The river was a major barrier and few good bridges existed across it. It was critical to both sides.

Saturday, the 7th, opened with bright sunshine and temperatures of about 60°F. Dry conditions would certainly help the Russians push forward their advance.

The 3rd Hungarian Army created a weak, improvised defensive line by 0700 from Mako- Földeák-Orosháza, which had absolutely no depth.

The 4th Guards Cavalry Corps reached the Sebes-Körö River by 0730. Some Russian units had also reached Körösladány. The 113th PG Regiment from the 1st Panzer Division attacked south from the bridgehead, just as the Russians began breaching other parts of the line elsewhere. Russian tanks seized Sarkadkeresztúr, and Vészto.

By midday, the Hungarian 3rd Army and the German 4th SS PG Division had withdrawn to the Csóka-Valcani—Nagyszent Miklós -Maros western line. But the Russians failed at taking Nagycsanád, which was held by the 4th SS PG Division. Further north, the 23rd Hungarian Division fell back to Hódmezovásárhely, Algyonél and Tápénéi. The 1st Hungarian Armoured Division withdrew to Mindszentig and created a bridgehead. The 8th Reserve Hungarian Division supplemented forces (2nd Regiment/1st Hungarian Cavalry Division) already at the Szentes and Csongrádi bridgehead. The German 13th Panzer Division continued to hold Mezotur. Neither the Hungarian 8th or 23rd Divisions offered much resistance.

In the afternoon the Russian 18th Tank Corps launched new attacks directed at Kurcza in the northwest. Its objective was the railway bridge spanning it. The Hungarian cavalry retreated from the Szentes bridgehead at 1600. The 1st Hungarian Armoured Division and 8th Hungarian Division counterattacked, since the bridgehead become endangered. 8th Hungarian Corps ordered troops from the 1st Hungarian Cavalry to reinforce. A motorized regiment of the 1st Hungarian Armoured Division remained in Szentes. However, later that night, these same units were ordered to withdraw to safer areas, which they did.

Of greater importance was the Szolnok Tisza-bridgehead. During the night the Germans sent the 66th PG regiment (13th Panzer Division) to ensure it remained under German control. The Regiment contained the 1st Battalion/66th PG Regiment (2,110 men), the 2nd Battalion/4th Panzer Regiment (14 Panther tanks), and elements of its artillery regiment. This group searched for a safe avenue starting at 1150, and by 1710, had yet to find Mezotur (15 km away) and Kisújszállás, but did find small groups of Russians. Many of the Russian troops had still not yet crossed the Sebe-Koros River. Only at Szarvast had Russian cavalry crossed. The German 1st Battalion/25th AA Regiment retreated from Gyoma and much of the 13th Panzer Division had not been caught up in the heavy fighting—yet.

One of the Russian groups the Germans stumbled upon was the 1289th Self-Propelled Artillery Regiment (SU–85s), which was in the area. Four of the Panther tanks opened up in an exchange of fire. The Russians lost several vehicles before the rush of battle carried both groups towards their own planned objectives.

The Russian offensive had caused much chaos on both sides. Battle areas at times had opposing sides just missing contact with one another. The Russians pushed northwards in an attempt to seize the critical Tisza River crossings. The FHH PG Division had easily swept away the Russian units at Tizafured and now it was transferred into the Debrecen area. Thus, one of its battalion arrived, the remaining parts of the Division remained on the march further north. The Russians did control Szarvast and much of the Harma-Sebe-Koros River. Its 53rd Army on the right flank had advanced 55 km in two days and aimed for Mezotur.

At 0500, the Russian artillery opened fire, saturating the opposing forces. Russian armour from the 7th Mechanized Corps moved forward as artillery and rockets flew overhead. Their destination was the German-held Gyoma. A few companies of the German 25th AA Regiment defended the immediate area. More Russian tanks and infantry appeared at 0645. Besides Gyoma, the Russians desperately wanted the few bridges across the Koros-Sebes River. The 1st and 3rd AA companies opened up destroying three T–34s. However, a nearby railway station was seized by the Russians. The pressure in numbers forced some of the German forces to fall back into Gyoma. The Russian 7th Mechanized Corps rolled through, seizing Gyoma and threatened the bridge over the Koros. The Russians continued to build pressure on the German bridgehead now held by the 2nd, 4th and 5th companies from 25th AA Regiment, equipped with 37mm, 20mm AA, and one 88mm gun. The intense and rapid fire stalled the Russian advance for a while. By noon, several Russian tanks were in flames. It was the dreaded 88mm that had ravaged eight T–34s. This one gun was the obstacle to the Russian advance! This 'stall' lasted until 1630, when finally, the 88mm was destroyed and infantry threatened to surround the Germans. After its destruction, the Germans fell back across to the north bank of the Harma-Koros River towards Dévaványa.

This particular battle had involved a few German AA companies against elements of the 7th Mechanized Corps (some 50 tanks and 1,500 men battled for Gyoma) and rocket artillery. The Germans destroyed 12 T–34s and killed 500 men. The Germans lost 26 men killed, 56 wounded. The German AA companies still had a combined strength of eight 88mm, seven 37mm MG, 14 2omm MG, two HMG and 85 vehicles.

The 9th Guard Cavalry Division from 4th Guards Cavalry Corps managed to move through one of the many gaps between 0800–0900 near Füzes-Gyarmat. The town fell by 0900. The 13th Guards Cavalry Division from the 6th Guards Cavalry Corps and a tank brigade easily took Biharnagybajom. From there, smaller cavalry units galloped towards Csökmore where the Hungarian 1st Armoured Division rested, which they soon routed.

The Sebes-Koros River had impeded the advance of the Russian 7th Mechanized Corps, slowing down their race towards Dévaványá. The commanders then ordered the cavalry from the 4th Guards Cavalry Corps to cross the river and surround any resistance at Ujiráz. German resistance was not light wherever met. By 2200, the 7th Mechanized Corps had crossed and engulfed and then seized Dévaványá. Their next goal was now Karcag.

The 113th PG Regiment from the 1st Panzer Division launched their attack against the Russian cavalry spearheads heading northwards along their eastern flank. It was then to strike southwards towards Körösön aiming at further heavy concentrations of Russians.

Leading the way was the 2nd Company/1st Panzer Regiment with 17 PzKpfw V tanks. These gathered near Csökmon. The attack initially made good headway but by 1400, it was in danger of being encircled. The Panzers and their supporting infantry became separated and communications were bad. The Panther tanks themselves caused an impact that created more chaos and hesitancy for the Russian troops advancing. However, Russian anti-tank guns knocked out three of the Panther tanks. By 1700, the encircling danger had become more serious to the Germans and the unit's headquarters. They soon halted and dispersed to safer ground, retreating away from Csökmore. It was during this time that Lt. Col. Streith received a very serious wound and taken to a field hospital.

The German troops in the nearby area were quite weak, some 350 men, totally inadequate to hold their lines or attack the enemy. Their counterattack had not achieved much in the way of stemming the Red tide. However, later in the evening, the same force regrouped and attacked again. This time, the 1st Panzer Division punched through the Russian lines northwards towards Berettyófalu and Biharnagybajom.

At dawn, the Russian 6th Guards Cavalry Corps controlled the Újiráz area, but due to a combination of resistance and apprehension, their attack stalled. German artillery fire attempted to destroy the bridge in vain. The 8th Guards Cavalry Division supported by tanks, likewise, attempted to cross the Koros River, only to be met with fierce German resistance.

In a separate action, the 23rd Panzer Division's 128th PanzerGrenadier regiment attacked towards the southwest at 0730. Their objective was Komadi. By 0830 the attack had pierced the Russian lines and they have achieved their objective. Resistance was surprisingly light. The battle continued to rage, as both sides' armour appeared. The German 51st Panzer Pioneer Battalion and 128th StuG Battalion also arrived, however, they had little impact.

Between 0900–0930, the German Panzer Grenadiers attacked the bridge across the Sebe-Koros River in an effort to cross southwards near Zsadány to rescue elements of the 22nd SS Cavalry Division, who were struggling to move northwards to safety. The 1st Battalion/128th PG Regiment reached Elorenyomulás and moved southeastwards towards a Russian crossing and bridgehead on the north shore. Although supported by a few PzKpfw V tanks, Russian T–34s appeared, ending any further advance. The force withdrew. Later, at 1530, the same units with conducted an attack from Komadi and reached the river's northern bank. The units then turned eastward and reached the bridge. Russian tanks barred any further advance. The 3rd and 11th companies from 128th Panzer Grenadier Regiment pressed their attack, as the 1st Company/23rd Panzer Regiment, with assault guns, attacked on the left flank. The 51st Panzer Pioneer Battalion, and 3rd Company/23rd Panzer Regimet (PzKpfw Ivs) were not attached. The German 126th PG Regiment and the 4th Reserve Hungarian Division secured east of Körösszakál.

The battle around Komadi continued into the night in vain. The Germans reinforced north of the river with the 228th StuG Brigade. At 1150, the staff of the 3rd Panzer Corps met to discuss how to prevent the Russians from moving northwards from the Sebes-Körös. The German counterattack was a success near Békés. It was hoped that the Germans could delay the collapse of Szeghalm, since Russian cavalry were easily moving though numerous gaps between the 1st and 23rd Panzer Divisions. It was decided to turn both Panzer units in a westerly direction towards Karcag and Dévaványa to link with the 13th Panzer Division. It was hoped to cut through the Russian rear lines. The Russians and Germans were virtually in chaos, with armour from both sides seemingly everywhere. No one was quite sure where the other side was and in what strength. In Karcag, Püspökladány, Földes and Berettyóújfalu, the only German units present were elements of the 15th Anti-Aircraft Division armed with only a variety of AA weapons and machine guns. Arriving was the 662nd Tank Hunter Battalion with 88mm guns.

On the 8th, a beautiful, warm sunny, dry day, the 4SS PG Division and the Hungarian 1st Armoured Division near Szentes were directed towards Szarvas in their attacks. Further, it was determined to hold the Tiszafured bridgehead, requiring one battalion from the German FHH PG Division. The 1st Panzer Division pushed through in a northerly direction with a new attack, while the 13th Panzer Division also combined with it near Karcag.

The Russian 46th Army was at Óbecsénél, while the Hungarian 3rd Army by noon continued to fall back, giving up Kiszombor to the Russians without a fight. Russian tanks were observed near Szarvas. 1st Company/25th AA Regiment retreated from the Gyoma area after its losses continued to mount from Dévaványá (which was in Russian hands) to Mezotur. Later, the 3rd Panzer Corps' Panzer divisions fought near Bárándo. Losses were heavy, mainly due to Russian armour. From Darvastól, Russian reconnaissance units moved northwards over the Berettyo River, then eastwards. 23rd Panzer Division elements continued to hold the Komadi bridgehead. The Russian 46th Army was directed to cross the Óbecse and near Ada, Martonos and Magyarkanizsa regions. The German 4th SS PG Division retreated towards Szeged.

The Russian units continued to advance east of the town with smaller groups crossing the western bank of the river. By evening, they were south of Szeged. The Hungarian 23rd Reserve Division could do little to impede the Russian juggernaut and soon it had become nearly surrounded. As the Russians approached the Hungarian bridgehead at Szentes, opposition to the Russian advance stalled, while other Russian units did, in fact, cross the Tisza and created small bridgeheads on the western bank. The small Hungarian force holding this critical bridgehead was augmented with the arrival of the 1st, 5th and 6th Companies from the Hungarian 2nd Cavalry Regiment at 0530. Also nearby were the 3rd and 4th Battalions of the 1st Reserve Cavalry Regiment, and a Heavy Weapons Company at Apponyi. At 0600, the Hungarian 13th Assault Gun Battalion arrived with only 2 vehicles. Hungarian attempts to remove a Russian bridgehead across the Tisza failed.

At 0800, the 3rd Company/Hungarian 2nd Cavalry Regiment ran into a Russian tank group. The cavalry fell back but the Hungarian assault guns managed to destroy six T–34s with their 75mm guns. However, numbers prevailed and the Russian armour continued freely north across the Tisza River and cut off the Hungarian retreat route. The Hungarian 1st Motorized Regiment from the 1st Armoured Division, likewise, was unable to advance to the northwest due Russian troops. The Hungarian 2nd Cavalry Regiment and 1st Reserve Regiment continued their tenacious defence. Elements of the 1st Hungarian Armoured Division found itself on the eastern side of the Tisza trying to reach the west bank, while 1st Motorized Regiment, 1st, 5th, and 6th Companies from the 2nd Cavalry Regiment, and a Heavy Weapons company attacked Russian units that had been pressuring the Division. This attack, although weak, did succeed in allowing the Hungarian units to escape by 1100.

Meanwhile the Russian 18th Tank Corps began its own attack with the 181st Tank Brigade upon the rear support units of the Hungarian 1st Motorized Regiment (1st Armoured Division). By noon, its 1st Battalion had destroyed seven Hungarian tanks, nine artillery guns, 37 cars. The Hungarian troops near the bridge did fight with resoluteness despite heavy Russian artillery fire. Cavalry (2nd and 4th Companies from the 2nd Hungarian Cavalry Regiment) retreated past their weak armoured screen as Russian tanks blasted away. The cavalry safely reached the western side of the river near Szentes. The Russian lost four tanks to anti-tank fire.

Northwards the Russian offensive rolled, hemming in the Hungarian 3rd and 4th Battalions from the 1st Reserve Cavalry Regiment in parts of Szentes. Along the wide avenues, north and south, urban combat raged. At their rear were elements of the Russian 18th Tank Corps, namely the 1438th Self-Propelled Artillery Regiment with SU–85s, destroying six Hungarian tanks, seven artillery guns, and 30 vehicles. One T–34 was lost. Along the riverbank, 1st Company/2nd Hungarian Cavalry Regiment retreated out of the city near the river's bank and forced a Russian unit to retreat. This was only a brief success for the Hungarians, arriving were 34 T–34 tanks along the river's banks. The Hungarians fired their *Panzerfäuste*, but caused little damage. Riding on the tanks were Russian infantry that quickly descended from the tanks and engaged the Hungarians.

3rd Company/7th Hungarian Assault Gun Battalion (4 StuG III) also participated in the defence of the Szentes bridgehead from the other side of the Tisza. The unit contained about 250 men and 15 officers and supported the 8th Hungarian Corps troops in also defending Csongrád. The 7th Assault Gun Battalion was one of the better Hungarian units serving in the operations since September 24. As a whole, the 7th Assault Gun had disabled or destroyed 67 Russian tanks and 14 other vehicles. Its own losses came to 10 disabled StuG III's and 30 vehicles. It had 12 operational StuGs. The unit had lost 140 men. Other Hungarian units were quite the opposite – many were panicky as they attempted to flee across the Tisza at various crossing points.

1st, 5th and 6th Companies from the 2nd Hungarian Cavalry Regiment fought off the Russians, who were attempting to seize another bridgehead; this bought time for the others to cross in strength until the Russian tanks appeared. Hungarian soldiers fired their *Panzerfäuste* from 20m away, two T–34's were destroyed. However, the 2nd and 4th Companies were ripped apart by the Russian armoured battalions.

This Regiment bore the brunt of more than 70 Russian tanks and battled for possession of towns and cities as it fell back towards the safety of the Tisza. But like most of the Hungarian units, the unit had been ravaged by the Russian offensive and eventually fell back to Szent-Miklos, which was deserted. There the remnants regrouped.

Located on the west side of the Tisza at Csongrád was the 1st Hungarian Armoured Division. The bridgehead there continued to be held by the 200 men from the 2nd Cavalry Regiment. This was evacuated and the bridge was blown later in the night. However, left on the east bank of the Tisza remained (in error) the 6th Company! It was struggling to get across, and any discipline gave way to chaos and panic. The Russian 228th Division remained in hot pursuit and was able to establish eight small (2km wide x 1 km deep) bridgeheads across the west bank of the Tisza near Csongrád. There was little to oppose them.

The Hungarian 1st Cavalry Division remnants stood at Kunszentmárton. The numerous small Russian bridgeheads further reduced the Hungarian morale inside the Szentes bridgehead because now the Russians threatened their own rear! Halting the Red tide seemed to be an impossible task.

Meanwhile, the Germans themselves were attempting to grasp control of the situation. As the Russians approached Tiszafüred along the Tisza, an Alarm unit (4th Company/21st Battalion) comprising 400 men waited. Their weapons included one 88mm, five 37mm, three 20mm AA guns and seven HMG. Also present was a ragged and worn Hungarian battalion poorly armed with captured weapons. It was of dubious value. The Germans had created adequate anti-tank defences and the Russian approach was rebuffed. This bridge was not seized. Outside the city, along the west bank, were another two 88mm guns and a labour unit of some 1,500 men, all lightly armed (200 were German). The bridge itself had been damaged by air attacks and it had not yet been decided whether to blow it up.

The German 741st Alarm Battalion with 800 men defended the Szolnok bridgehead. This was a polyglot unit with a variety of troops. Their weapons included 13 MG, 17 HMG, one 88mm, eight 1.5cm Drilling flak guns and the 147th AA unit. The bridgehead also contained some 500 Hungarian soldiers armed with rifles and machine guns.

At Csongrád, the bridge was defended by 1,000 men, which included the 201st Hungarian Defence Battalion, and the 1st Independent artillery unit with two 105mm and two 88mm guns. Also present were 16 88mm guns from the 844th German AA Regiment. The 203rd AA Battalion defended Dánielfy Tibor. The Hungarian 8th Corps units continued to fight 12km west of there.

During the day, the Russian 53rd Army had advanced up to 25 km, its 27th Corps by 1800 was at Tiszaföldvár—Kunszentmárton and a regiment was heading for the Sznolok area.

The shattered 20th Hungarian Division had been reduced to a shell of its former shelf (only a few battalions remained) as it fled towards Tiszaföldvár. Many of its small rearguards attempted to shield the remnants. The Russians T–34 tanks continued their rout.

In the morning The German 13th Panzer Division was in the Szent Miklós area and was assigned to the 3rd Panzer Corps. It was ordered to secure the Karcag area and clear the Russians there and remain southwest of Debrecen. The 1st Panzer Division was ordered to remain the Püspökladány area. It was hoped that both divisions would somehow link up. As the 13th Panzer proceeded, it was in danger of being surrounded, so it was ordered to halt at Kunhegyes.

The German 1st Battalion/66th Panzer Grenadier Regiment, together with a company of PzKpfw V tanks proceeded to move east towards Karcag. However, it was not very long until these units ran into the Russian 7th Mechanized Corps in the environs of Kisujszallas. Some 30 Russian tanks to be exact. Both sides fought desperately to hold the area. The German PzKpfw V company had six tanks remaining. Nearly undisturbed, in the late afternoon the Russians invaded the Karcag area supported by infantry only to meet elements of the 13th Panzer Division, whose infantry dismounted from their tanks. The Russians destroyed one group with its 78th Guards IS–2 Regiment, whose heavy armour made them unstoppable.

The Russian IS–2 tanks could not be penetrated by direct fire from the German PzKpfw V Panther tanks, at least not from the front. Nevertheless, the Germans remained stoutly holding the area with the 66th PG Regiment and halted the Russian advance towards the northwest. However, again, there were just too many gaps and the Russians continued pushing through gaps further to the south. By nightfall, the German PzKpfw V company had only four operational tanks! The Germans eventually had to fall back in the Kenderes area as the Russian advances cut more and more of their retreat routes. This was especially so after Kenderes was seized. Hampering the Germans were their own communications, which were failing at a critical time. The commander of the 13th Panzer Division could no longer communicate by radio to his subordinates and was forced to use messengers on motorcycles to issue commands. Of course, the Russians, too, were in the dark about the German movements and mistakenly allowed the 13th Panzer Division to regroup in the Kunhegyes-Kunmadares area, when they could have continued decimating it. This regrouped 13th Panzer Division was to connect with the 1st Panzer Division further east in a counter-attack.

By early morning, the Russian 4th Guards Cavalry Corps continued its own blitzkrieg, and easily took Biharnagybajom and Sárrétudvari using the 152nd Guards Anti-tank Regiment, which destroyed two 88mm guns. The Corps tanks had reached Püspökladán. This area was held by German Alarm units armed with only anti-aircraft guns. The Russian 66th Rocket Regiment also had arrived but before they could fire their weapons, the German Alarm unit counter-attacked, disrupting the Russian fire. From the air, German Fw 190 aircraft squadrons disrupted and scattered the 10th Guards Cavalry Division. This unit suffered heavily. The divisional commander himself was killed. Russian fighters then appeared and an aerial battle ensued. Protecting the Fw 190s were Bf 109s, which now intercepted the Russian aircraft.

Seizing Püspökladány were the 9th and 30th Cavalry Divisions from the 4th Guards Cavalry Corps. Numerous street battles reduced the small city to rubble. However, it was the reorganized 10th Cavalry Division that sealed its fate by arriving at 1300 and encircling it, trapping the remaining German troops. Russian tanks arrived by nightfall.

Meanwhile, the 1st Panzer Divisional group, Huppert, comprising the 1st PG Regiment, 37th Panzer Pioneer Battalion, 1st Panzer Regiment and an artillery battery, moved eastwards through Berettyóújfalun – Bihartordát at 0800. The Russian tanks and cavalry had already taken Nagyrábét, Bihar and Füzesgyarmat. Thus, the Huppert group moved northwards with their tanks.

The 37th Panzer Pioneer Battalion along with 1st Company/1st Panzer Regiment (12 PzKpfw V) led the way and in a short time became engaged with the 8th Cavalry Division from the 6th Guards Cavalry Corps and six T–34s from the west. By 1030, Nagyrábét was German again. But the commander of the 1st Panzer Division was not aware of this and the balance of the division remained at Berettyóújfalu.

The 113th PG Regiment was ordered towards Bihar by the 1st Panzer Division's commander. It comprised the 1st Battalion/113 PG Regiment, which moved southwards, 10th Company/113 PG Regiment moved north and behind them 1st Company/73rd Panzer Artillery Regiment's self-propelled artillery with 150mm Hummels. None of the German units made much progress due to Russian anti-tank and rocket fire and clogged roads. The Russian rocket fire proved deadly, killing the commanders of both the 1st Battalion/113th Panzer Grenadier Regiment and 73rd Panzer Artillery. These losses furthered delayed the German movement, but by 1700, the 1st Battalion/113th PG Regiment was also approaching Nagyrábé from the west and southwest. The other battalions from the 113th PG Regiment deployed towards the north and threatened the Russian-held Biharnagybajom area. The German deployments had not been easy and due to the enemy and losses, it was decided to halt any further movement until night, specifically, at midnight under the cover of the moonlight. In this same area were 25 Russian tanks, which hopefully could be avoided.

The German reconnaissance unit found a railway at Derecské free of Russians and this was quickly taken by the 1st Panzer Division. Meanwhile, at dawn, the 23rd Panzer Division was fully engaged in a series of tank battles a few kilometres southeast of Komadi. The Russian infantry did not realize that the German 11th Company/128th PG Regiment had redeployed the previous night over the Sebes-Körös River's north bank. In one case, German infantry captured an operational T–34 tank. Germans manned the tank and operated it until the T–34 developed engine problems, after which, it was blown up. The Russians kept coming and the German 128th PG Regiment found itself seriously engaged at 0700 in the Komadi area. Russians arrived from the southeast and engulfed the Axis bridgehead. Along the north bank of the river, the 128th fought tenaciously against large amounts of Russian armour crossing. The 1st and 3rd Battalions/128th PG Regiment managed to destroy five tanks. By 1130, the Russians had created their own bridgehead near Komadi and both sides were determinedly preparing for combat. A company of PzKpfw Vs arrived, as did anti-tank guns. These were deployed against the Russian threat.

The 51st Panzer Pioneer Battalion and the 1st Panzer Reconnaissance Battalion moved through numerous gaps in the lines northeast of Csökmo, and Darvas, attacking and causing chaos to small groups of unaware Russians. The Russians had not been aware that their bridgehead at Komadi had been expanded to 5 km wide, and did not know the Germans continued to possess one at Ujirázró.

The two German Panzer divisions of the 3rd Panzer Corps were small plugs trying to stop a dam breaching. The water continued to move through, in this case, Russian troops of the 13th Guards Cavalry Division from the 6th Guards Cavalry Corps managed to reach Hajdúszoboszló by 1000. In this area, lay a company of tanks from the 23rd Panzer Division. Its Panzer Regiment was nearby recuperating and awaiting the arrival of tanks from the workshops. The arrival of the Russian troops disrupted their relatively relaxed mode. First to greet the Russians were the 44 men, 4 damaged tanks and 2 StuGs from the 2nd Company in the south west. Part of the company occupied the nearby railway station. The railway station was important as it contained 12 PzKpfw V tanks on flat cars still unloaded. The Germans hurriedly rushed to unload them and all suffered some damage as the Red storm moved closer. Eventually, these were sent to Debrecen.

In Debrecen, the Hungarian 16th Assault Gun Battalion stood idle. 3rd Company contained one infantry platoon armed with 2 HMG, 3 LMG, 2 cars. It departed for Hajdúszoboszló, then moved onto Naduvar. One StuG platoon moved to Balmazújváros. Much of Debrecen's infrastructure and administration had fled. Some 200 police remained as well as the 3rd Panzer Corps. For the time being, Hajdúszoboszló remained in Axis hands, however, the right flank was thinly defended and the Russian 8th Guards Cavalry Division attacked Bihartorda from the east, capturing it. The Pliyev cavalry-mechanized group had advanced 100 km and reached Hajdúszoboszló – Püspökladány and its spearhead was pointing at Karcag. It had secured an area including Kisújszállás and the main road between the Szolnok-Debrecen. It had taken 4,220 Axis POWs. By the end of the third day, the Russian 'Operation Debrecenyi' had bagged 8,220 POWs (many became casualties).

During the day, the Germans and Hungarians continued to repulse the much stronger Russian armoured formations at Nagyvárad, some 29km to the southeast. Six Russian formations that broke through in a northerly direction were all stopped and disrupted. Hungarian artillery observers could watch as large Russian and Romanian forces gathered. The Russian 53rd Army also became subject to more Axis counterattacks. These were conducted by the Hungarian 48th Regiment, 12th Reserve Division. The 7th Hungarian Corps near Nagyvárad fought with AT guns, AA guns, and Hungarian tanks.

The German Fretter-Pico Army Group prepared to encounter the Russian attack at Nagyvárad from the Kolozsvár area. The 72nd Corps received the 1776 StuG from the 76th Division, and the 1054, 3/844, and 9/140 anti-tank battalions. From 3rd Panzer Corps, it received StuG battalions 1257 and 1179 with Jagpanzer 38t tanks, armoured infantry and a Heavy Weapons company. Germans conducted night attacks with 50 aircraft upon the Russians. The Russian reconnaissance units fanned out seeking gaps in the defences, of which there were plenty to be found.

The Russian 5th Air Army had flown 1,313 missions in the two days. They flew in groups of 6–8 aircraft. The Germans claim to have shot down 30 aircraft. As for the German 4th *Luftflotte*, it had flown 600 missions. About 150 of these were flown by the 1st German Fighter Divisions and the 102nd Hungarian Fighter Division, mainly over Debrecen. Many of these air attacks targeted enemy tanks and other formations.

Strike against Debrecen

The original concept for the Russian attack was to simply strike and take Debrecen using the 46th, 53rd Armies and the Pliyev Group. It was now decided to take Nyíregyháza once Debrecen fell. The German 8th Army much further east could then be trapped. So far, the 6th Guards Tank Army attack upon Nagyvarad had been a fiasco due to the terrain and defences. Since the city had to be taken, it was decided to encircle it. The plan called for the 6th Guards Tank Army to bypass Nagyvarad and push towards Kismarja-Nagykereki-Bihar-püspöki –Csatár. The Pliyev Group would strike for the Tiszafüred bridgehead, Nagy Károly-Nyíregyháza. However, the STAVKA demanded that Nagyvarad be taken and given top priority. Their orders indicated that the Pliyev group strike for the city with at least one cavalry corps and the 7th Mechanized Corps. The other cavalry corps would take Debrecen. The 6th Guards Tank Army would then strike westerly across the Sebes- Körös River. The 33rd Corps of the Tank Army would attack from Mezosás-Köröstol towards Biharkeresztes. The 4th Guards Cavalry Corps at Püspökladány and the 7th Mechanized Corps at Karcag were ordered to turn 180 degrees and strike southeast towards Nagyvarad. These units would separate the 3rd Panzer Corps and take Pocsaj, Kismarja, Biharfélegyháza and Bihar. The 49th Corps of 53rd Army would turn north and attack to join the cavalry towards Balmazújváros-Tiszafüred. The 6th Guards Cavalry Corps was to take Debrecen, thus incidentally exposing its rear to the Panzer divisions. The 18th Tank Corps and 53rd Army would continue their north-west advance.

The northern direction was the main axis of the Russian offensive. It steamrollered along, excepting periodic stalls, moving up the eastern bank of the Tisza River. The Germans had shown their quick ability to regroup and fall back and then strike back. This ability complicated the whole affair as the Russians were hoping to somehow cut off the German lines of withdrawal. The mission of the Russian 2nd Ukrainian Front was to strike and advance towards Budapest crushing the Hungarian resistance. The Russian 46th Army was also to move in a western direction. The German 8th Army far to the east could be trapped if the Russian attack northwards was not stalled. Of course, the only units able to stall them were three weak Panzer divisions (1st, 13th and 23rd). The strongest German unit in the area remained *Kampfgruppe* Ameiser. The numerous rivers and canals in the Russian area of attack all helped weak Axis groups to stall Russian units much stronger than themselves. It was not uncommon for a company to hold up a regiment. These restricted the avenues of approach for the Russian armour.

Both the German FHH Panzer Grenadier Division and the 109th Panzer Brigade were some of the freshest units available, principally assigned to defend the Budapest area, more so for the 109th Panzer that had arrived in part (15 tanks) in Budapest on the 8th. All of the German Corps demanded that the Luftwaffe provide greater support, although fuel availability was an issue.

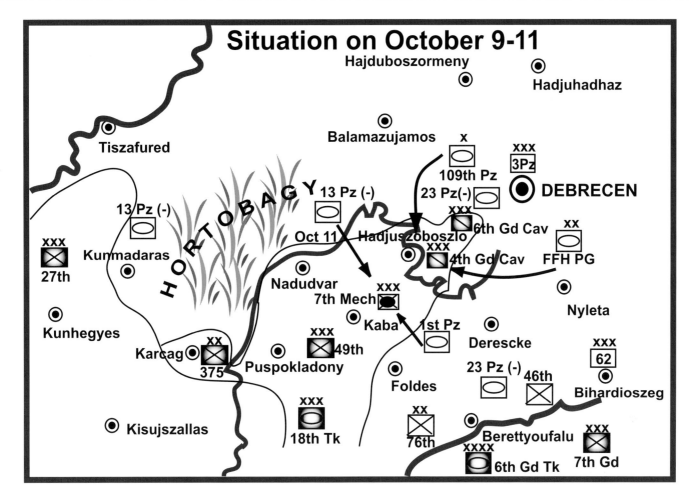

Situation on October 9-11

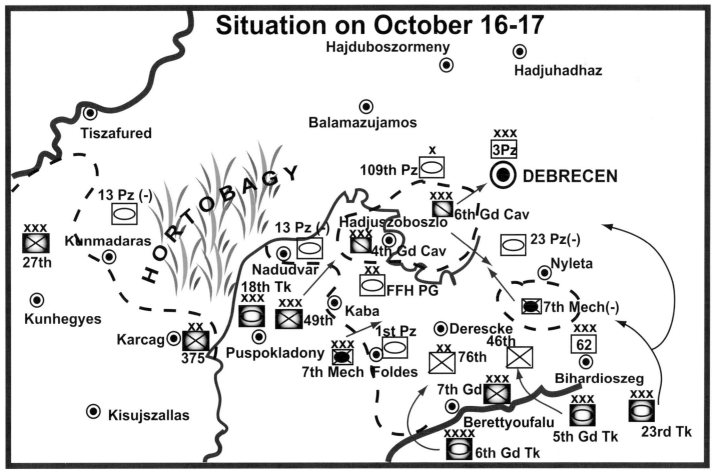

Situation on October 16-17

Operation Debrecen

A SdKfz 8 half-track towing a 17 cm Kanone 18, autumn 1944. Note the tactical marking on the rear wheel arch of the gun, indicating a towed mortar (the full designation of the weapon was '17 cm Kanone 18 in Morserlafette'). (Bundesarchiv 101I–244-2312-19)

Soviet troops enter Szeged, 11 October 1944. (RGAKFD Moscow)

Romanian mortar team in action, Transylvania, Autumn 1944. (Photo archive of the Bulgarian Ministry of Defence)

Soviet machine-gun team in action, Transylvania, September 1944. (Photo archive of the Bulgarian Ministry of Defence)

A Soviet artillery unit equipped with M 1927 76mm regimental guns moves through the streets of Szeged, October 1944. (RGAKFD Moscow)

Fine study of a Soviet infantry unit in recently-liberated Szeged, October 1944. All are armed with the Shpagin PPSh–41 submachine gun. (RGAKFD Moscow)

Soviet infantry unit marching through the streets of Szeged, October 1944. (RGAKFD Moscow)

Colonel-General Johannes Friessner, commander of Army Group South, October 1944.
(Military History Museum Budapest)

Soviet anti-aircraft troops, Szeged, 1944. The weapons are 7.62 mm SG–43 Goryunov
medium machine guns on anti-aircraft mounts. (RGAKFD Moscow)

German 3.7 cm anti-aircraft gun knocked out by Soviet forces, Szentes area, October 1944.
(Military History Museum Budapest)

A destroyed Hungarian Turan M41 tank, Szentes area, late October 1944. (Military History Museum Budapest)

Destroyed Hungarian Nimrod 40mm self-propelled anti-aircraft gun, Szentes area,
late October 1944. (Military History Museum Budapest)

The German Fretter-Pico group together with the Hungarian 3rd Army continued to shield along the Tisza River from Szeged, Algyon, Szentes and Szolnok. The 4th SS PG Division and the 1st Hungarian Armoured Division attacked into the Russian rear areas south of Szeged. The Hungarian 1st Cavalry Division also conducted minor attacks near Kunszentmárton and along the Hármas-Körös River. The German 6th Army's task was to use the 1st and 13th Panzer Divisions in the Püspökladány area to attack and cut-off the Russian spearhead forces further north. The cooperation between the 6th and Hungarian 3rd Army was strained for a variety of reasons and there was a lack of communication between the commands. The 3rd Hungarian Army area of responsibility was at Cegléd-Sarvas, while the German 6th Army was from Békéscsaba.

It was decided to have the 8th German Army withdrawal from the Carpathians and fall back to Nyireghaza while the 6th Army also pulled back more slowly and held the line long enough for the 8th Army to arrive safely. This was decided by 1430. The 8th Army would begin the withdrawal first.

The 44th Reserve Regiment (1,000 men, 20 HMG, 68 LMG, 67 MMG, 12 cm rocket launchers, five 7.5mm PAK 40 guns) remained at Baja. The 277th Division was a shell with only 300 men, 33 LMG, 150 sub-machine guns. It remained at Érsekújvár. At Siofok, stood a SS Brigade. This had 1,500 men and 30 MGs. The 1st and 38th SS Regiments were near Dunaföldvár. This force had 400 men and 12 LMG. These units were mechanized. The 18th SS PG Division and the 22nd SS Cavalry lacked the standard issues for weapons. The 22nd Cavalry Division had 12,453 men, the 18th SS PG had 10,063 men. However, their combat value was in question. Many of the units were still training. Many had no weapons.

When Tuesday, October 10th arrived, the weather continued to favour the Russian juggernaut with sun and warm temperatures.

The Debrecen Operation had totally ripped up, consumed, and spat out the remains of the Hungarian 3rd Army. Much of the countryside was now in Russian control, along with many stretches of the Tisza River. The cities of Szeged and Szolnok remained contested.

The 2nd Ukrainian Front attempted to secure a bridgehead on its left flank across the Danube-Tisza for a strike towards Budapest. Nayvarad was now encircled. The German 3rd Panzer Corps was really the only viable opposing force as was the German 6th Army. Both struggled to get a handle on the situation rapidly overwhelming them. They continued to hold a small bridgehead over the Tisza at Szolnok. The Russian 27th Army Corps continued westward, approaching this bridgehead until German units attacked into their rear. The Pliyev Group continued to move southeasterly and reconnected with other Russian units. The German forces also felt the results of the Red offensive when many of their supply dumps in the forward areas were captured by fast-moving enemy forces. This is in addition to the loss of armour being repaired in various workshops.

In the area of Biharnagybajom, a German Reconnaissance Company from the 113th Panzer Grenadier Regiment and two StuGs found themselves being overwhelmed as the Russian 7th Mechanized Corps moved into the area. At Pocsaj, the Russian 9th Guards Cavalry Division arrived and was challenged by the German 1st PG Regiment from 1st Panzer Division. Later, tanks of the division also arrived, which preserved the area for the Germans. By 1030, a battalion from the 1st PG Regiment conducted an attack towards the northwest in the direction of Sárrétudvari. This area was not defended and was a security threat between the 13th and 1st Panzer Divisions. Joining them was a Panther company with eight tanks. After a brief clash with T–34s, in which several were destroyed, the Germans reach their objective. After which, the Germans advanced towards Püspökladány.

A paradox now occurred. The German 1st and 13th Panzer Divisions had now cut-off the Russian Pliyev Cavalry-Mechanized Group. However, it also meant that the German units' rear, to some degree, faced the advancing Russian forces from the south! The question was how long could the Germans afford to remain this precarious position? The two Panzer Divisions did not have the ability to destroy the trapped Russians. In fact, the opposite was really the truth. Also, the Germans had only cut off the Russians with weak reconnaissance forces between Sárrétudvari and Püspökladány. It was a very tenuous, almost symbolic encirclement. By noon, the area was secured as far as Kabá. The Germans had one PG battalion from 1st PG Regiment and four PzKpfw V tanks at Sárrétudvari, the 1st Battalion/113th PG Regiment at Biharnagybajom with four Marders of 37th Panzerjäger Battalion some two miles away! The 2nd PG Battalion/113th PG Regiment sat at Nagyrábé, the remaining units of the 37th Battalion held Bihartordá. Elements of the Panzer Pioneers attempted to take Dancsházára, but were repulsed. The 1st Panzer Regiment moved northwards towards Sárrétudvarit and ran into Russian units. Now, it faced a fierce counter-attack against Biharnagybajomon with only four Panther tanks.

At 1300, the Russian 8th Cavalry Division and the 1st Romanian Division with 22 self-propelled guns attacked the area between the 1st and 13th Panzer Divisions near Bihar- Nagyrábé in an attempt to break through. The 1st Romanian Division did so near Darvas, across the Berettyó River.

Oddly, the Russians did not attack from the west towards Püspökladány during the day, but continued moving towards capturing various key bridges. The Germans sent 20 tanks towards Nagyivánon to secure the area, leaving one weak tank company to defend Püspökladány. The 1st Panzer Division did this as it was clear the Russians were attacking from the east and towards Karcag. Several tanks were lost, which were simply left behind. There was no ability to repair them.

Near Karcag, the 93rd PG Regiment was attacked, which, with the help of German 13th Panzer Regiment, repulsed the Russians. The 4th Panzer Pioneer Battalion secured the northwest of Karcag-Kunmadara-Kunhegyes areas. The PG Regiment from the FHH PG Division finally departed from Tiszafüred for the embattled Hajdúszoboszló area. Under orders, this German combat group at Tiszafured and Balmazújváros, 25 km NW of Debrecen, were to reinforce the Debrecen area. By 1300, the group began its advance and was almost immediately under attack from Russian reconnaissance troops of the 6th Guards Cavalry Corps. The German Regiment fought off the Russian units, eventually arriving at Hajdúszoboszló by nightfall with 28 StuG III assault guns. The other reinforcement, the 109th Panzer Brigade had still yet to leave for Debrecen. Its 33 tanks (many PzKpfw V) were still awaiting orders to move!

Two cavalry divisions from the 6th Guards Cavalry Corps continued attacking all around Debrecen to the southwest and west. Russian T–34s approached Debrecen from the west only to be thwarted by the Hungarian 16th Assault Gun Battalion from 1000 yards away. This Hungarian unit also had fired at the fast-approaching Russian cavalry, which quickly changed direction and went elsewhere. This unit was then attacked by 14 Russian T–34s supported by infantry. A brief armoured clash resulted in a loss of three Hungarian Túrán tanks and one Russian T–34. The Russians failed to continue with the attack. If this had not been enough, at 1600, the Hungarian unit came to face to face with 45 Russian tanks! For some reason, the orders received were thought to indicate a retreat, so one company did. This weakened the defensive position. In reality, the orders were to redeploy into terrain with better observation. Luckily, this error was corrected just as the Russians came within firing range. The Hungarian position was held.

The 23rd Panzer Division remained south of Komadi, repulsing many of the Russian troops filtering through the numerous gaps. The situation seemed rather hopeless. The Russians tossed in 50 tanks and 800 men to capture the key river bridge there. Enemy artillery saturated the German positions. A PG Company from the 128th PG Regiment became surrounded- only seven men returned to Komadi. The remaining companies of the Regiment established river line defences and the 23rd Panzer Regiment with 16 tanks attacked a gathering Russian force southwest of the city. The 16 tanks demolished the opposing Russian armour: 11 T–34s and 10 M2A2 US Sherman tanks (10 anti-tank guns also). But, the Germans had lost three very precious Panthers during the duel.

This was the German problem: numbers. The Russian had plenty of numbers in men and tanks. They took heavy losses from small numbers of German men or tanks. During the exchange, they would suffer high losses. Losses the German could not afford. If the cycle continued long enough, the Germans would be wiped out.

The German 128th PG Regiment conducted a number of probing attacks southwards towards a key bridge at Komadi, one company opened up with their anti-tank guns but the Russians failed to scatter. The 126th PG Regiment and the 51st Panzer Pioneer Battalion advanced northwest of Darvastó, Kórósszigetmajor, Csökmo, and by noon were west of Ujiráz. The Russians counterattacked, seizing Csökmot.

During the day, the 23rd Panzer Division had destroyed 28 T–34/76s, 12 T–34/85s and two IS–2 tanks. Yet, the Russian 7th Mechanized Corps continued to advance towards Derecsk- Berettyóújfalu-Poscaj and launched attacks towards Kismarja. In the Berettyóújfalu area, the 1st Panzer Division waited. This Division had been constantly fighting and slowly withdrawing. Eventually, both opponents halted their movements near Debrecen. Numerous German supply troops and rapidly repaired tanks helped saved Debrecen for the moment. These ragtag Axis forces continued to advance on Nagylétát – Sáránd and Derecske against Soviet lines, causing grave losses to them.

Regardless of the minor successes, the Russian 9th Guards Cavalry Division from the 4th Guards Cavalry Corps had encircled and taken Kismarja by 1600. It then took Bihar and proceeded to advance towards the Germans at Nagavarad. Joining them were the motorized elements of the 10th Guards Cavalry Division. The 7th Mechanized Corps had turned towards Berettyóújfalu and its 64th Motorized Brigade seized Bojt. The Hungarian 12th Reserve Division had recently retreated from the same area!

The German 72nd Corps continued to struggle, moving towards the northwest. Its 76th Infantry Division had repulsed many of the Russian attacks near Nagyvarad. The Hungarian 12th Reserve Division followed to Bihar with three 75mm AT guns, a battalion from the 48th Regiment, the 176th Supply Battalion, the 325th StuG Brigade with 26 StuG and the 228th StuG Brigade with 34 StuG AFVs. All of these forces ended up southwest of Debrecen. Near Biharkeresztes, a main German supply based was overrun by Russian troops and armour. The German rear area personnel fled.

Within the German 6th Army High Command many felt the earlier suffering of the 3rd Panzer Corps and dividing of the 1st and 13th Panzer Divisions by the Pliyev Mechanized-Cavalry Group had been unnecessary and

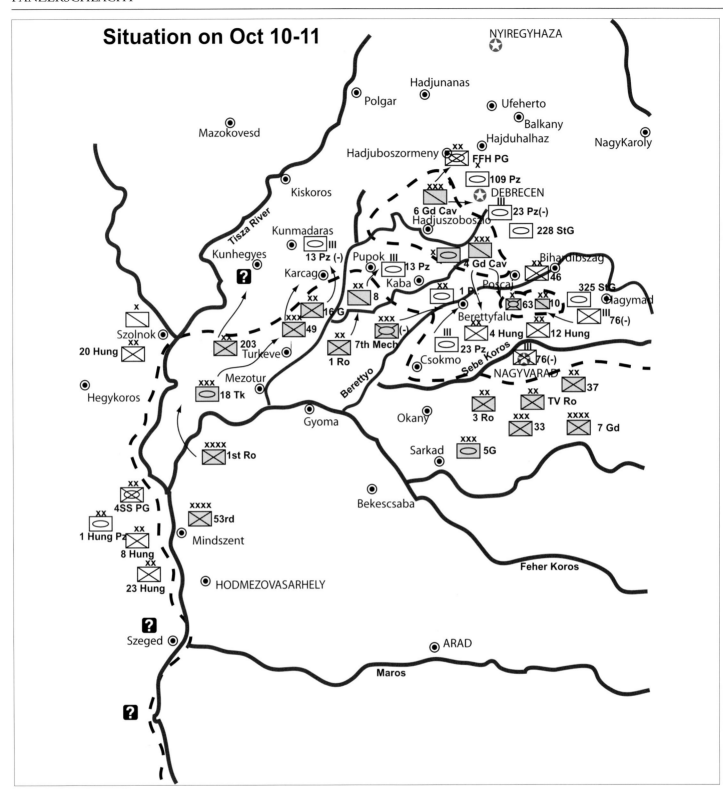

Situation on October 10th–11th

could have been avoided. In addition, the handling of the Russian pocket created by the same Panzer Divisions was questioned. Some felt the pocket could have been reduced, others thought the whole situation made such a move rather moot and pointless.

The German 6th Army defences had been breached at Hajdúszoboszló, Báránd, Hajdúszovát, Derecske, Konyár, Szent Péter, Gáborján, Hencida, Kismarja and Pocsaj, by 5000 Russian cavalrymen, one tank brigade, two motorized brigades and many smaller sized units. The German supply base there had fallen. This made the German situation more precarious during the heat of battle when ammunition supplies or fuel suddenly became an issue. Thus, the Germans were forced to consolidate and use or supply their resources when the tactical situation dictated they should. Later in the day, the German 203rd Regiment from 76th Division loaded into trucks and moved to Nagyvarad. This was at 1900 hrs. The 72nd Regiment from 46th Division reached Szerétfalvárói around the same time. Also arriving was the FHH Panzer Grenadier Division – a unit that was needed everywhere, but could not be! It was needed at Hajdúszoboszló and Debrecen. The 3rd Panzer Corps command relocated to Almosd, the 4th Panzer Corps was at Hajdúnánás. Meanwhile, Russian aircraft attacked at will Axis troops seeking refuge on the western bank of the Tisza.

To the commanders in the two Corps headquarters the situation ominous: the Russians had 450 armoured vehicles southwest of Debrecen! Pliyev had 170, the 6th Guards Tank Army had 100, the 18th Tank Corps had 80, the 23rd Tank Corps had 100. Still not accounted for was the 5th Guards Cavalry Corps. It was a numbers game. One the Germans could not win. Even though the 3rd Panzer Corps alone had destroyed 81 tanks, more came! In the past three days, 162 Russian tanks had been destroyed.

The 3rd Panzer Corps contained 59 operational tanks and 66 StuG, totalling 125 AFVs. The FHH PG Division contained 28 StuG III, while the 109th Panzer Brigade contained 33 PzKpfw V tanks and Pz IV L/70. 6th Army had approved but had not sent the 1176, 1179 and 1257 Panzerjäger Battalions, which in reality were only company strength, as all together they possessed only 25 Jagdpanzer 38 assault guns. The Hungarians had 12 tanks remaining. The FHH was just now entering the battle area and the 109th Brigade had yet to arrive. Some books indicate that the Germans had 104 tanks and 120 assault guns, however these numbers do not distinguish between those that were operational and those that were not. That is a big difference!

The 3rd Hungarian Army and the 4th SS PG Division had cleared the Szentes and Szolnok areas of Russian troops, forcing them back over to the east bank of the Tisza. The 8th SS PG regiment stood at Csongrád.

Wednesday, the 11th, finally brought clouds and showers. The temperature remained mild. The rain forced the Russians to stick to the few passable roads.

At Szolnok, the Hungarians attempted to attack from their bridgehead against a solid and strong Russian defence. This attack consisted of the Hungarian 20th Reserve Division remnants consisting of three battalions, totaling 2,320 men with three AT guns, and elements of the Hungarian 1st Cavalry Division. The attack utterly failed. Later, the Russian 409th Division from the 27th Corps attacked from the Szent Miklos area towards the bridgehead and nearly encircled much of the key bridge over the Tisza. As for the Romanian 1st Army, its 7th Corps containing the 9th Cavalry and 19th Infantry Divisions had been given the mission to establish a bridgehead over the Tisza River near Mindszent. Defending in the area was the Hungarian 1st Armoured Division (which had battled the same units near Arad on September 13th) and the 23rd Infantry Division. The Romanian 4th Corps, containing the 2nd and 4th Divisions, had been given the task of creating another bridgehead near Sznolok. The Romanian units went into action and were immediately attacked by the weak Hungarian 1st Infantry Division and 1st Cavalry Division. When this failed, the Germans tossed in their 24th Panzer Division (regimental strength), some Tiger Tanks from the 503rd Battalion, and the 4th SS Panzer Grenadier Division! This rapidly became a deteriorating situation as the Russian 20th Division and Romanian 4th Division became encircled, lacking anti-tank weapons; both finally surrendered after 30 hours of resistance. As time went on, the Romanian 7th Corps retreated to the right bank of the Tisza for safety and advanced northwards and eventually seized Ocsod and Szarvas. The Romanian 19th Division finally succeeded in winning a bridgehead at Alpar.

The German 1st Panzer Division redeployed from Sárrétudvariból to Bihar leaving only a weak rearguard of company strength while the Russian 203rd Division (49th Corps) attacked north towards Kunhegyes and then towards Szent Miklos. The 110th Guards Division and the 16th Brigade from the 7th Mechanized Corps struck the right flank of the 1st Panzer Division near Sárrétuvari and Biharnagybajom. Finding itself in a near-encirclement, the German 66th PG Battalion (13th Panzer Division) burst out from Püspökladány, moving in a southwesterly direction to reconnect with the 1st Panzer Division. This was a desperate decision of last resort. In their way was the Russian 18th Tank Corps and 49th Corps, which held the Karcag area. These enemy units continued to apply heavy pressure towards the bridge over the Hortobágy and Berettyó Rivers. By 1130, the Russian 53rd Army's commander was instructed to use the 18th Tank Corps and the 49th Corps to attack Bihartorda, Biharnagybajom and Püspökladány. The 6th Guards Cavalry Corps would assume control of the Hajdúszoboszló-Hajdúszovát-Karcag area.

To counter this, the Germans sent the 1st Battalion/66th PG Regiment towards Karcag to intercept from Püspökladány. Such an order was rather silly in the face of the size of the enemy facing them! Nevertheless, the German unit moved southeasterly and despite the losses reached Sárrétudvari in an exhausted state due to Russian units constantly attacking. The unit repulsed these attacks but further advance was halted. Meanwhile, at Püspökladány itself, the Germans were having a very difficult time in holding the area and bridges. Russian units were just too many and their tanks captured the bridges. In this game of chess, the Germans had no choice but to fall back northwards. A large group of Russian armour faced only four Panther tanks!

The Russian 18th Tank Corps crossed over to the western bank of the Tisza River, as the 49th Corps (53rd Army) with the 6th Guards Cavalry Corps seized the Püspökladány area. However, the battle was not yet over. The

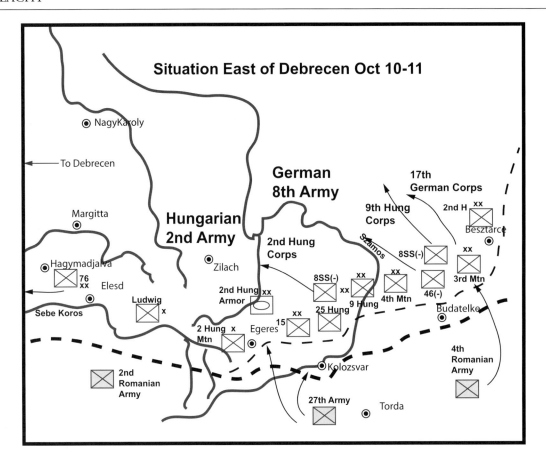

Situation East of Debrecen Oct 10-11

NagyKaroly

To Debrecen

German
8th Army

17th
German Corps

9th Hung
Corps

2nd H

Besztarce

Margitta

Hungarian
2nd Army

2nd Hung
Corps

8SS(-)

Zilach

Hagymadjava

76

Elesd

Sebe Koros

Ludwig

2nd Hung
Armor

8SS(-)

25 Hung

9 Hung

4th Mtn

3rd Mtn

46(-)

Budatelke

2 Hung
Mtn

Egeres

15

4th
Romanian
Army

2nd
Romanian
Army

Kolozsvar

27th Army

Torda

East of Debrecen

bridge's value there lured the German 13th Panzer Division and two PG companies to attack, and by afternoon, the Germans had retaken the bridge from the Russians after a bitter battle! The town itself also was narrowly retaken and garrisoned by two PG companies, 3 PzKpfw V tanks, a few AA MGs, and a PG unit with 1.5cm Drilling MGs. The 13th Panzer Division remained southwest of the town repelling numerous Russian attacks the rest of the day and night. The Russian 6th Guards Cavalry Corps continued to probe, attempting to sever the German lines. Because of this, by midnight, the 66th PG Regiment once again had to evacuate Püspökladány and Sárrétudvarit. Small rear-guard units remained to delay their eventual loss. Likewise, the 1st Panzer Division also pulled back from Sárrétudvariban and Biharnagybajom. At Karcag, the Russian 1st Guards Airborne Division with the 18th Tank Corps attacked and trapped the German 2nd Battalion/66th PG Regiment, and 2nd Battalion/93rd PG Regiment plus other miscellaneous units.

From the northeast, the 2nd Regiment of the 1st Guards Airborne Division pushed into Karcag, held by the 93rd PG Regiment. This attempt stalled in the urban environment, with the Germans holding the northwest portion of the city. The 66th PG Regiment attack also failed to dislodge the enemy, however, the streets were impassable due to debris from artillery barrages. When the Russians attacked the polyglot group of soldiers nearby, they broke and fled down the road towards Kunmadaras, which meant the two PG Battalions were nearly surrounded! Their only hope was to retreat north. Supporting this breakout were 15 PzKpfw V tanks from the 13th Company and a company of armoured infantry in APCs (10 in all).

In the city of Karcag, the Russian 1st Guards Division, armed with numerous anti-tank and artillery guns fought house-to-house with the German Panzer Grenadier battalions in bitter battles. Eventually, the Germans were forced into the centre of the city by 1700. By 1800, Karcag was in Russian hands. Some of the German units slipped out and escaped, others were caught and destroyed 3 km from the city. Some German infantry slipped out and reached Tiszafüred but suffered severe casualties. Ten of the Panther tanks were destroyed, along with SPWs (armoured half-tracks) and other vehicles. Whatever remained of the original German defenders arrived during the night of October 12th at Nagyiván, where they regrouped and reformed. Püspökladány was also evacuated for the last time. The FHH PG Division assembled at Balmazújvárosban and finally joined the 3rd Panzer Corps. It had been a long, arduous road. Upon its arrival in the morning, the armoured regiment with 28 StuG IIIs, together with other AT and tank hunter units, conducted its own attack upon the 6th Guards Cavalry Corps, which then counter-attacked with high losses. The German attack continued but stalled as it approached Hajdúszoboszló (although some sources indicate Germans actually reached the town).

The German 6th Army issued the 3rd Panzer Corps an order stating that the panzers should attack and create a breakthrough point in order for the Panzer Grenadier units of the FHH Division to advance southwest to Hajdúszoboszló. The FHH Division did not have artillery support, thus, the order was difficult to follow. The 13th Panzer Division was ordered to attack towards the Püspökladány-Sárrátudvari area again. The 4th Panzer Corps was completely halted between Tiszaszentim – Kunhegyes. Between these two Corps was a gap of about 12 km.

Meanwhile, the 1st Panzer Division at Bihar was battling the Russian 8th Cavalry Division and the Romanian 1st Division. These two units conducted several attacks in vain, supported by several rocket artillery regiments.

Near Debrecen, the 6th Guards Cavalry Corps managed to reach the city limits. This was grave news to the Axis command. Russian lead units faced only four Panther tanks just arriving from the 23rd Panzer Regiment and a battalion of Panzer Pioneers! These German units entered the city environs from the southwest and were joined by two more PzKpfw Vs. Russian cavalry-tank elements found themselves suddenly encircled. The battle continued for some time and by 1400 ended up in a brick manufacturing complex until the Russian armour was partially destroyed. A lull then commenced but at 1530, the Hungarian 16th Assault Gun Battalion conducted its own attack against the Russians using their Turan tanks. Together with the Germans, who had three Panthers, they regained control of the area and repulsed the Russians in house-to-house fighting. The German Panzer Pioneers from the 23rd Panzer Division with only 8–10 guns proved to be the turning point. The Germans and Hungarians were able to re-establish a defensive line a few miles south of Debrecen. The Russians made a subsequent attack with armour. This was thrown back.

Pliyev was ordered to take Nagyvarad. He sent two cavalry divisions from the 4th Guards Cavalry Corps and the 7th Mechanized Corps east of Berettyóújfalu, southwards. The 30th Tank Brigade also conducted an attack from the southeast. The 10th Guards Cavalry Division advanced north and northwest with two tank companies towards Jákóhodos. The German 76th Division was under heavy pressure from the Russians and being gradually compressed by enemy forces from a variety of directions at Bihar. The supply base for the 76th Division was seized.

Meanwhile, the Russians took Biharkeresztest. The Germans were unaware of this. When this was found out, the 1176 StuG Battalion with Jagdpanzer 38 Hetzers also joined with several Alarm units in an attack to retake the town. During the day, a portion of the 76th Division was placed under 3rd Panzer Corps control, which instructed it to defend northwest of Nagyvarad. The Hungarian 4th Reserve Division remained in positions along the Sebes-Koros River. The 7th Hungarian Corps occupied Micskén.

The 7th Mechanized Corps advanced during the afternoon and took Biharpüspökit, the 30th and 9th Guards Cavalry Divisions from the 4th Guards Cavalry Corps bypassed the town. Both Russian combat groups continued to attack that night, however, the Germans halted these, although not before the 152nd Guards Regiment, with tanks and self-propelled guns, captured 19 artillery guns, of which eight were 105mm. This was a hard loss. The Russian wave then rolled towards Nagyvarad, the thorn in side of the Russian 6th Guards Tank Army since October 6th. While the bulk of the two Corps rolled forward, to secure the rear areas they had captured, two cavalry divisions, one motorized and tank brigade remained behind. This weakened the Russian strength. The 23rd Panzer Division's left flank was then hit by the 6th Guards Tank Army again at Csökmo, the latter engaging the 2nd Battalion/126th PG Regiment. East of this, was the 3rd Panzer Battalion/128th Pz Regiment, which halted any further Russian advance. Even though they had failed, the Russians tried yet again with a larger force in a northeast direction. The 7th Company of the 128th PG Regiment repelled this attack as well. At Komadi, a massive Russian attack began with artillery and rocket barrages and by noon this began to make serious headway until the 23rd Panzer Regiment with PzKpfw IV and V tanks arrived. As the day wore on, the Russian attempts continued with numerous armoured battles in and around Komadi. The 1st Battalion/126th PG Regiment was engaged in battles all day; by the afternoon, the Russians achieved some success northeast of the city. This was to be the only small success the 6th Guards Tank Army would have – it had lost 17 tanks. German sources indicate the Russians had lost 17 T–34/76s, five T–34/85s.

Elsewhere, the German 230th Regiment of the 76th Division (72nd Corps) was engaged in heavy fighting in and around Nagyvarad. It had managed to repulse many Russian attacks but the enemy did penetrate the lines near Biharugra. This was partly due to the Hungarian 4th Reserve Division routing when it was attacked some two miles to the left of the 230th Regiment. When this event unfolded, the enemy 33rd Corps seized Rojt and Romanian troops with Russian tanks moved through the gaps until a German battalion stalled them. By late night, the 76th Division sent a message to its Corps HQ stating that it was being overwhelmed with 200 AFVs, that the lines were very porous.

The Hungarian 12th Reserve Division fought a hopeless battle near Hajo with the 53rd Russian Army. The Russians easily took Püspökfürdo. By noon, the 7th Hungarian Corps commander filed a report stating that the 12th Hungarian Reserve Division had only four battalions with no reserves. Its defensive line was simply too long and the German 178th Regiment/76th Division was near Nagyvarad. It was suggested that the city be evacuated.

A Sturmgeschütz III Ausf G rumbles through the streets of a Hungarian town, October 1944.
(Bundesarchiv 101I–244–2304–30)

A Panther Ausf A passes a 15 cm schwere Feldhaubitze 18 in a Hungarian town,
October 1944. (Bundesarchiv 101I–244–2306–12)

Above and below: Soviet troops move through a Hungarian town, autumn 1944. (RGAKFD Moscow)

Soviet anti-tank gun crew in action, 18 October 1944, Hungary.
The gun is a 45 mm battalionanti-tank gun M1937 (53–K). (RGAKFD Moscow)

Fine close-up of a Hungarian Toldi I light tank. Small numbers remained in service, despite being hopelessly
obsolete compared to the modern Soviet vehicles encountered on the battlefields of 1944. (The Tank Museum)

View of a Hungarian M40 Turan tank, having crossed an
improvised field bridge. (The Tank Museum)

A PzKpfw V Panther Ausf A with German infantry riding on it,
Hungary, late October 1944. (Ullstein Bilderdienst)

A Sturmgeschütz IV moves along a road in Hungary, early October 1944. (Ullstein Bilderdienst)

German Sturmgeschütze move forward to launch a counter-attack in Hungary, bypassing captured Soviet soldiers. (Ullstein Bilderdienst)

The view within a Hungarian village shortly after its recapture by German troops, October 1944. (Ullstein Bilderdienst)

The Hungarian and German commanders met and conferred. It was agreed that to remain Nagyvarad would not be prudent since Russian forces were wearing the Axis units down and succeeding in isolating the city. During the night, the 178th Regiment from the German 76th Division quietly withdrew from besieged Nagyvarad. By nightfall, much of the unit had evacuated but left behind four 7.5cm PAK guns. By 2000, the city was in Russian hands. The thorn had finally been pulled! Some of the Hungarian 12th Reserve Division had been trapped, but most made it out and acted as a rearguard during the retreat. Some of the units sought defences along the Pecze River. Northwest of the city, the Germans deployed at a railway station with two pioneer companies and a Panzerjäger Battalion. On the left flank, Hungarian cavalry with *Panzerfäuste* and the 2nd Motorized Battalion deployed. The German 76th Division was exhausted from continuous fighting – this unit moved towards Nagyvárad. German supply troops also fled from the area as well as Biharpüspöki and Berettyóújfalu. The rear areas had become front lines!

The Russians continued to press their attack and came close to trapping both the 23rd Panzer Division and 76th Division during the confusing night evacuation. The Axis path to a more secure front line was fraught with danger and enemy units, all pressing their attacks. The road being used had also been cut by Russian machine gun units, some 16 km away. Because of this, the easiest line of withdrawal was not viable. Thus, the Germans retreated across muddy ground, across open country, and across minor rivers towards Nagyvarad (Elesdet) some 34 km to the east. Once there, they turned northwest towards Debrecen to rejoin the 3rd Panzer Corps. However, fast approaching to the Germans east flank was the Gorskov Tank-Cavalry Group. Its lead units were already being engaged! Part of the 23rd Panzer Division moved east from Szaránd through Mezosza, while others moved from Nagyvárad through Kolozsvár. In both cases, they had to fight their way through to safety. There was no easy way out.

The Russians now unleashed the 5th Guards Cavalry Corps with 15 tanks from the east of Nagyvarad. During the day, the German and Hungarian air force units appeared overhead, making some 50 sorties over the Szeged and Debrecen areas. Their arrival was a morale booster.

On the far left flank at Sznolok, the German 24th Panzer Division arrived near Budapest and was being unloaded. The 503rd Tiger Battalion also began to arrive and was preparing for action. Neither were ready for operations and the German commanders discussed how best to use them.

The Germans would soon unleash their own counter-attack, the so-called Operation 'Gypsy Baron', with the 4th SS PG Division and the 503rd Tiger Battalion. However, none of the units were ready and the 4th SS deployed

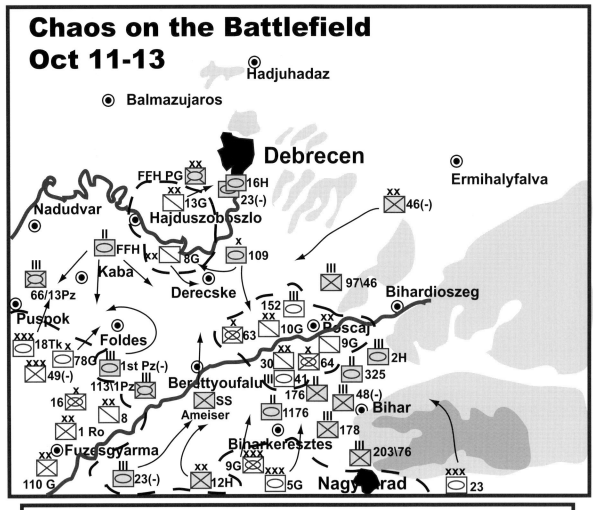

Chaos on the Battlefield
Oct 11-13

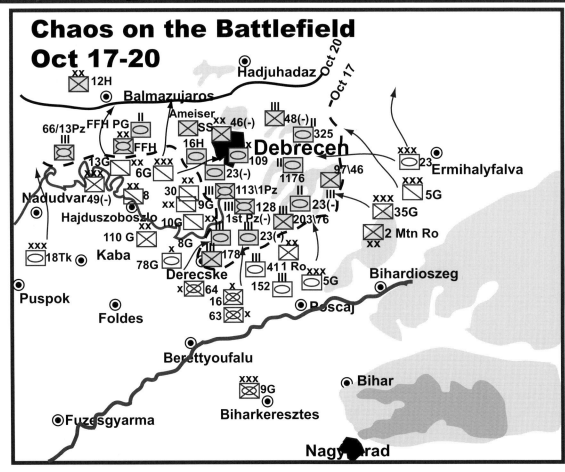

Chaos on the Battlefield
Oct 17-20

one combat regiment towards its launching spot at Sznolok. Meanwhile, Russian armour rolled towards the railway line and Kolozsvár. The German 13th Panzer Division fought desperately in the Karcag area and elements of the 46th Division finally reached Mihály. A composite group of Axis forces managed to create a weak defensive line comprising the Hungarian 2nd Armoured Division, elements of the 76th Division and the 1176 StuG Battalion (Jagdpanzer 38s). And a thin line it was!

The German 6th Army now went into survival mode and provided the following reserves to the front line troops:

114 Arko (Artillery Command), 1335 StuG Battalion with Panzerjäger 38s, 661st Anti-tank, 663rd and 721st (7.5cm gun) battalions.

Hitler was informed of the situation and during the day, the 3rd Panzer Corps with the 1st and 23rd Panzer Divisions and 72nd Corps defended the Nagyvarad area extremely tenaciously, but the Russian 4th Guards Cavalry Corps, 7th Mechanized Corps and 6th Guards Cavalry Corps had made holding it extremely difficult. Around Debrecen, there were a variety of German and Hungarian troops. The Russian 18th Tank Corps supported by the 49th Corps broke through in the area of Püspökladány and Sárrétudvari. These units were running around freely. There was little to oppose them! Many of the Hungarian units had simply melted away. Faced with this, Hitler approved the retreat order but demanded Debrecen be held. This was hard to swallow.

On October 12th, the Russian units continued to latch onto and fortify their hold on key cities. At Karcag and Kunmadaras, the 203rd Division (49th Corps) did just that and then moved towards Tiszaszentim. As they approached the marshy areas near Biharnagybajom, German units counter-attacked, repulsing them.

The German Counter-Attack begins

The Germans continued gathering bits and pieces for the 'Gypsy Baron' attack from the Sznolok area with the 4SS PG Division at Csongrad. At noon, a battalion from the 8th SS PG Regiment attacked eastward from the Sznolok bridgehead supported by tanks and assault guns. The 8th SS Regiment contained three battalions, and was supported by the 4th SS Panzer Pioneer Battalion, 4th SS Panzer Reconnaissance Battalion (minus two companies), 4th SS Panzerjäger Battalion, a company of 75mm AT guns and supply troops.

The German assault met only token resistance from the Russian 409th Division of the 27th Corps. The SS troops easily took Szent Miklos and advanced an additional four kilometres. So far, so good.

The 13th Panzer Division was about 3 km northeast of Püspökladány. The situation remained unclear, so the divisional commander ordered the 1st Battalion/66th PG Regiment to reconnoiter the area towards the town. It did not get very far—the unit ran into a large Russian tank unit. After an exchange of fire, the Germans continued south of the railway and stumbled upon a parked supply column of the Russian 6th Guards Cavalry Corps! Long columns of trucks with fuel and ammunition sat in the open. Both sides frantically scrambled into firing positions, the Russians AT guns fired the first rounds and destroyed four German APCs. The supply column quickly detoured to safer lines further south. The Russians now attacked. Due to low fuel, the Germans were forced to fall back prematurely to avoid running out and being stranded themselves. Many of the German infantry dismounted and acted as a delaying force. The town of Kaba remained in German control.

Near Püspökladány, the Russian 110th Tank Brigade from the 18th Tank Corps clashed with ten German Panther tanks during their attack. Four PzKpfw V were destroyed. During this attack, the tanks used were from the newly arrived FHH PG Division, moving towards Hajdúszoboszló. Germans encircled the town from the east and suddenly became embattled. The 3rd Panzer Corps then immediately ordered the 13th Panzer Division to halt in the Nádudvar area. Reports indicated the Russians were also encircling Hajdúszoboszló! The thin defensive line between the 13th Panzer and 1st Panzer divisions had been broken by the Russians and the only German units in their way were the 1st Battalion/66th PG Regiment and the divisional headquarters of the FHH Division! The break in the German lines ran from Hajdúszovát-Tetétlen south-east of Báránd. The Germans did reinforce their defences at Kaba but the Panzer Pioneers were unable to link up with the FHH Divisional units. It was just too much to ask.

At Kaba, German reserves and assault guns deployed, a Panzer Grenadier battalion and more StuGs were sent to hold Bárándon from the 1st Panzer Division. Counter-attacking towards Hajdúszoboszló from Debrecen was the 109th Panzer Brigade with 18 PzKpfw V tanks (out of 36) and StuGs from the 3rd Panzer Corps.

North of Hajdúszovát, the Russian 30th Cavalry Division from the 4th Guards Cavalry with the 134th Tank Regiment engaged various counterattacking German forces. Meanwhile, the German FHH unit (28 StuGs) and the 109th Panzer Brigade eliminated the threat posed by Russian 6th Guards Cavalry Corp. Although up to six PzKpfw Vs had been lost, the danger for the time being was gone and the FHH fell back towards Kaba. However, the breached lines in the German defences remained.

General K. Beregfy, Hungarian Minister of War after the extremist Arrow Cross Party took the reins of power in Hungary on 15 October 1944. (Dénes Bernád)

Hungarian infantry on the march, 18 October 1944. (Bundesarchiv 146-1980-100-14A)

Soviet ISU-152 self-propelled guns move through a Hungarian village, autumn 1944. (RGAKFD Moscow)

The remains of a Sturmgeschütz III ripped apart by an internal explosion,
Western Transylvania, autumn 1944. (Dénes Bernád)

Soviet officers from a Guard Cossack unit chatting with the inhabitants of a Hungarian
village liberated from the Germans, October 1944. (RGAKFD Moscow)

An infantry unit commanded by Captain E.F. Pavlichev on the attack, Hungary 1944. (RGAKFD Moscow)

Troops from Captain E.F. Pavlichev's unit manhandle a M1910 Maxim machine-gun during combat in Hungary, autumn 1944. (RGAKFD Moscow)

German armoured vehicles move along muddy roads in Hungary, late October 1944. In the foreground a radio vehicle, note the Sturmgewehr 44 leaning by the soldier. (Ullstein Bilderdienst)

Excellent rear view of a Hungarian Nimrod self-propelled anti-aircraft gun. (The Tank Museum)

A knocked-out Soviet SU-76M self-propelled gun. (Dénes Bernád)

Good view from the rear of a Hungarian Turan medium tank, autumn 1944. (The Tank Museum)

Elsewhere, the 1st Panzer Division held the Biharnagybajom area where it was attacked by the Romanians after a thunderous artillery barrage of 300 rounds. A single reconnaissance unit of the division fought a heavy battle until Panzer Grenadier battalions arrived to stabilize the area within two hours.

Much of the afternoon was spent by the German 1st Panzer Division units repulsing and counterattacking numerous Russian attempts aiming for the environs of Biharnagybajom. The German 1st PG Regiment held the western side of the town and was subjected to several strong Russian attacks. These were repulsed but German counterattacks failed. Close combat with the Russian 110th Guards Division became fierce. The last German reserves were consumed to ward off the attack. The Germans sent in their Panzer Pioneers and the small 160-strong SS *Kampfgruppe* Ameiser. The 1st Panzer Regiment battled with 26 Russian tanks, while another 44 were further back and approaching. However, with night fast approaching, the large Russian tank force refrained and did not press their attack. Near Foldes, weak Panzer elements from the 1st Panzer Regiment were facing the 78th Heavy Tank Regiment from the 7th Mechanized Corps equipped with IS–2 tanks.

The Russian 8th Guards Cavalry Division launched an attack with rocket artillery support during the day towards Sznolok. The Hungarian 16th Assault Gun Battalion with Turan tanks and additional German support defended a line along a railway embankment, and repelled the attack with the cavalry suffering heavy losses. The Russian retreated towards Kishegyes.

At Debrecen, up to 300 Russian troops had penetrated into the city. These were surrounded – 80 were killed and 42 became POWs, the balanced escaped. Rumours among the Hungarian troops had spread since so many had fled during the previous days. There were rumours of court-martials and executions. The 23rd Panzer Division sought refuge in the city and refueled. This ended when a company with seven Panther tanks was ordered to move south of the city to clear the road. The 2nd Battalion/23rd Panzer Regiment had seven PzKpfw V, one StuG, an AA section and Panzer Grenadiers. At Mikepércs, some weak Russian resistance was encountered and destroyed. The Germans also rebuilt a bridge for armour to cross and occupied the town then continued and retook Derecske, which had been vacated by the Russians. With the roadway open, the Germans were able to resupply mechanized units with fuel.

The Russians tossed their men against the lines held by the German 23rd Panzer Division,. The battles were brutal. Each was a life and death situation. Attacking from the west were 18 Russian tanks and mechanized troops near Mihály. The German PzKpfw Vs repulsed yet another attack – 12 American M4A2 Sherman tanks were destroyed (these were part of the massive lend-lease programme to the USSR). Then, the Russians attacked towards Komádi, where another bitter struggle ensued. The 1st Battalion/128 PG Regiment knocked out a further six T–34s. By late afternoon, the Russians had backed off from Komadi. However, the battles had also weakened an already battered German unit, and orders were received to withdraw from the town to another defensive line Darvas-Vekerd—Nagynyesta – Kömösd. There, the 23rd Panzer Division regrouped. The Panzer Division had battled with the Russian 6th Guards Tank Army for the past six days. The Panzer Regiment had destroyed 60+ Russian tanks out of some estimated 130 tanks and self-propelled guns used during this time. Of course, the Panzer Division was down to the bare bones—it had less than 30 tanks and some of those required repair! Russian sources indicate that the 6th Guards Tank Army had 71 tanks (not including self-propelled guns) before the operation began.

The Hungarian 12th Reserve Division continued to hold along the minor river, the Pecze. Hungarian artillery units with 150mm guns from its 7th Corps blasted the area northeast of Nagyvarad. The German 178th Regiment also arrived there to hold the line. Russian- Romanian attacks were weak and repulsed. Elements of the 76th Division occupied the Nagyvarad city hall. The building was important because it directly stood at the base of a critical Sebes-Körös River bridge on the south shore. Possession of the building could delay enemy crossings.

The Pliyev Cavalry-Mechanized group attacked towards Biharpüspöki with 20 tanks. Opposing them was the 53rd Battalion, two Hungarian engineer companies and other rear area German troops. The defences held for over an hour before breaks began to appear. Attacking the bulk of the German 178th Regiment was the Russian 33rd Corps. The Russian 78th Heavy Tank Regiment with IS–2 tanks from the 7th Mechanized Corps suddenly appeared on the north side of the bridge. German engineers were unable to blow the bridge or block it. The IS–2 tanks began a systematic shelling of the city hall. The Germans evacuated. The chaos was complete. Russian units appeared along both sides of the Sebes-Körös River. Military discipline began to break down as units became more and more mixed up. Events rapidly unfolded and soon the German and Hungarian units were faced with either breaking out to the west along the Koros Valley, or standing and facing destruction. Communications with the 76th Division commander had ceased and German troops frantically tried to reestablish them. The commanders discussed in which direction would be best to breakout. Some suggested towards the west, along the south shore of the Sebes-Körös at night when valley fog would help hide their movement. In the end, the Germans began their breakout in the early morning, marching along the river towards the northwest. Six StuGs of the 325th StuG Battalion were leading the way, plus 10 *Schwimmwagen*. Along the north shore of the Pecze, 22 7.5cm were hauled along the road from Biharszentandrás, as well as Panzer Pioneers. The 178th Regiment withdrew as the 230th Regiment screened the rear area, as the German forces withdrew from the city. The Hungarian 12th Reserve Division began its own withdrawal, leaving the remaining 50,000 inhabitants (originally, 100,000) to fend for themselves in the horrible conditions.

The 76th Division marched from Nagyvárad and by 1100, despite Russian air attacks, reached Körösgyéres. From there, it moved northwards. The front lines were to their southeast.

The 178th Regiment marched along the right bank, while the 230th Regiment moved along the left bank. The 12th Hungarian Division was less orderly; it moved southwards and then turned west. Much of its men had scattered. Left behind was the trapped 57th Battalion of 38th Hungarian Regiment and three 75mm AT guns.

By the time the fog had been burned off by the October sun, Nagyvárad had been evacuated. The Russians seemed to be unaware as what had taken place. They had waited for the visibility to improve before unleashing another volley of attacks.

The Pliyev group did, indeed, launch another offensive with the 4th Guards Cavalry Corps approaching Nagyvarad from the north using the 9th, 30th Guards Cavalry Divisions, as the 41st Tank Brigade and 64th Motorized Brigade entered from the northwest. The battles fought were with the rearguard troops and those previously trapped. These spasms kept Pliyev occupied for the day as the 76th Division walked into safety. Oddly, Hitler had ordered the city to be retaken, and the 3rd Panzer Corps HQ ordered it so. The 76th Division then launched its counterattack in a southeast direction breaching the Russian rear area! The attacked, however, failed to reach the river.

The 76th Division, once again, fell back and marched towards Körösgyéres and then to Artand and finally, Debrecen. While much of the 12th Hungarian Division had scattered, small groups continued to help seal the gaps that the Germans could not. By the afternoon, the following Hungarian units were deployed as follows:

The 53rd Border Battalion at Körösszakálra

The 2nd Battalion/36th Regiment at Körösszegapátira

The 2nd Motorized and 57th Border Battalions, the 1st Battery/89th Independent Artillery Battalion, the 12th Anti-aircraft Company, the 48th Regiment, and four 75mm AT guns at Berekböszörménybe.

The 12th Hungarian Reserve Division was a shell with six infantry companies, three MG companies, one artillery company, four 75mm AT guns and one cavalry platoon. The division was then ordered to move to Váncsod and Mezopeter and secure the north shore of Berettyótól. The 4th Hungarian Reserve Division remnants moved west towards Köröstarjántói.

The Berettyóújfalu and Derecské Battles, October 13–17

The 4th Panzer Corps with the 4th SS PG Division stood at Ujszász and 15 km NW of Sznolok. Its 8th SS PG Regiment attacked with a number of Panther tanks assaulting enemy positions in the Kenderes area and managed to seize the town. The operation was proving a success. However, a Russian attack recaptured it later in the day, although the SS continued to hold Fegyverneke. In the air, Luftwaffe aircraft flew numerous ground support missions, which greatly helped the whole counterattack and troop morale. The 13th Panzer Division repulsed another serious attempt by the Russian 1st Guards Parachute Division and 18th Tank Corps, which contained only 43 (out of 88) tanks and self-propelled guns by this time.

The 2nd Ukrainian Front strength at this point consisted of 367 tanks and 202 self-propelled guns. The Front had begun the operation with 481 tanks, and since October 3rd, the Front had lost 256 armoured vehicles (tanks and self-propelled guns). Clearly, the opposition was having an impact.

Heavy battles continued 8km east of Karcag and in the vicinity of Püspökladány, where another 17 Russian tanks had been destroyed. However, the Russian 1st Guards Parachute Division proved to be too strong and held onto the area. The German 13th Panzer Reconnaissance Battalion was unable to hold Kunmadaras despite the arrival of the 2nd Battalion/63rd PG Regiment and 2nd Battalion/93rd PG Regiment near Nagyivánnál. Further west, the 13th Panzer Division repelled another Russian foray. Meanwhile, the FHH PG Division continued to defend the Kábá – Kabat area, but it failed to reconnect with the other German units on its left flank. More gaps to seal! The 1st Panzer Division's defences came under attack at 0300 in the Biharnagybajom area. Much of the Russian force managed to encircle part of the town, forcing the 1st PG Regiment to evacuate from it. The evacuation was costly to them although it did succeed and by sunrise, the 1st PG Regiment had reached safer ground.

More Russian attacks upon the same area occurred a few hours later, launched by the 1st Romanian and 110th Russian Guards Divisions between Biharnagybajom and Nagyrábé. They were supported by the 1815th Self-Propelled Artillery Regiment (SU–76 Self-propelled guns). This was repelled. Yet, another attack in the same area resumed using infantry and 25 tanks from the east. This attack proved to be the most serious since the early light, as it fell upon a thin German line between the two towns.

Lt. General Szokolov, the commander of the Russian 6th Guards Cavalry Corps, quickly redeployed his forces and withdrew his 8th Guards Cavalry Division west of Debrecen to join his others in the Hajdúszoboszló-Hajdúszovát area. The 13th Guards Cavalry Division held Szepes. Both units had suffered considerable casualties and were tired. The Corps had tried a raid towards Mikepércs, which failed.

West of Debrecen, Hungarian and German AA guns and elements of the Hungarian 16th Assault Gun Battalion managed to thwart further Russian attacks. The Germans counterattack with 11 Panther tanks but their allies, the Hungarian 16th Assault Gun Battalion, failed to provide any support—their crews had fallen asleep! Along the outskirts of Debrecen, numerous *ad-hoc* soldiers and other able-bodied men managed to create a thin defensive line. Elements of the 22nd SS Cavalry Division came under an air attack from roving Russian aircraft. As for the 23rd Panzer Division, it moved into a new defensive line between Darvas and Told, making preparations at Furtánál.

The Russian 6th Guards Tank Army remained in the area of Komadi and Magyarhomorog where the 5th Guards Tank Corps and the 9th Guards Mechanized Corps were directed to Mezosast. The German 128th PG Regiment stood at Körmösd. In the Mezosast area, the German artillery fired upon the arriving Russian units. A small unit from the 23rd Panzer Division with five PzKpfw Vs repelled a very weak incursion. Obviously, the Russian attack was a mere probe. However, German supply troops did evacuate from the area and fell back to Zsáka. Elements of the Division also occupied Bagamér, 25 km southeast of Debrecen. The 6th Guards Tank Army had only 71 tanks and self-propelled guns remaining. Thus, it had greatly been reduced in strength since the operation had begun! In reality, this 'Army' was only equal to a full-strength brigade. Of course, the 23rd Panzer Division had only six tanks in the Mezosast area!

The Germans had set up huge tank repair facilities in Debrecen on Rosza Street. This facility was nearly two stories high, and filled with shops and men feverishly working around the clock. Gigantic cranes were used to lift out tank engines for repair. Numerous Panthers needing repair sat on the street – engineless.

During the day, the 33rd Corps of the 6th Guards Tank Army assembled in the Nagyvarad area as did the 7th Mechanized Corps. The Russians still had in their reserves two fresh corps.

The Hungarian 4th Reserve Division continued its retreat to the north. A small Russian bridgehead was observed and reported near Köröstarjántói. The Germans probed it and amazingly, the Russians evacuated it. In the area of Váncsodra, the Hungarian 12th Reserve Division had a variety of units including the 53rd Border Battalion, 2nd Motorized company, the 1st Company/89th Assault Gun Battalion with obsolete guns, 12 AA guns, and the 48th Regiment with four 75mm AT guns. The Hungarian 2nd Armoured Division had three Tiger tanks, although these had only been temporarily assigned to it.

The Russians attacked Beregböszörmény held by 24 Hungarians and the German 809th 21cm gun unit, which had just arrived from Komadi. The attack continued towards Váncsod and was met by the 48th AT Regiment (one company). The Russian tanks dispersed and their attack fizzled out.

By afternoon, some Hungarian troops at Mezopeterd became surrounded by the Russian attack. Armed with four 88mm guns and two companies, the Hungarians managed to repel many of the attacks. The 53rd Battalion also became encircled. The Hungarian troops fought well and were becoming exhausted. The 57th Battalion and the German 809th came to their rescue. The Russians now sent hundreds of rockets into the battle zone. Meanwhile, the Hungarian 12th Reserve Division remained in the Vancsod area, and the arrival of the 4th Reserve Division saved the situation. Both of the Hungarian divisions had been on the 'run' since the 6th, both suffering greatly from loss of men and material, lacked fuel and food. Eventually, both would be subordinate to the 3rd Panzer Corps.

The Russian 4th Guards Cavalry and 7th Mechanized Corps were ordered to attack towards Berettyóújfalu and Derecske. These corps' began their attack advancing from Biharkeresztes and Berettyószentmárton. The 10th Guards Cavalry Division began the attack at 1300 in an assault on Esztar, while the 7th Mechanized Corps advanced quickly to cut off the retreat route of the Germans by taking Berettyóújfalut. The 30th Cavalry Division advanced via Nagyszántó, Nagykereki and towards Bojt, then Berettyószentmárton. The 9th Guards Cavalry divided and sent one regiment to Bihar and another to Biharkeresztes and towards Berettyószentmárton.

When the 10th Guards Cavalry reached Berettyóújfalu, the 7th Mechanized Corps moved on towards Bors-Biharkeresztes-Berettyószentmárton. Its 16th Mechanized Brigade also reached the same area near Berettyóújfalu. All of the Russian units had received food and fuel to last three days.

Heading towards Vancsod was the 41st Guards Tank Brigade and the 64th Mechanized Brigade. These units quickly moved though Biharkeresztes and continued north to Borso and by 0700 had encircled Bojt. The advance had taken over seven hours. The 4th Guards Cavalry Corps began its attack between 0100–0200. Its 9th Guards Cavalry by 0900 had reached Biharszentjános, the 30th Cavalry had arrived near Bojt. The 10th Guards Cavalry and the 63rd Mechanized Brigade attacked together northwards from Berettyóújfalu.

The 41st Guards Tank Brigade invaded Berettyóújfalu, while the 64th Mechanized Brigade seized Váncsod and continued on towards Berettyóújfalu. The Pliyev Corps had been slowed down as the German attacked with up to

30 tanks. The resistance was fierce, as expected. The Russian attack stalled, causing the attack to lose its concentration, as units were fought to a standstill. Objectives were not achieved. So frustrated, Lt. General Pliyev regrouped the forces and decided to strive for Biharkeresztesre, Tóidra, Mezosasra, Berettyószentmárton and thereafter Berettyóújfalu. The size of the attack had called for a massive amount of units to maneuver in an area where rivers caused bottlenecks and crossings and good roads were few. Even the adjustments failed to yield success by nightfall. Pliyev had lost another 17 tanks. The 9th Guards Cavalry had only taken Borsnál, while the 10th Guards Cavalry Division and 63rd Motorized Brigade had only inched closer to Berettyóújfalu. The Hungarian 12th Reserve Division had, to their own surprise, managed to survive and held on with token resistance. The occupation of Berettyóújfalu had failed, as the 10th Guards Cavalry Division and 63rd Brigade were still 8 km away. Pliyev had also suffered 700 casualties. Regardless, he ordered the 41st Guards Tank and 64th Mechanized Brigades to join with the 9th Guards Cavalry Division to capture Biharkeresztes and Ártánd.

In the Nagyvarad area, the German 76th Division counterattacked towards Bors. It eventually reached the Told-Bojt line. The Hungarian 4th Reserve Division fell back when its right flank was suddenly exposed, when the 178th and 230th Regiments retreated towards Berettyóújfalu. The German 97th Regiment from the 46th Division fell back northwards though Kismarján and Nagykereki quickly establishing a small bridgehead south of the Berettyó River.

The Gorshov Cavalry-Armour group (this unit had 88 tanks and self propelled guns) advanced towards the Biharpüspöki-Csatár area. Its 5th Guards Cavalry Corps moved northeast of Nagyvarad. At Mezotelegdre, the Germans' Ludwig Group (a few battalions) had captured numerous AT guns and three T-34s.

In the afternoon, the Russian aircraft flew 150 missions in the Debrecen area destroying three tanks and 50 other vehicles.

The failure of the Pliyev attack was partly because of the misuse of cavalry attacking tanks and rapid-firing weapons. Added to this was fatigue. It seemed that Pliyev had forgotten the lessons learned in the First World War. The German front lines extended from Biharkeresztes-Pocsaj-Derecske-Berettyoufalu.

On the 14th, the attack conducted by elements of the 8th SS PG Regiment from 4th SS PG Division (namely, a PzKpfw V company and 2nd Battalion/8th SS PG Regiment) continued their attack eastwards from the Sznolok area towards the northeast, taking Kunhegyes and striving for Kenderes. By noon, the units were close to Kenderes but faced increasingly stiff Russian opposition. The Russians took Kenderes and the small SS force had to be content with what they had achieved for the time being. The Panther tanks attacked in a northerly direction along the Dévaványa railway line only to be met by Russian AT guns, which destroyed a few of them. Meanwhile, a Russian supply depot was encountered and seized by elements of the 13th Panzer Division after it had battled with the Russian 203rd Division from the 49th Corps. It was a minor, yet, important setup for the Russians. The German FHH PG division strived to contain the fierce attacks from the 18th Tank Corps and the 1st Airborne Division which originated from the west, southwest and south. The FHH Panzer Regiment failed to maintain their positions and gave ground.

General Breith of the 3rd Panzer Corps then ordered elements of 1st Panzer Division towards Kaba, but these were repulsed by Russian infantry. Barand also fell to the Russians. The Russian armour appeared lethargic in their approach, taking their time to reach Barand. German StuGs counter-attacked, destroying several. The Hungarian 16th Assault Gun Battalion with Turan and StuG tanks, sent the 1st and 3rd batteries towards the Gyula area; the raid quickly dispersed. By now, the 6th Guards Cavalry Corps, which had done much of the attacking towards Debrecen from Hajdúszoboszló, began to weaken its forward movement. Two Russian spies dressed in civilian clothing were caught and hanged.

During the morning, the Panzer Grenadiers from the 1st Panzer Division fought a fierce battle with the 110th Guards division in the Sárrétudvar and Bihar. The fighting spread to Dancsháza and Barand. The 73rd Panzer Artillery Regiment with 105mm guns supported the operations, while 150mm guns fired from the Sáptól area. The Russians had conducted attacks to take Nagyrabe, however all failed. The Russians had lost another 18 tanks during the fighting. The 23rd Panzer Division struggled to control the situation in the Berettyóújfalun area. Here, the Russian 9th Guards Mechanized Corps had begun its own offensive towards Mezosast, starting with a torrential rocket barrage. The attack petered out and became dispersed southeast of the town. The 128th PG Regiment and anti-aircraft guns cut into the Russians from the south. The German counter-attack advanced a few kilometres before it ran into an anti-tank front, which quickly ended any further advance. Near Verkerd, the German 51st Panzer Pioneer Battalion and the 126th PG regiment counter-attacked, destroying a large quantity of Lend-Lease American military equipment and numerous tanks. Russian aircraft arrived over the area and at Bakonszeget, forcing the Germans to pull back. By afternoon, the Russians still had yet to take Mesosast. Likewise, Russian attacks toward Berettyóújfalu from the northeast and southeast all failed.

The 23rd Panzer Division units in this area fought well into the night as the Russians attempted to encircle the town. The 128th PG Regiment and numerous tanks held to the south and west. The Russians continued to probe against the 25 tanks and StuGs the Germans had. Also in this area was the 228th StuG and 109th Panzer Brigades. The battered 76th Division struggled in their retreat towards Mezosas. The Hungarian 12th Reserve Division in the Mezopeter area began to evacuate when a Russian attack approached. The Russian 30th Cavalry Division from the 4th Guards Cavalry Corps eventually took the town as the 5th Guards Tank Corps and 6th Guards Tank Army advanced towards Biharkeresztes. Germans continued to defend Berettyóújfalu. However, at Berettyószentmárton, the town was nearly encircled in the morning. The town was in chaos despite the presence of Hungarian and German troops. Weapons and other military gear had been abandoned. The Hungarian 2nd Motorized Battalion was ordered to the town but only reached the eastern outskirts before turning back itself. The Hungarian 53rd Battalion managed to escape.

The German 76th Division came under attack from 7–10 Russian aircraft in the Bakon area. The aircraft conducted numerous strafing attacks in shallow dives. These attacks continued for sometime. Other aircraft then bombed the town. The Germans were totally helpless and at their mercy.

The 4th and 12th Hungarian Reserve Divisions remained in a scattered state and their commanders found it difficult to concentrate them. What units there were to create new units did so near Bihartorda, and Sáp. Of course, the Germans needed the Hungarian manpower and helped gather 14 75mm AT guns for the Hungarian units and recombined them near Foldes. Some of the fleeing Hungarian units had been confronted by German troops or tanks. There was a certain amount disrespect between these men and the German troops, as well as between Hungarian officers and German officers. Little things were representative of this, such as a German officer not saluting a Hungarian officer. This was true even if the German officer was of a lower rank. The Hungarian officers were always expected to obey the German officer, regardless of rank.

The 178th Regiment/76th Division repelled a Russian attack on its southern flank. At Mezopeter, the Hungarians had vacated the town and the Russians quickly occupied it. The German then counterattacked with elements of the 1176 StuG Battalion armed with Jagdpanzer 38s and supported by Panzer Grenadiers. This attack was joined by a Panzer company armed with PzKpfw IVs from the 23rd Panzer Division. The attack eventually failed and the 76th Division retreated back to their beginning positions. The panzers continued through a breach near Bakon.

The 109th Panzer Brigade halted another Russian attempt to break into Debrecen from Hajdúszoboszló. Part of the brigade with 14 tanks joined the 23rd Panzer and moved through Konya towards Berettyóújfalu. This counterattack failed. The 2109th PG Battalion, which participated in the attack, was a marginal combat unit. Much of the equipment was lacking or obsolete for 1944.

By nightfall, the 3rd Panzer Corps had ordered the 1st Panzer and 23rd Panzer Divisions, 109th Panzer Brigade and 2109th PG Battalion to secure and defend east and northeast of Berettyóújfalu – there were no Axis forces between the Sebes-Koros and Berettyó rivers.

According to Russian sources, the Axis had suffered a major blow losing 1,200 men, 9,650 taken prisoner, 115 tanks and SP guns, 85 armoured vehicles, 395 infantry weapons and 91 aircraft, since October 6.

The German 97th Regiment from the 46th Division defended Kismarját until it was heavily attacked and forced to withdraw westward. Some 15 tanks were lost by the Russians.

During the night, 12 Russian tanks and 50 other vehicles crossed the Kosmo River at Paptamási, while others advanced towards Kismarja. In the area was 176th Reserve Battalion of the 76th Division. It consisted of 380 Hungarians and 200 Germans holding a line Paptamásit to Jákóhodost.

The 203rd Regiment of the 76th Division held a wooded area northeast of Nagyvarad. The Russian attack in this locale breached the line and unravelled the defences at Kovagig-Borzeg. The Russians continued taking Kolozsvár and the road and railway line to Nagyvarad.

Both sides' aircraft were busy during the day. The Russian air force primarily focused on the Nagyvarad area, while the German 1st Luftwaffe Wing flew 180 missions focusing on Hajdúszoboszlo and Debrecen. The German air attacks destroyed 100 vehicles and six large rail tankers.

According to German sources, since October 8th, the 2nd Ukrainian Front had lost 344 tanks and self-propelled guns. The German 138th Regiment from the 3rd Mountain Division attacked along the road to Margitta.

The German attempt to take Karcag failed and the 23rd Panzer and 76th Divisions retreated from along the Berettyó River. The remnants of the decimated Hungarian 4th and 12th divisions were regrouped in the Debrecen area.

The Germans remained hopeful that even with the sustained losses they had received, they could somehow weaken the Russian juggernaut.

On the 15th, the 8th SS PG Regiment from the 4th SS PG Division continued with its counter-attack, which by noon made small gains – Russian counter-attacks from the north continued. The SS attack towards the southeast and Kenderes made little progress. The SS also struck for Törökszentmiklós, meeting Russian resistance. Little had been achieved.

Along the Szolnok-Mezotúr railway and from the south and southeast the Romanian 2nd Division and Russian 243rd Division approached and controlled the road from Törökszentmiklós- Szolnok. The Romanian 2nd Division reached Szentmiklos, held by one German battalion. One of the Romanian battalions crossed the Tisza in the south and linked up with the Romanian 4th Division and the 409th Russian Division in the afternoon.

Russian attacks upon the 13th Panzer Division all failed in the morning, while Russian attacks upon the FHH PG Division did succeed in removing elements from Kaba. Continued Russian attacks upon the FHH during the day in the Kaba area all failed. The 73rd Artillery Regiment from 1st Panzer Division supported the FHH during the day. Both sides lost armour, but for the Germans this was irreplaceable. Between Földes and Berettyóújfalu, the Russians attempted to breach the defences. The German Panzer Pioneers of the 23rd Panzer Division prevented this and captured 12 anti-tank guns. A German Panzer Pioneer Company stalled a Russian attack near Foldes.

The commander of the Hungarian 16th Assault Gun Battalion attempted to surrender to the Russians by ordering his men not to fight on the German's side. An attempt was made to contact the Russians and declare a Hungarian surrender near Derecsk. Upon the German's hearing of this, a force of 65 men and two PzKpfw V tanks arrived to 'persuade' the Hungarians near the Tisza bridge to remain loyal.

During the day, some of the Hungarian troops fled the battle area in the Derecsk area, which made the Germans suspicious of the Hungarian 7th Corps leadership. The Hungarian 12th and 4th Divisions remained somewhat intact as a result of their commanders. The 23rd Panzer Division units were also a strong deterrent! Of course, the thought of deserting the frontlines while Russians troops were ever-present, also was a deterrent. Damage was held to a minimum.

Attacking towards Berettyóújfalu was the 10th Guards Cavalry Division and the 63rd Mechanized Brigade from 7th Mechanized Corps from the northeast. To the east and northeast, the 23rd Panzer group Rebentisch, the 109th Panzer Brigade and the 228th StuG Brigade battled with the Russians. Much of the Russian cavalry dismounted and the infantry infiltrated through gaps. Russian tank regiments also were involved and despite their defences the Germans were forced to fall back. This was just too much. Part of the problem was that the Germans lacked infantry support. The German 178th Regiment arrived from the southeast. Together both German groups attacked a Russian force that bitterly defended itself near Berettyóújfalu. The three Russian cavalry divisions and two motorized brigades that assaulted Berettyóújfalu refused to give much ground. The 16th Mechanized Brigade of the 7th Mechanized Corps had failed to arrived there and had stalled at Rétszentmiklós. The 64th Mechanized Brigade and 30th Cavalry Division had seized Berettyószentmárton. The German 128th PG Regiment managed to repulse an initial attack conducted by two Russian cavalry regiments. However, these units simply crossed the Berettyó River elsewhere and began their own attack towards Berettyóújfalu. This was in the morning. The 41st Tank Brigade from the 7th Mechanized Corps and the 9th Guards Cavalry advanced in the afternoon south of Berettyóújfalutól. Axis artillery managed to stall further incursions.

In the afternoon, the Russian began to toss in the 6th Guards Tank Army, namely, the 5th Guards Tank Corps attacking Gáborján, and the 9th Guards Mechanized Corps towards Berettyószentmárton, the latter being taken by 1500. Likewise, the 5th Guards Tank Corps also seized their objective.

The Pliyev Corps Group was ordered to continue northwards and assaulted the area of Berettyóújfalun. The 41st Guards Tank Brigade was also ordered to Gáborján. This corps had attacked with the 4th Guards Cavalry Corps from Berettyóújfalu-Derecske. Only Derecske had been reached by noon. The 7th Mechanized Corps was ordered to break though defences between Szent-Gáborján-Konyár—Derecske in a northerly direction. This was accomplished. The 6th Guards Cavalry Corps also attacked towards Derecske.

These attacks fell upon the German 76th Infantry and 23rd Panzer Divisions. The Germans were forced to fall back to their second defensive positions. The line of withdrawal for elements of the 76th Division had been cut between Berettyóújfalu and Derecske, and other German units attempted to draw off the Russians so the encircled Germans could move northwards. The German 46th Division had taken Kismarjáná and blown the main road and rail bridges. The Russian Gorskov Group entered the Szalárd area from the southwest. At Esztárn and Pocsaj, the 46th Division fought bitter battles from the west and south against the Russian 33rd Corps. Eventually, Gorskov Group's armour had secured Berettyón, Biharvajdá, Hegyközszentimré and Szalárd.

In the air, Russian air activity was steady, with over 280 missions being flown over Debrecen and Hajdúszoboszló by the 4th Air Group supporting the Russian- Romanian troops that advanced from the southwest. The 3rd Panzer Corps units gradually fell back to the Tisza River under some Luftwaffe protection. The Russian spearhead penetrating between Kaba and Berettyóújfalu was of great concern to the Germans. It was proposed that the 13th Panzer Division strike east towards the 23rd Panzer. Division. The Feldherrnhalle Panzer Grenadier Division, which was one of the freshest units, would move south from the Miskloc area.

By afternoon, some of the battered German 8th Army (138th Mountain Regiment, 2nd Hungarian Armoured Division) were able to move west into the Margaritta area. There was the Hungarian 3rd Battalion/1st Armoured

Regiment with eight Turan tanks, one PzKpfw V, one motorized infantry battalion, 2nd Reconnaissance Battalion, divisional artillery, three 4 cm AA guns, and the 2nd Assault Gun Battalion with six 75mm. It combined with other elements, which brought the 2nd Hungarian Armoured Division strength to 1 PzKpfw V, 16 PzKpfw IV, four Turan 75mm, and 10 Turan 40mm.

Hungarian units did not wait for the Germans to issue orders; some units like the 25th Hungarian Division withdrew on their own and without German knowledge, heading for Polgar. This was because the Russian Gorskov Combined Corps had advanced northwards directly to the rear of some German and Hungarian units. The commander of the Hungarian 2nd Army, Lajos, issued orders to his troops to retreat around 1400–1500 hours, seeking the protection of the Tisza, which was a long way off. Some Hungarian units struck out for Tokay or Nagy Károly. Most of the German 8th Army did not begin to retreat from the Carpathians until late afternoon. The Germans did not like the fact that the 2nd Hungarian Army's commander had issued these orders and by 2100, the German 8th SS Cavalry units had full control of this allied army.

The 4th SS Panzer Grenadier Division was ordered to the Török -Szent Miklós -Fegyvernek line so that Sznolok area would remain German control. Close by in the Budapest area lay the weak 24th Panzer Division and the strong 503rd Tiger Battalion. But the 6th Army made it a priority to seal the many gaps in the front lines between Pocsaj and the Berettyó River. Its commander, Fretter Pico, threw all available troops into this area.

PART III

The Final Curtain Drops on the Hungarian Plains

The German Counter-Attack continues

The mid-October morning dawned foggy. Local weather forecasts indicated a balmy 70°F with no rain sight. For the time of year in Hungary, this was unusual.

The German attack originating from the Sznolok area continued to struggle, with the 4th SS PG Division repulsing counterattacks from the 2nd Romanian Division as they moved eastwards from the Törökszent Miklós area. Joining this attack force was the 2nd Battalion/8th SS PG Regiment. Russian troops fought with tenacity against the SS troops near Kisujszallas-Torok and succeeded in reaching the railway and German positions near Törökszent Miklós. The Russians managed to also control Kunhegyes and Kunmadaras. The 24th Panzer Division arrived near Sznolok along German supply lines, which relied on the railway. The railway was greatly affected by Russian air attacks.

The battered 3rd Panzer Corps was at a full stop from Debrecen to Hajdúböszörmény. Its 66th PG Regiment / 13th Panzer Division attacked towards the southeast to aid the FHH PG Division, which itself, was under heavy attack. The two divisions in the Nadudvar-Kaba area attacked eastwards toward Hajdúszoboszló and Kaba, halting a few kilometres from both. Several hours then passed until the FHH Division managed to retake Nadudvar exploiting a gap in the line west of the Russian 53rd Army. Just arriving was the Russian 1st Guards Airborne Division, about 4 km south of Nadudvar to halt the Germans at Kaba. The 6th Guards Cavalry Corps was nearby, in a damaged condition.

This corps badly needed fuel resupply after six days of battle. The FHH continued to defend Kaba from the north, south and southwest against numerous Russian assaults. The Russian 18th Tank Corps with the 1st Guards Airborne Division attacked and were quickly repulsed, however, as the day wore on, the German line cracked and Russian units penetrated. Only so much could be done.

The German 1st Panzer Division fought a series of deadly battles that forced them to retreat from the Sáp-Berettyóújfalu area, as well as, Bihartord, Kaba, and Derecske, which were to be defended. During the battle, a gap developed between the 1st Panzer and 23rd Panzer Divisions. Holding Derecske was the 1st Panzer Reconnaissance battalion. The 1st Panzer Division received 10 new PzKpfw IV tanks. These replenished the threadbare Panzer regiment.

At Berettyóújfalu, the German 109th Panzer Brigade's battery joined a company of tanks from the 23rd Panzer Division. In turn, they joined Panzergruppe Rebentisch. Also defending were elements of the 23rd Panzer Division's reconnaissance battalion. This group contained six PzKpfw V tanks and 12 StuGs, and began an advance towards Pocsaj. Joining in the attack was *Kampfgruppe* Fischer from the east. The objective was yet another critical bridge. Infantry from the 46th Division joined and the town was seized in the morning. Only weak Russian forces had resisted. The defending force consisted of a cavalry regiment from the 30th Cavalry Division (dismounted), a few AT guns and four self-propelled guns. However, this success was fleeting as the Russians struck towards Derecske and the German combat groups were ordered northwards to meet the attack. The town was already under attack and the Panther tanks arrived in the Russian rear. The Panther tanks fired upon the Russian 152nd Guards SP Regiment. This unit had 57mm guns. Entering into the fray came the Russian 9th Guards Cavalry Division and 30th Cavalry Division, which attacked the German armoured forces. The battle scene was very chaotic as opposing troops mingled. The German 76th Division near Berettyóújfalun retreated and the 23rd Panzer followed with the 178th and 230th Infantry Regiments (76th Division) arriving safely, however, the 126th and 128th PG Regiments (23rd Panzer Division) lagged far behind and were forced to moved towards Derecske to breakthrough. Eventually, the 76th Division reached Foldes to join the 1st Panzer Division after a march lasting at least six hours! Foldes itself came under Russian air attacks, as it was a temporary German supply depot.

A PzKpfw V Panther Ausf A travels along the streets of a Hungarian town, October 1944. Note the additional spare track lengths added to the turret and hull to provide increased protection. (Bundesarchiv 101I–244–2306–14)

Soviet infantry in action, Transylvania, autumn 1944. (RGAKFD Moscow)

The crew of a ISU–122 self-propelled gun from 2nd Ukrainian Front discuss a forthcoming attack. (RGAKFD Moscow)

Romanian aircraft, with an anti-aircraft gun in the foreground, Sibiu airfield.
(Photo archive of the Bulgarian Ministry of Defence)

Cossack unit passing through a Hungarian village, 25 September 1944. (RGAKFD Moscow)

Hungarian M40 Turan medium tank, followed by a field car. (The Tank Museum)

Later model Hungarian Turan medium tank undergoing field repairs. (The Tank Museum)

Soviet Cossack cavalry in Hungary, October 1944. (Military History Museum Budapest)

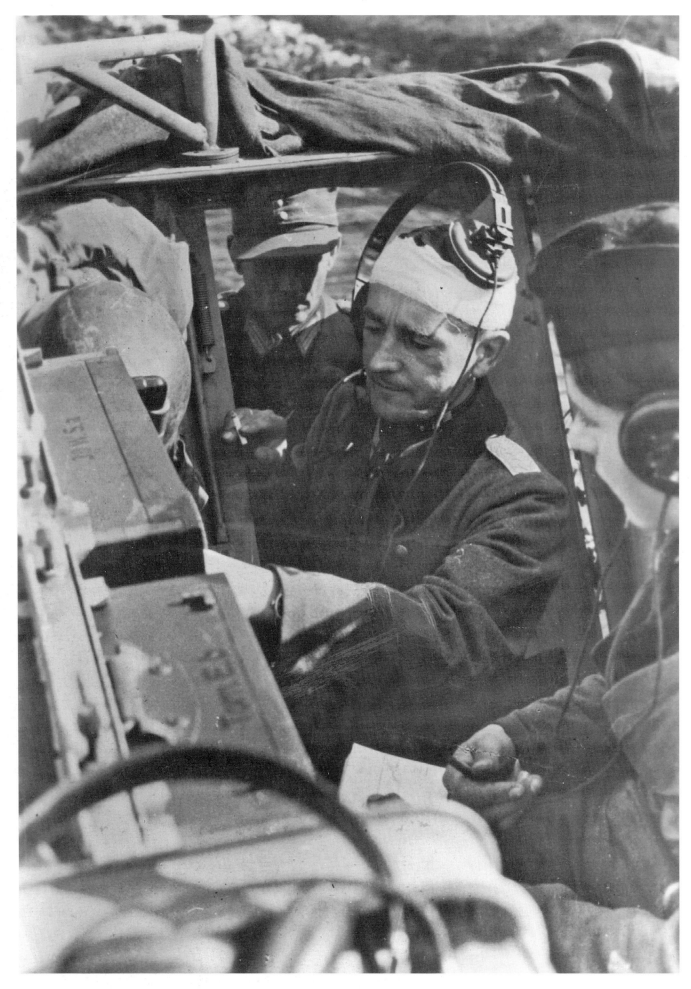

Major Wilhelm Schöning, battalion commander in Panzer Füsilier Regiment Feldherrnhalle, Panzer Grenadier Division Feldherrnhalle, Hungary, late October 1944. (Ullstein Bilderdienst)

Waffen SS troops supported by a Sturmgeschütz move towards Soviet positions, Hungary, October 1944. (Ullstein Bilderdienst)

Russian attempts to seize Konyar all failed. Meanwhile, the 23rd Panzer Division group, Fischer, occupied a nearby hill of 106m in height. Also in the group were the 2109 Panther Battalion and the 228th StuG Brigade (battalion strength). Fischer battled with the Russian 7th Mechanized Corps.

Fischer himself was nearly killed when his Panther was hit, wounding him. He bailed out and occupied another nearby tank. The Germans continued to battle, but despite their ability to handle the Russians, their losses increased. The group had only three PzKpfw V and StuG's that remained operational! These units were attempting to advance against nine Russian tanks, three of which were IS–2 tanks.

When the Russians broke through south of Konyar, they raced towards the bridge just as a German Panzer company attempted to prevent them. The Germans reached within two kilometres of the bridge before Russian troops halted this advance. By now, only four tanks remained of the Panzer company. The Russian armour with infantry support moved to within 500 m of the bridge. The four German tanks continued to move ahead despite the enemy fire. They refrained from stopping. Russian tanks on the south shore, instead they aimed and fired at the moving targets. The German tanks blindly moved through the weak Russian infantry and seized the north end of the bridge. Russian tanks fired from the other side. In all, *Kampfgruppe* Fischer had destroyed 16 Russian tanks but at the cost of nine German tanks. Tanks that were hard to replace. Fischer's success was fleeting – he only had a weak company of PzKpfw V and remnants of one company (25 men) of Panzer Grenadiers from the 128th PG Regiment. Thus, it was all for nothing. The Romanian 1st and 3rd Divisions took control of the area, including Konyar, when the Germans withdrew. Other elements of the Russian 33rd Corps moved onwards. More lives were lost for absolutely nothing. No victory was in sight.

At Derecske, the 23rd Panzer Division had fought fierce battles most of the day. The Russians attacked with cavalry, rocket barrages and up to 50 tanks, from all directions. The battles were bleeding an already weakened Panzer division, which had to be reinforced with the 278th AA battalion armed with 88mm guns. These guns destroyed seven Russian tanks within a minute. Bitter infantry battles very close to the town engulfed both sides. The arrival of the Rebentisch *Panzergruppe* allowed the Germans to retain control of the town. In this battle, the Russians lost 28 tanks and SP guns during the day. German forces consisted of 29 tanks, 20 SP Guns and 15 AT guns.

The German 46th Division was also engaged in bitter combat when the Russian 33rd Corps attacked with overwhelming force near Bihardiószeg. This became particularly serious since the arrival of an armoured group from 23rd Panzer kept division failed to arrive. The Russians penetrated with armour east of the town, forcing elements of the German division to retreat. The division had lost a large amount of equipment.

By afternoon, a new German defence line was created from Balmazújváros to the Tisza River and orders allowed troops to pull back into Debrecen. Much of the civilian workforce in Debrecen had vanished and holding the city was not an easy task for the 3rd Panzer Corps in its weakened state (i.e., a Panzer division with 20 tanks!). Debrecen was a large city.

The Hungarian 7th Corps was also in Debrecen and issued orders to the Hungarian 12th Reserve Division to join the German armour forces moving towards Derecske. The remaining Hungarian units would march to Balmazújváros- Hajdúböszörmény to create a porous defensive line of some sort. These units amounted to 800 men in two battalions. Each battalion had three infantry and one machine gun company, two artillery guns, and three 75mm AT guns. There was also a Hungarian Alarm regiment under German control.

The German 72nd Corps was surprised by the Russian Gorskov Group between Bihardiószeg –Székelyhídra. The German Corps was able to remove the seal the penetration using its 75mm guns.

In the air, both air forces operated successfully.

The German High Command, far removed from the battle area, decided that continued fighting south of Debrecen would result in excessive losses to the army group that it could not afford. Thus, the German 8th Army was ordered to withdraw to Margitta-Szatmár and eventually to the Tisza River to prevent the army's destruction. Hitler was more obsessed with holding Budapest than saving his 8th Army.

Much of the 503 Tiger Battalion and the 24th Panzer Division had by now gathered near Sznolok. The 6th Army suggested that the 24th Panzer be used to assist the 4th SS PG Division in attacking towards the east, since the 4th SS had not made sufficient headway against the Russian 18th Tank Corps and four Russian divisions in the area. This was rejected as the 53rd Army was south along the east bank of the Tisza. To their north, the Germans were unopposed.

Without opposition or German permission, the Hungarian 2nd Armoured Division freely tried to move through Nyíregyházá and towards Tokaj. However, the 'fleeing' armoured division was halted by three German tanks and SS troops at Nagykároly. Its leading officer was arrested. More SS troops quickly surrounded the long convoy. The German 6th Army tried to seal the gap between Derecske and Nagyléta. It proved to be impossible.

The Russian Pliyev Group had yet to take Derecske as of 1600. Large groups from the 4th Guards Cavalry Corps and 7th Mechanized Corps were ordered to strike for Hajdúszová and merge with the 6th Guards Cavalry Corps then attack Debrecen on the 17th. By evening, the 6th Guards Cavalry Corps had managed to take Hajdúbagos-Sáránd.

Meanwhile, the Russian 6th Guards Tank Army continued to strike towards Hajdúbagos-Sáránd from Berettyóújfalu. The 53rd Army was ordered to join and connect with the 18th Corps and together advance towards Hajdúszoboszló-Hajdúszovát, where it was to join with the 6th Guards Cavalry Corps. Russian reconnaissance forces had, by now, reached Etyek-Tiszafüred-Abádszalók-Fegyvernek—Tiszapüspöki. The 33rd Corps of the 7th Guards Army was instructed to advance to Hajdúszoboszló. Further, the Gorskov Group was ordered to Nagykároly to cut off the German 8th Army withdrawing from the east. Two more infantry corps of the 7th Guards Army had also advanced northwest near Nagyvarad. The Russian moves were bold and aggressive!

It looked as if the Russian steamroller was about to move northwards. Numbers prevailed and the offensive had always been a numbers game. The problem for the Russians was how to orchestrate the rush northwards fast enough to cut off the Germans. It would prove a difficult task for the Red Army.

Tuesday, the 17th, was like the day before. On the right flank of the German 6th Army, the 4th SS PG Division continued with its eastward pursuit in a series of bitter battles with the Russians and Romanian 2nd Division. A long cancerous bulge had been created. The Romanian 4th Division, which was further south, also applied pressure on the SS troops. Both the Russian 409th and 243rd Divisions counterattacked the SS regiment at Törökszentmiklós towards Szolnok. This attack was repulsed by the SS artillery and anti-aircraft guns firing from a distance of 200 m. Still, the SS division was forced back. To the left of the SS, Russian attacks in the Kunhegyes area from the Russian 203rd Division occurred. These attacks did succeed in the Russians seizing this town and much of the area.

The 1st Panzer Division began to pull back from Dancsháza, Nagyrábé and Bihartorda. Its reconnaissance battalion secured south of Sáp. The Division had attacked with its 1st Panzer Regiment, 1st PG Regiment and the 73rd Panzer Artillery Regiment (towed artillery) towards Hajdúszovát. The attack was down a narrow single-track road and through a wooded area. The Russian 72nd Guards Heavy Tank Regiment was waiting for them, well camouflaged. The unit, armed with IS–2 tanks, ripped into the unsuspecting German force. Turrets went flying. German artillery opened up and the panzers rapidly redeployed. The town could not be taken. Thus, the German unit and others used the cloak of night to avoid combat, negotiating narrow roads and muddy conditions from Derecske to Debrecen. Russian units could be heard during the night. Eventually, both the 1st Panzer and the 23rd Panzer units moved through Sarandon towards Debrecen.

The German High Command had issued its withdrawal order – for the Russians it was clear that Debrecen would soon be theirs. Many of the Russian troops celebrated as they entered the outskirts of the city, firing their weapons wildly. The German engineers were busily destroying their manufacturing, stores, railways, etc. Overhead, Russian aircraft buzzed over. German rearguard units contested when they could. Black smoke filled the air towards Nagyverdo. This was not a Stalingrad or Breslau situation, the Germans were not determined to hold Debrecen, in fact, they were too weak to do so. The local populace struggled with the lack of food and the Red soldiers, who committed numerous rapes and other killings upon them.

Ironically, the remains of the Hungarian 12th and 4th Reserve Divisions conducted a minor counter-attack around Derecske without much German assistance and gained a few kilometres before the Russians halted it with the 33rd Regiment of the 8th Guards Cavalry Division. The Hungarians had used a few captured T–34s in the attack, originally from the 136th Tank Regiment.

Once the Hungarian attack failed, the Hungarians, like the Germans, withdrew towards Hajdúböszörmény and Hajdúnánásra. The 53rd and 57th infantry battalions were to secure the river crossings. The Hungarian troops upon their arrival were totally exhausted.

The Pliyev mechanized and cavalry group was ordered to send the 7th Mechanized Corps from Derecske-Sarand-Mikepercs area into Debrecen. The 4th Guards Cavalry Corps was ordered to attack towards Hajdúszováton and through it to occupy the countryside adjacent to the city. The 6th Guards Cavalry Corps was ordered to advance from Hajdúszoboszló towards Debrecen ending on the northwest side of it.

Earlier, the German 23rd Panzer Division managed to seize Tepet in the morning and later, the 178th and 280th Regiment from 76th Division retook Derecske. The Russian counterattacks were all repelled northwest of Hosszúpály. With the 23rd Panzer and 76th Division acting as a rearguard, the remaining German units in the area were able to withdraw, moving northwards through Debrecen.

The 3rd Panzer Corps withdrew in safety. The 1st Panzer Division also received orders to withdraw at around 0900.

Of course, the 4th Guards Cavalry Corps attacked this 'shield' frequently with armour. Some of its troops were able to block the main route but this was temporary. The German 76th Division continued with its superb performance and by nightfall, it, too, left Derecske. Both the German 72nd and 3rd Panzer Corps withdrew and marched 80 km behind the front lines and the 23rd Panzer continued to screen the area between Sáránd and Hosszúpályi.

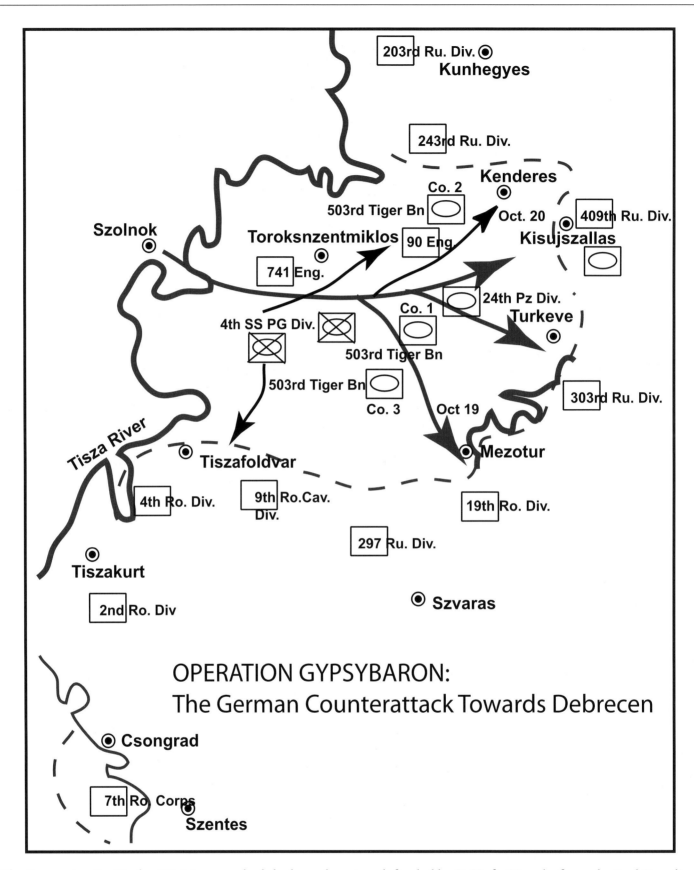

The Romanian 1st Tudor Division attacked the latter location defended by PzKpfw V tanks from the 2nd Battalion, 23rd Panzer Regiment, armoured engineers and reconnaissance troops. This was repelled. However, the town of Monostorpály was lost.

At Sarand, the 128th PG Regiment of the Division also came under attack. The 2nd PG Battalion/126th Regiment retook Hajdúbagost and southeast of there; by afternoon, the German battalion came under a bitter attack from the tank brigade from the Russian 7th Mechanized Corps including some of the IS–2 tanks of the 78th Guards Heavy Tank Regiment. A total of 27 Russian tanks were in the attack. This attack was also repulsed with the help of nearby German SP artillery. The Russians lost six tanks. The Russians continued to toss their abundant armour at the 23rd Panzer Division near Hosszúpályinál, where over 30 tanks assaulted. Here, they lost 12 tanks and failed again. But the massive Russian use of artillery, rocket and on some days, air support from the 5th Air Army, hampered and made difficult any threatening German response.

Fierce combat also engulfed the German 46th Division along the Sáránd-Vértes railway line. The Division used the embankment to buffer such attacks. It too, was forced to retreat in towards Debrecen.

During the day, the German situation became critical, when the Russian Gorskov cavalry and tank group burst through east of Debrecen and advanced towards Mihályfalva. This was a smart Russian move to outflank the German defences surrounding Debrecen. It was a serious issue – for between the German 6th and 8th Armies some 40–50 km was NOT defended at all! Only vacant land and cows lay between them.

This became such a threat that some Russian units had reached the 3rd Panzer Corps rear positions, sending non-combat troops into a frenzy. Quickly, supply issues arose for the Germans and they called upon air supply drops for those isolated units. This emergency actually created a situation where elements of the 24th Panzer Division and the newly arrived 503rd Tiger Tank Battalion were ordered to join the struggling 4th SS PG Division attacking east from Sznolok.

The Germans gather their strength

The 24th Panzer Division left from the Dukla Pass on the 11th and arrived in Budapest to quell the potential Hungarian betrayal. The 503rd had also arrived from France for the same purpose. When the 24th Panzer Division departed from the Dukla Pass, it had an assortment of tanks in the Panzer Regiment, only 20 PzKpfw IV and StuGs. Its 2nd Battalion/21st PG Regiment and 2nd Battalion/26th PG Regiment were transported in various types of trucks. Like most of the Panzer divisions in Hungary, it was threadbare. Some sources indicate the 24th Panzer Division actually had only three PzKpfw III, 18 StuG III, and 22 PzKpfw IV. The PzKpfw IVs were in Panzer companies 10 and 12, while the StuGs were in companies 9 and 11. Its divisional artillery, the 89th SP Artillery Regiment, had two light batteries and one heavy battery. The 26th PG Regiment had only one such battalion. The 26th PG Regiment contained 31 Sd.Kfz 250 and 25 Sd.Kfz. 251 armour personnel carriers, while its 24th Panzer Reconnaissance Battalion. contained 10 armoured cars. Its actual strength was a full company. On October 1, the division could deploy the following vehicles operationally:

14 PzKpfw IV
4 StuG III
3 PzKpfw III Command tanks (*Befehlswagen*)
86 APCs
7 armoured cars with 150mm guns

On October 8 the Division received 17 Panzer IV L/70, this greatly increased its firepower. Thus, by the time the Division entered into the battle area, its real operational value was equal to an Panzer brigade. Thus, the need to commit the 503rd Tiger Tank Battalion in the counter-attack was very strong!

The 503rd Tiger Battalion arrived from Germany. While in France, the unit fought the British near Caen in July. At that time, it contained 33 Tiger I and 12 Tiger II. It fought there until September when it was transferred to Paderborn for refurbishment. There, it received 45 new Tiger II, and arrived in Hungary to help suppress the Hungarian 'coup d'etat' on October 13–14. Its presence was a definite psychological edge for the Germans and helped Hungary remain a German ally instead of surrendering to the Russians. Its arrival at the 4th Panzer Corps near Budapest was welcome but none of the troops had trained together. While there, it was decided to have the Tiger unit support both the 4th SS PG and 24th Panzer Division in the proposed counter-attack.

The battalion commander was Rolf Fromme. Its 1st Company was commanded by Joachim Oemler, 2nd Company by Wolfram von Eichel-Streiber, and 3rd Company by Richárd Freiherr von Rosen.

Its organization was as follows:
Each Panzer company contained 113 men, 14 PzKpfw VI B.

Each Panzer company contained three platoons. Each platoon had 70 men and 4 PzKpfw VI B (the additional two vehicles were directly under the command of the company commander).

Thus, one Tiger tank company contained 14 PzKpfw VI B. The battalion also contained a workshop company. The battalion contained 35 officers, 274 NCOs, 694 soldiers, 90 Russian volunteers. The total battalion strength was 1093 men. Clearly, this unit had more tanks than two Panzer divisions in Hungary!

Strength:
47 PzKpfw VI B Tanks
4 20mm Wirbelwind SP Flak
4 37mm Möbelwagen SP flak

A Soviet anti-tank rifle team (Ya. Pustovit and K. Shevchik) equipped with a PTRS–41 semi-automatic weapon in action, 2 Ukrainian Front, Hungary 1944. (RGAKFD Moscow)

Guards Captain A.G. Belonogo corrects the fire of artillery from his observation post, 1944. (RGAKFD Moscow)

A Soviet cavalry unit in Transylvania, autumn 1944. (RGAKFD Moscow)

Hungarian Turan M40 tanks. (The Tank Museum)

Soviet motorcycle reconnaissance party equipped with DP light machine guns,
Hungarian plains, October 1944. (Military History Museum Budapest)

Soviet 76 mm anti-tank gun engaging enemy troops on the Hungarian plains,
October 1944. (Military History Museum Budapest)

Two Jagdpanzer IV Panzerjäger pass German infantry, including some carrying Panzerfäuste over their shoulders. Hungary, late 1944. (Bundesarchiv 146–1976–039–09)

German 3.7 cm flak gun in position in a Hungarian town square, autumn 1944. (Ullstein Bilderdienst)

PzKpfw V Ausf G Panthers, Hungary, autumn 1944. (Ullstein Bilderdienst)

A fallen German soldier, his belongings lying spread about him, Hungary, autumn 1944. (Dénes Bernád)

3 20mm flak half-tracks
11 SdKfz 251 APCs
5 T–34s
7 18 ton tractors
13 1 ton tractors
14 half-tracked motorcycles (Kettenkrads)
6 motorcyles
38 cars
6 Maultier half-tracks
84 trucks
123 LMG
136 MG
480 rifles

The German 6th Army was informed that both the 24th Panzer Division and 503rd Tiger Battalion would attack with the 4th SS PG Division in an effort to relieve the struggling and weakened 3rd Panzer Corps commanded by Breith. The Germans were confident they could burst through a Russian line consisting mostly of infantry. But the Germans were already withdrawing from Debrecen, so any success would be very problematic since the battle remained a numbers game, one that the Germans simply could not win at this stage. Time or resources were not on their side. Militarily, it was a spoiling attack-one to siphon and draw off Russian units striking at Debrecen, diverting forces so the German 6th Army could regroup and the 8th Army could escape.

As the German counter-attack force gathered, the real battle continued with the Russian 23rd Tank Corps breaking through towards Mihaly—unobstructed. The only German forces in the vicinity were weak reconnaissance forces.

The downside for the Russians, and their rapid advance and penetration of the German lines, was that their units now also needed to be re-supplied and refuelled. This was not easy as the Germans were weak but daring. The Russian spearheads had fragile supply lines, which tenuously stretched farther and farther. While the Russians created havoc for the 3rd Panzer Corps units trying to flee, by the same token, because of a lack of supply, the Russians did not take advantage of the gaps between Kába, Derecske, Sáránd, and Nagylétá. The Russian success was now starting to hinder them. This allowed some breathing space for the Germans to regroup. Both the German FHH PG and 1st Panzer Divisions needed this.

By late morning, both the 76th Division and 1st Panzer Division had been cut-off from their supply. It was not long before both divisions began to experience critical ammunition and fuel shortages. The 76th Division had no more rations. These units were ordered to create a tightly combined group and retreat northwards from Hajdúszoboszló and Derecske. The FHH PG Division was ordered to do the same. The 3rd Panzer Corps hoped to delay the Russian attacks long enough south of Debrecen, awaiting the German counter-attack from the west scheduled for the 19th. However, this was not to be.

Facing the German counter-attack would be five Russian divisions. The Russians had lost 400 armoured tanks and other vehicles since October 6th. The Pliyev Corps sat 15 km south of Debrecen.

Terrain and conditions played heavily in favour of the weakened Germans. In the Derecske vicinity lay an area that was marshy with small lakes dotting it. This forced the tanks and mechanized troops to stick to roads, which were narrow. Muddy countryside also contributed to the Russian inability to exploit across a vast area. All these events forced them to stay close to the main paved roads. The Germans deployed small groups and tanks at all the crossings and in all towns and villages, especially along the main roads. The Russian advance was fast until it was halted at one of the strong points and stopped until cleared. The German troops were daring and struck back with skill. The Germans would resist until they were in a dangerous position and then withdraw. This made the advance slow. At one time, the Russian 2nd Cavalry Division and other mechanized forces attempted to outmanoeuvre the Germans at Derecske and wasted much of the day dealing with various small German counterattacks. Pliyev ordered his troops to remain close to the roads and concentrate their strength.

On the 18th General Malinovski, who was impatient about taking Debrecen, was told of the problem and how the German forces had intercepted the Pliyev Corps some 15 km south of the city using weak rearguard forces. STAVKA issued new orders for the Russian 2nd Ukrainian Front to the 6th Guards Tank Army and the Gorskov armour and cavalry group, as Debrecen still was not in Russian control. The Gorskov group was instructed eastwards to Szatmárnémetinek, but not Nagykaroly, since that might endanger the group. The 4th Guards Cavalry Corps would attack towards Derecske and then proceed to Hajdúszovát and merge with the 6th Guards Cavalry Corps. Once Derescke was taken, the weakened 6th Guards Tank Army would be reinforced with the 5th Guards

Tank Corps and 7th Mechanized Corps. These two corps would then strike straight to Debrecen. Part of these units would meet the Gorskov Group at Mihályfalva. Depending on developments, some of the Russian forces would advance to Bagamér-Vámospércs.

The German 503rd Tiger Battalion spent much of the morning unloading, preparing and being issued orders for the upcoming attack. The 2nd Company was assigned to help the 4th SS PG Division. Supporting the 24th Panzer Division were 22 Tiger II, however, only 11 actually managed to arrived at their start positions due to a variety of reasons. The Germans attempted to camouflage this upcoming event from the eyes of overhead Russian aircraft; they were only partially successful. The 4th SS PG Division continued to strive to move south of Törökszent Nicholas, however this was not very successful and the Russian counterattacks towards the Sznolok bridgehead followed the same course. The 4th SS was instructed to conserve its strength. The 24th Panzer Division launched its attack eastwards towards Túrkeve supported by elements of the 8th SS PG Regiment and 4th SS Artillery Regiment. South of the bridgehead sat the Romanian 4th Division, which gave warning of the German build-up.

The German 3rd Panzer Corps' right flank and the area between the Tisza River and the Russian 53rd Army was undefended. The Russians attempted numerous attacks towards the Axis bridgehead which failed. The commander of the 53rd Army sent some of his forces towards the northwest. Its 409th Division and the Romanian 7th Corps would conduct an attack towards Fegyvernek and Szapárfalu and then towards the 4th SS PG Division. The 13th Panzer Division also assaulted a small Russian bridgehead at Nagyhortobágyi. Another Russian bridgehead some 14 km to the southwest was also removed at Balmazújváros by elements of the FHH PG Division. As for the Hungarian 12th and 4th Reserve Divisions, these units attempted to run across to the west bank of the Tisza River from Hajdúdorog and Hajdúnánás. However, the Hungarian corps' commander, Col. Tömöry, prevented this. He personally arrived with the 2nd Motorized Battalion and arrested the Lt. Colonel of the 12th Division. The Hungarian 16th Assault Gun Battalion, now with only a handful of vehicles, combined with a German battalion on the outskirts of Debrecen.

The German 1st Panzer Division remained in the rearguard and was by now, exhausted from continual days of heavy combat. The 113th PG Regiment had arrived from south of the city by noon. Likewise, the 73rd Panzer Artillery Regiment (towed artillery). The Headquarters took up command in the university area. Its reconnaissance battalion continued to explore south of the city. The 1st PG Regiment was east of the city to counter the Russian Gorskov Group northwest of Vámospércs. This Regiment could not stop them, only delay them, and they were pushed backed from Vámospércs.

The Russian 6th Guards Cavalry Corps remained at Hajdúszoboszló, while the 4th Guards Cavalry Corps attacked unsuccessfully towards Hajdúszovát. The Corps was able to move to within 6 km of the city suburbs by the afternoon.

The 6th Guards Cavalry now assaulted the city from the west and arrived 5 km from it by mid-morning. The local population was harassed by strafing Russian aircraft. Actual German resistance was light, as many of the units had already evacuated north of the city.

The Germans destroyed a large gun and car manufacturing factory during the day, sending toxic chemicals and black smoke into the sky. They also destroyed railway lines, bridges and other key buildings.

The 23rd Panzer Division continued to repulse numerous Russian attacks in the Sáránd area, which was amazing due to how weak the Division was. It eventually was forced to fall back in the late afternoon. The Russian 7th Mechanized Corps had reached Hajdúbagos, defended by the 1st Battalion/23rd Panzer Regiment and the 51st Panzer Pioneer Battalion. The battle continued for sometime until Russian numbers prevailed once again. The Germans had to retreat through Mikepércs. This Russian Corps had intercepted the 23rd Panzer Division elements to the northeast. Other 23rd Panzer divisional units remained some 10 km southeast of Debrecen.

The Red storm was fast approaching Debrecen. According to Russian data, some 100 tanks, assault guns and other vehicles were headed towards the Germans from Derecské, Hosszúpályiba, Hajdúbagos and Sáránd.

Russian units also penetrated and outflanked the German 46th Division some 10 km to the northwest on their left flank, and in the southeast around Vámospércs. The Red cavalry closely followed the tanks from the Gorskov Group at Nyíradony, which was defended by the German 721st AT Battalion with 75mm guns. Several T–34s were destroyed, but many more came. As usual, the tide was strong and the Germans were forced to retreat to Nyíradony by noon.

Also fast approaching Debrecen was the 35th Guards Corps, which included the 2nd Romanian Division, from the southeast near Bagamér.

On the 19th, Thursday, the German counter-attack continued at 0500 with a brief artillery barrage and tanks of the 24th Panzer Division crossing the Sznolok railway bridge. The 3rd Battalion/24th Panzer Regiment with PzKpfw IV tanks and StuG III assault guns, 24th Panzer Reconnaissance Battalion and 26th PG Regiment all rumbled forward. The 3rd Panzer Battalion now contained 40–50 operational tanks and StuGs. Behind this unit, came the 503rd Battalion's 3rd Company with 11 Tiger II tanks. Following further back was 1st Company of the same Battalion.

At this time, the 24th Panzer Division contained 40–50 tanks and assault guns, and this force assaulted the Romanian 4th Division. The Romanians were overwhelmed by this attack and the rest of the 4th Panzer Corps' assault. The Romanians had only six battalions forming a defensive line along the west bank of the Tisza River. Further south, only rear area troops existed, amounting to two companies. The appearance of the Tiger II tanks, in addition to the other German units, caused many, many Romanians to simply raise their hands and surrender. The Germans took few prisoners, they were in no mood to do this and this was a desperate time. Some Romanian units did oppose the German armour with numerous types of AA guns, minor damage occurred to a few tanks. However, the Tiger II tanks simply ran over and destroyed most of the Romanian 1st Heavy Gun Regiment and the breach opened the way for German troops to advance through. The advance continued for 20 km, Company 3/503rd Battalion advanced to the Szolnok-Mezotur railway line. There, it found a cargo train approaching and one Tiger II took aim and fired at the monster target. The train quickly became a wreck. Romanian troops and horses dismounted, scattering to a nearby wooded area. Apparently, the train was carrying supplies for a cavalry division.

The German attack had captured the towns of Tiszaföldvárt and Cibakházát by 1700. The Romanian 4th Division was then consumed by the attack and their supply line had been cut.

The Hungarian 20th Reserve Division from the 3rd Hungarian Army attacked with the 4th Panzer Corps. Its two regiments invaded the Tisza-várkony district and proceeded to the Szolnok railway line, where Romanians continued to surrender or retreat eastwards. The Romanians had so far lost 179 officers, 272 NCOs and 4,680 enlisted men during the German attack, either as POWs or killed. They had lost 23 artillery guns, 79 LMG, 82 MG, 20 AA guns.

By noon, the 24th Panzer Division and Company 1/503 Tiger Battalion had arrived at Mezotur. They were joined by the 3rd Company in the afternoon. The German tanks had consumed a large amount of fuel and needed to refuel, supply for which was brought up. Opposing them was the Russian 409th Division, located in various places. Arriving just in time near Gyoma was the Russian 303rd Division from the 7th Guards Corps. Of course, not that far way was the 6th Guards Cavalry Corps with the tired 8th Cavalry, 8th Guards Cavalry and 13th Guards Cavalry Divisions. Closer, arriving south near Szarvas in the Mezotur area, was the Romanian 9th Cavalry Division.

After refuelling the 24th Panzer Division continued advancing towards Túrkeve, in the northeast, which it seized by nightfall. It was here that the first Russian tanks were encountered and armoured engagements flared. Russian air units attacked the Tiger tanks to no avail. Most of their bombs missed the tanks by 60–100 m. The Russians conducted numerous small infantry delay that attacks against the 4th Panzer Corps spearhead, all to no avail. It was just like the old days again, so the Germans thought.

While the 24th Panzer and Tigers rampaged, the 8th SS PG Regiment of the 4th SS PG Division stumbled at Szapárfalu and Fegyvernek against the Russian 243rd Division, which fought a resolute battle. This unit had a plethora of AT and AA guns. Forced to redeploy, the 7th SS PG Regiment swung towards the southeast and arrived 10 km northwest of Mezotúr. The division contained only two PzKpfw V and 10 StuG IV.

The 13th Panzer Division continued to repel most of the Russian attacks, however, it was not aware that the Russian 53rd Army troops had outflanked some of its defences and moved further north from Tiszacsegé about 9 km. The Division was under a lot of pressure. It had only three operational tanks! At least 10 tanks needed repairs. The Russians had caused it severe losses in the previous days and while the Germans continued to fight with their usual resolution, the unit was simply too weak to stop Russian infiltration. The Russians threatened Balmazújváros. The FHH PG also repelled Russian attacks 9 km north of Hajdúszoboszló. The 1st Panzer Division counterattacked towards Balmazú jvaros west of Debrecen and FHH PG units also defended the left flank.

The 2109 PG Battalion and 109th Panzer Brigade helped support the 23rd Panzer Regiment east of Debrecen, fending off numerous Russian advances and attacks. Their own counter-attack failed and eventually they moved towards Hajdúhadház. This group had a total of 46 operational tanks (20 tanks in the 109th, 26 in the 23rd).

Thus, the 13th Panzer, FHH and the Hungarian 46th Divisions created a solid defence line towards Polgar-Észak-Erdélybol. This allowed both the German 8th Army and Hungarian 2nd Army, for the time being, a safe route to the Tisza River. German forces also approached Balmazújváros and Hajdúböszörmény.

More armour was now available to the Germans: The 1335 StuG with 7, 1176 StuG with 4, 1257 StuG and 1179 StuG Battalions with 11 Jagdpanzer 38 each. Together with the 228th StuG Brigade (30 StuG), and 325th Brigade (with 12 StuG), there were 55 operational assault guns in the Hajdúböszörmény area. The Hungarian 2nd Armoured Division sat 6 km from Polgar.

Meanwhile, both the 12th and 4th Reserve Hungarian Divisions from 7th Corps finally received orders to march across the Tisza River. The German 76th Division and Hungarian 12th Reserve Division held a 35km gap between Tiszatarján- Tiszafüred. The 3rd Panzer Corps focused its attention on its left flank as the Russians approached from the southwest and east of the city. The Hungarian 16th Assault Gun Battalion had already left Debrecen moving towards Nyíregyháza. It contained 300 men out of the original 600 and had lost all of its 16 StuG. It continued along the Tokaj-Miskolc Egerbe road towards Polgar.

Hot on the German heels were the 4th and 6th Guards Cavalry Corps approaching Debrecen from the west and southwest, while the 7th Mechanized Corps entered a vacated Hajdúbagos and Sarand in the morning. The 5th Guards Tank Corps also arrived at the southern edge of the city by 1500. Pliyev was not aware of that the Gorshov Group was east of Debrecen. Pliyev ordered his troops to assault the Debrecen suburbs with the support of the 3rd Guards Air Corps (consisting of the 7th, 297th, 13th, 3rd Guards, and 14th Air Divisions) flying numerous missions. The German rearguard units continued the fight, but this was quickly fading.

The Soviets continue their thrust towards Debrecen and the Tisza River battles

The Russians continued to order cavalry to attack well-prepared German defences situated in buildings in and around Debrecen. The 8th Cavalry Division made several attempts and were mowed down by German fire. The Cossack units fired while mounted as if this was the year 1915. Some did dismount and fought as infantry with artillery support. The first to penetrate into Debrecen was the 9th Guards Cavalry Division. These units fought a series of street battles with the German rearguards in the western suburbs. Following was the 8th Guards Cavalry Division, which forced the Germans back towards the centre of the city. The arrival of the 8th and 13th Guards Cavalry Division on the eastern outskirts allowed the Russians to surround the city. These units were supported by 50 tanks from the northern area. These carefully navigated their way into Debrecen's streets against some of the German 76th Division, which stopped them cold.

The German elements of the 46th Division also were present. Other Russian units continued northward, thus, by early afternoon, Debrecen had been surrounded and penetrated by the Russians. Finally! It had taken six hours for this to be accomplished. It would be another six hours before Debrecen was in Russian control. The 20th Urban Military Command established itself in the Debrecen financial section near Kossuth Street. Fighting inside the city continued and would finally end at 0400 on the 20th.

In the morning on October 20, Debrecen was occupied. The first of the 5th Guard Tank Corps units to enter were the 20th and 22nd Guard Tank Brigades. Their swift daring flank attack devoured enemy rearguards on the outskirts of city. The commander of the 20th Guard Tank Brigade, Colonel F. A. Zhilin, displayed such bravery and skill he was rewarded with the Order of the Red Banner!

The Russians, indeed, had tried to stay one step ahead of the German evacuation, but were continually slowed by the presence of German rearguard units. The 1st PG Regiment, which was 10 km east near Vámospércs, retreated towards Józsára, fighting Red troops all the way.

The German 6th Army retreated over the Tisza. The 1st Panzer Division had lost 19 of their 32 operational tanks. The 1st Panzer Regiment did receive 7 PzKpfw IV during the chaotic day near Magyarország. The 23rd Panzer Division moved through Mikepércs in the early morning on the northeast side (it only had one tank battalion). It combined with other divisional troops and held the area for a while. Its 1st PG Battalion/128th PG Regiment attempted to move towards Hajdúsámson but found it was occupied by the Russians. Other 23rd Panzer units filtered in and joined to create a force to blast their way northwards. The 126th PG Regiment was just north of the city, holding until it was forced to pull back. Meanwhile, the Russians conducted large scale artillery bombardments and intense air activity all directed at the German units. The 2109 PG Battalion with 22 tanks attacked the Russian troops to their north and burst through, linking up with friendly forces 5 km north of the city.

Elements from the 135th Tank Brigade of the Russian 23rd Tank Corps, which was situated a few kilometres west of the city, came under attack from German units supported by three PzKpfw V tanks. Amazingly, the 10 Russian tanks fell back in an easterly direction! The arrival of elements from the Russian 5th Guards Cavalry Corps did not help a great deal, and their losses were once again heavy, including a loss of five tanks.

The German 23rd Panzer Division had suffered greatly in their withdrawal throughout the day. In particular, the 128th PG Regiment, which had to fight one battle after another in its attempt to reach safety north of the city. The Division eventually received additional tanks, 1st and 2nd companies receiving a total of 21 Jagdpanzer IV tanks from Germany!

According to Russian sources, between the 15th and 19th October, the 3rd Panzer Corps, had lost 133 tanks and StuGs, 37 various armoured cars, 287 guns, 9,000 KIA and 1,000 POWs. The German Luftwaffe had lost 61 aircraft.

Friday October 20th – weather: sunny.

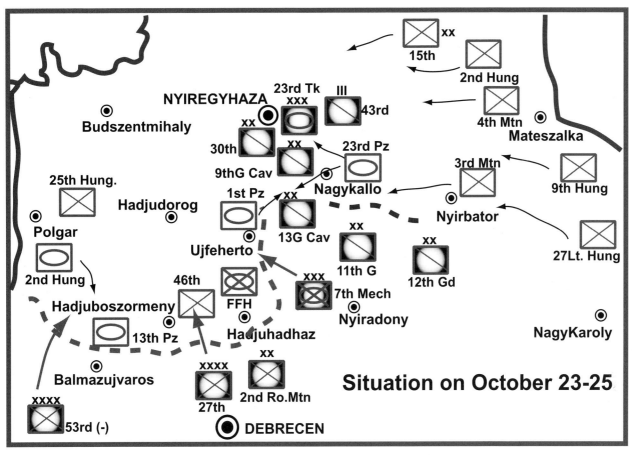

Situation on October 23-25

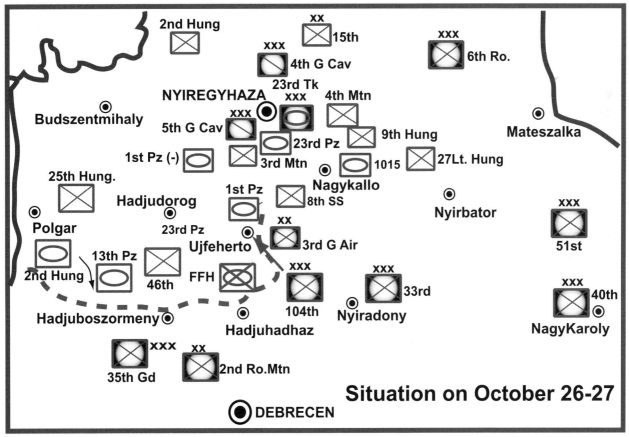

Situation on October 26-27

Waffen SS signals troops using a field telephone, Hungary, autumn 1944. (Bundesarchiv 146–1977–138–35A)

Field fortifications thrown up by Waffen SS troops to halt continuing Soviet advances,
October 1944. (Bundesarchiv 146–1982–090–17)

Above and below: Hungarian anti-tank gun, carefully camouflaged commanding the approaches to an unknown town, Hungary, October 1944. (Bundesarchiv 146–1986–064–14)

Soviet tanks moving through Debrecen, 19 October 1944. (Military History Museum Budapest)

Soviet troops across the River Tisza, autumn 1944. (Photo archive of the Bulgarian Ministry of Defence)

Above and below: Soviet military vehicles motor along Hungarian roads, autumn 1944. (RGAKFD Moscow)

Cossack unit moving along Transylvanian roads, 28 September 1944. (RGAKFD Moscow)

This extremely rare shot shows Hungarian paratroopers and German soldiers with captured Soviet prisoners in the Tiszafüred bridgehead, late October 1944. (Military History Museum Budapest)

Hungarian infantry equipped with 8mm M31 light machine guns in firing positions on the banks of the River Tisza, October 1944. (Military History Museum Budapest)

A Soviet T–34/76 tank, knocked out and abandoned by its crew, Hungary autumn 1944. (Dénes Bernád)

A German soldier lies dead beside his MG 42, Hungary, late 1944. (Dénes Bernád)

The commander of Army Group South, Colonel-General Johannes Friessner, confers with a Hungarian general. Late October 1944. (Ullstein Bilderdienst)

During the day, the Russian 53rd Army combined its forces and tanks, and struck against the 24th Panzer Division in the area between Mezotur and Püspökladány. The divisional flank was a weak point in the overall German defences. The Romanian 2nd and Russian 297th Divisions conducted their attacked towards Tiszakür-Kunszentmárton, and were ordered to seize Öcsöd and Tiszaföldvár. The 24th Panzer Division followed 3rd Company of the 503rd Tiger Battalion along the roads towards Kisújszállás. This was the main direction of the German operation, other units of both groups struck out towards Túrkeve and succeeded in taking it by nightfall, although their position was not all that secure. As the Tigers approached Kisújszállás, Russain AT guns fired; their shells did little damage and the Tigers destroyed all of them within 10 minutes. The 3rd Tiger Company encountered fierce resistance from Russian infantry defending in trenches and other defences. These infantry groups used bazookas, Molotov cocktails and hand grenades. The Tigers received many, many hits. Most did little damage. The Tigers were stuck to roads due to the muddy conditions and fired at point blank range. They penetrated the defences and proceeded a few more kilometres.

As the other group approached Turkeve, the Germans faced more resistance and stalled. The armour also approached from the city's rear. Three Tigers managed to break through the defences. By 1700, the Tigers had eliminated 36 Russian AT guns defending the area. The battle was expensive, the Germans losing heavy casualties. Even three of the Tigers were sufficiently damaged to need repair. This left six Tigers in the company that remained operational.

Despite the success, the Germans were aware that some of the objectives seemed elusive. Thus, the combat group spent the night preparing for the reported approach of Russian tanks and bringing up their supplies.

Part of the problem for the Germans lay in the fact that the counter-attack's southern flank was weak and being attacked. Elements of the 24th Panzer Division fought a series of heavy battles with the Russian 303rd Division southeast of Mezotúr. The 2nd Romanian and 297th Russian Divisions also headed for Tiszaföld.

The 4th SS PG Division together with 14 Tiger II tanks managed to take Torokszentmiklós and Kenderes. However, from the north, the Russian 18th Tank Corps attacked. The battle ebbed back and forth. The Germans faced 20 AT guns and tanks, yet despite the resistance, the Germans managed to prevail.

The 7th SS PG Regiment from the 4th SS PG Division moved into defensive positions some 10 km southeast of Torokszentmiklos, while the 8th SS PG Regiment, with Tigers and StuG IV assault guns, attempted to break through northwest of Kenderes – Kisújszállás. This was not entirely successful. However, the SS StuGs did penetrate into Kenderes and fought the Russian 243rd Division in that area. Some of the division's supply depot was taken.

The Hungarian 20th Division from the 3rd Hungarian Army battled with the 4th Romanian Division and succeeded in eliminating the enemy Tiszavárkonyi bridgehead.

General Malinovski was going to commit his last reserve force, the 7th Guards Army, northwards through Debrecen, but the German attack from Mezotúr-Kisújszállás concerned him and the army was sent in that direction instead. The 6th Guards Tank Army had been put into reserve status to refurbish and replenish, except for the 5th Guards Tank Corps and 9th Guards Mechanized Corps, which approached the Kisújszállás area by nightfall with orders to halt any further German advance eastwards. The remaining 23rd Tank Corps, 5th Guards Cavalry Corps now combined with the Pliyev Group in the Debrecen and north of Debrecen area.

The Pliyev Group was battered after 14 days of combat. Now, the five corps were ordered to Nyíregyházát-Gáva-Nyíregyháza. The 5th Guards Cavalry Corps and 23rd Tank Corps were occupying the Hajdúsámson area, while the remaining units were near Debrecen.

The 33rd Corps of 27th Army was ordered to advance to Nyírbéltek-Nyíregyháza area, while the 53rd Army occupied the Tisza River line. The 7th Guards Army and the 1st Romanian Army were ordered to destroy the German counter-attack from Sznolok. The Russian 5th Air Army would support mainly the Pliyev Group with minor support to the 7th Guards Army.

For the Germans, the counter-attack had only obtained the minimum of objectives. That would be about the best they could hope for. It was simply a case of 'numbers'.

Part of the 13th Panzer Division attacked from Balmazújvárostól towards the north-west and was able to re-establish a defensive line with the Hungarian 2nd Armoured Division near Tiszacsegé. Tiszafured had fallen to the 53rd Army. Elements of the German FHH PG Division were also in the area, which repulsed Russian attacks all day long. If the Russians could reach the Nyíregyháza area, the German 8th Army would be cut-off. Trapped! Pliyev now ordered the 23rd Tank Corps, 7th Mechanized Corps and 4th Guards Cavalry Corps to the city in the north. He planned the offensive from two directions. The 23rd Tank Corps would advance through Balkány and Geszteréd from the southeast, the 7th Mechanized Corps would advance from the southwest towards Hajdúhadház—Újfehértó. The 4th Guards Cavalry Corps would be the second echelon. The 5th Guards Cavalry Corps would screen the right flank and the 6th Guards Cavalry Corps, the left flank. The target city was expected to be reached and taken within 24 hrs. However confident Pliyev was in his troops, he misjudged the wily German forces. The distance to the objective was a good 50 km and three of the corps were exhausted.

The attack began at 0400. By 1700, the 5th Guards Cavalry Corps had taken Nagykállót, but failed in taking Demecser and Nyírbogdány. The 23rd Tank Corps reached Nagyszállá but failed to reach Nyíregyháza, the 7th Mechanized Corps seized the eastern section of Nyíregyháza. It then continued and occupied south of Nyírbogdány and Kemecsét on the next day. The 23rd Tank Corps was also to occupy the area west of the city to the Tisza River. The 6th Guards Cavalry Corps arrived at Kálmánháza at 1700. It then advanced toward Nagycserkesz-Nyírtelek-Buj-Paszab-Vencsello. The 21st Corps moved to take Rakamazt and Tiszalököt.

The second stage began at 0600, with the 4th Guards Cavalry Corps following, but it failed to keep pace with the 7th Mechanized Corps south of Nyíregyházá. The 10th Guards Cavalry Division remained at Pallag, with the 9th Guards Cavalry Division of the 6th Guards Cavalry Corps remaining in Debrecen. The 30th Cavalry Division had arrived at Hajdúhadház.

Throughout the day, the 23rd Panzer Division attempted in vain to delay the Russian forces racing northwards near Hajdúhadház and Pallag. Luckily, muddy conditions hampered the Russian units moving forward.

Meanwhile, the 2nd and 3rd battalions from the 128th Panzer Artillery Regiment supported the right flank of the 126th PG Regiment northeast of Debrecen. These units bombarded the Russian logistical routes. South of Pallag, the 1st Battalion/128th managed to dismantle a sloppy Russian attack (consisting of 3 T–34s and 20 armoured cars) moving along the railway. The Russians eventually did force the Germans to retreat as they advanced towards Hajdúsámson. The Germans fell back towards Nagyerdo and Hajdúszentgyörgy. On its right was the German 46th Division. The 1st Panzer Division attempted to disperse and attack the Russians moving along the main roads. The 1st Panzer Division seized Teglas and Hajdúhadház with *Kampfgruppe* Bradel. The Russian – Romanians maintained a porous line towards the south and southwest.

The Russian advances continued, making the battlefield a very chaotic place. They approached Hajdúsámson and seized Hajdúhadháza with the 7th Mechanized Corps and its spearhead pointed towards Nyíregyháza. *Kampfgruppe* Bradel (113th PG Regiment) failed at retaking them. The 73rd Panzer Artillery battalion held at Hajdúböszörmény, along with Bradel.

The Russian attacks met with varied success. Arriving was the 1009th PG Regiment (700 men). In the afternoon, the 1st Panzer Reconnaissance Battalion and 37th Panzerjäger Battalion battled with the Russians at Hajdúhadház and Téglás. The Russian 5th Guards Cavalry Corps and the 23rd Tank Corps with 40 tanks advanced through Nyíradony towards the north.

The Hungarian 25th Division and the 10th Assault Gun Battalion then attempted to move westwards toward the Tisza River, as did the 7th Hungarian Corps. These units had been moving for several days across the countryside from Tiszaluc, Sajóhidvég and Kesznyét. However, the Russians had arrived at Nagykálló, and Russian tanks had reached Nyírbátor. At Nagykallo, two 75mm Hungarian-manned AT guns defended against approaching armour. These units fired a few shots before fleeing. Russian units continued to pour though Ujferto along the highway towards Nagykallo. Many crossed the countryside through fields of corn. In such confusion, there were several 'friendly-fire' incidents, when Russians could not tell friend from or foe. This happened while Russian units, taking different routes encountered one another in their approach to Nagykallo.

Part of the Hungarian 25th Division was *en-route* between Nagykálló and Kállósemjén. The Russian attack in this area was a total surprise. Tanks dashed forward and fired. Cavalry arrived and the civilian population panicked. Russian tanks simply ran over cars. Hungarian troops either fired or ran. It was complete pandemonium.

The city of Nyíregyháza fell at 2300, despite the Hungarian 25th Division's weak defence (it had one regiment and three 75mm AT guns).

Meanwhile, Pliyev Corps had only advanced 22 km, its advance slowed by small German forces counter-attacking. Nyíradony fell to the 5th Guards Cavalry Corps, while the 23rd Tank Corps held Geszteréd. The 7th Mechanized Corps defended southeast of the 23rd Tank Corps. It had yet to begin its advance to Nyíregyháza and this left a gap in the Russian right flank. According to sources, the Russians had 180 tanks and assault guns in the area between Debrecen and Nyíregyháza.

During the day, the Russian 5th Air Army flew 2,200 missions. The Axis air forces flew 1,770 missions and lost 26 aircraft.

Attack and Counter-attack

Saturday October 21

The 4th Panzer Corps counter-attack was now a few days old and was now facing strong Russian opposition on the south and northern edges of the bulge it had created. From the southeast, the Russian 303rd Division struck near the 24th Panzer Division near Mezotúr. These units succeeded in entering the town. Heavy combat ensued upon the arrival of elements from 1st Company 1/503 Tiger Battalion. American Lend-Lease 57mm AT guns were prominent in this combat. This attack ultimately failed. In the north, small Russian attacks continued throughout the day towards Turkeve. The 24th Panzer Division, after receiving a few replacements, continued in vain to make progress. The 503rd Tiger Battalion continued to make small gains in the Turkeve area. Some of the Tigers from 1st Company were left behind to help defend the supply units bringing up ammunition and fuel.

Heavy fighting continued into the streets of the conquered towns against 13 Russian AT guns. Due to the thick armour, the Tigers seemed to be immune to their fire, although the intensity of Russian fire did manage to hinder their attack and response. In one case, three Russian AT guns fired at a Tiger with nearly no effect. A small wound from a metal splinter was received by one its occupants. 3rd Company of the 503 Tiger Battalion became involved in heavy combat in the Turkeve area with numerous tanks from the Russian 18th Tank Corps. Numerous Hungarians lost their lives attempting to remove or repair tanks and vehicles during the fighting.

Elements of the 24th Panzer Division tried to hold onto the Torokszentmiklos area against increasingly heavy Russian attacks. They faced much of the Russian counter-attack against the German right flank of the spearhead. Russian air attacks made resupply for the Germans very difficult until nightfall; even then, supplies could only trickle in. The 7th Corps from the Romanian 1st Army succeeded in retaking Csongrad and passing through Koroshoz. The 2nd and 19th Romanian Divisions and the 19th Cavalry Division managed to reconnect with the struggling Russian soldiers near the Tisza River close to Mezotur. The 4th SS PG Division made little progress. Thus, for the most part, the 4th Panzer Corps eastward attack had been stopped.

Elements of the 72nd Corps and the Hungarian 48th Regiment/12th Reserve Division held along the Tisza and Aroktonel. The 1st Battalion/89th Artillery with three 75mm had also arrived. Also arriving were the scattered remains of the Hungarian 10th Division with a total of 350 men. German forces defended the small bridgeheads near Tiszafured and Polgar. Arriving also was the 1st Battalion/36th Regiment between Tiszabábolnára and Tiszadorogmára.

The 3rd Panzer Corps had been torn apart and scattered. The Hungarian 2nd Armoured Division attacked and made small meaningless gains south of Polgar. Elements of the 13th Panzer Division moved west along the railway near Balmazújváros. As it did, Russian units were encountered and repulsed. It continued to remain this area defending it for as long as it could.

Similiar Russian attacks fell upon the FHH PG division in the same area. One battalion had been reduced to 433 men. Part of the 23rd Panzer Division was in the Hajdúhadház area and attacked along the railway line towards Nyíregyháza. This made good progress. The other group attacked south through Hajdúdorog and towards Ujfehértó. This group succeeded by nightfall in reaching north of the city despite a Russian presence on their left flank. The 1st Panzer Division moved west from

Hajdúhadház and ran into the Russian 7th Mechanized Corps. Heavy combat developed and the Panzer division soon found itself repelling its foe for most of the day using the 12 PzKpfw IV tanks from 6th Company/1st Panzer Regiment.

The Russian 23rd Tank Corps seized Gesztere and Nagykálló and continued northwards towards Balkany. This unit had numerous American-made vehicles armed with AA guns, which assisted the cavalry units moving in the same direction. By 1300 hours, the 3rd Tank Brigade (20 tanks) and the 56th Motorized Brigade had reached Nyíregyházá. By 1500 hours, the 10th and 30th Cavalry Divisions from the Russian 4th Guards Cavalry Corps had advanced past Nagykálló. The city was taken by evening.

The Hungarians were the only units attempting to repulse the Russians, with a battalion from the Hungarian 25th Division supported by one rocket artillery company, two 88mm guns, and 3 StuGs from the 25th StuG Battalion. A regiment of the 25th Division was south near Nagykallo. Most of this unit scattered when Russian cavalry approached, thus, only one artillery company stood and fought. A few Panther tanks from the 23rd Panzer Division eventually arrived and fought within the city. Some of the Panther tanks conducted ambushes upon the Russian tanks, however, some of the Panthers themselves were damaged, requiring workshop units to repair them while under fire.

Forced to withdraw, the Germans and Hungarians moved rapidly towards the northwest some eight kilometres, as the 2nd Battalion/241st AA Regiment covered the withdrawal. The town of Kállósemjén changed hands numerous times as the first of the 8th Army units began to arrive: the German 15th Division. This unit counterattacked the Russian 5th Guards Cavalry Corps, which had also arrived in the area.

Thus, the Pliyev Group had captured Nyíregyháza, and by doing so, had cut off 150,000 men of the German 8th Army. The question was – as the Germans who had cut off the same corps' earlier had experienced – could Pliyev actually continue to encircle the Germans?

Pliyev ordered his 23rd Tank Corps to continue and seize Kotaj and Ibranyt, after which they were to hold their positions. The 4th Guards Cavalry Corps was partly to move and hold an area west of Nyíregyháza, whilst another part of it held Büdszentmihály. Units were ordered to keep the roads open between Újfehértó and Nagykálló. The

Waffen SS grenadiers move along a ditch, Hungary, late October 1944. (Bundesarchiv 146–1971–033–27)

Romanian and Soviet soldiers celebrate the complete liberation of Transylvania, Karei,
25 October 1944. (Photo archive of the Bulgarian Ministry of Defence)

Soviet submachine gunners equipped with Shpagin PPSh 41s fire through a
window during street combat, Northern Transylvania, October 1944. (RGAKFD Moscow)

Members of a German Signals unit rest beside their vehicle during the bitter
defensive fighting, late October 1944. (Ullstein Bilderdienst)

Above and below: Soviet troops moving along North Transylvanian roads, Hungary, 1944. (RGAKFD Moscow)

Excellent view of a German 8.8 cm Flak 36 gun in an anti-tank role. The original caption records that this crew had already accounted for 11 Soviet tanks and six aircraft. (Ullstein Bilderdienst)

A German PzKpfw IV moves through the streets of Debrecen, October 1944. (Ullstein Bilderdienst)

A destroyed PzKpfw VI Ausf B 'King Tiger' from sPzAbt 503, Hungary, November 1944. (Dénes Bernád)

The wreckage of war: a destroyed Hungarian Turan II tank, November 1944. (Dénes Bernád)

A Soviet SU–76M self-propelled gun and its crew, late 1944. (Dénes Bernád)

Column of Soviet T-34/85 tanks, Hungary, end of October 1944. (Dénes Bernád)

5th Guards Cavalry Corps was ordered to seize Nyírtura—Kemecse-Székely-Berkesz-Demecser. This would secure the northeast area. The 7th Mechanized Corps was unable to move due to German attacks in the vicinity of Hajdúhadház and Téglás. The 9th Guards Cavalry Division from 6th Guards Cavalry Corps garrisoned Debrecen. The Russian 27th Army was also moving closer, but still some miles away. The bulk of the 6th Guards Cavalry Corps was a few miles southeast of Nyíregyháza.

In Debrecen, the Russians forced the Hungarian population to enact various civic duties, occupied most of the key buildings, and repaired damaged or destroyed city infrastructures.

At first, when the Russians had cut-off the 8th Army, the Germans were inclined to disperse and attempt to escape by moving northwards towards the Tisza River. However, another decision had been made to simply attack westwards southeast of Nyíregyháza as the Panzer divisions of 6th Army attacked towards them. The 8th Army also now commanded the Hungarian 2nd Army.

The 8th Army created two offensive groups. The 29th Corps with the 3rd Mountain Division, 15th Division and all of the assault guns. These were near Nyirbator. Near Mátészalkától were the 9th Hungarian Division, German 27th Jäger Division and the Hungarian 2nd Reserve Division.

The day was noteworthy because Tiger tanks had advanced 70 km through enemy lines. The unit had also destroyed 36 AT guns – the Romanians had no effective weapon against the Tiger.

On Sunday, the 22nd, the 4th Panzer Corps counter-attack had stalled. A thick fog and mist caused the heavy Tigers of the 503rd Battalion to only advance a few kilometres in the Törökszent Miklós area. The Tiger tanks had also been aware of the Russian presence throughout the area. The Russian 7th Guards Army had counter-attacked in part towards the northeast, towards Tiszaföldvár and Torokszent Miklos with the 297th Division and 303rd Divisions near Mezotur. The 1st and 3rd Tiger Companies acted as breakwaters, anchoring their defences against the Russians in the local farms, which dotted the countryside. Each company sent five Tiger II tanks. However, observation was quite to 100 metres.

The Tigers of the 3rd Company advanced slowly, each tank spaced 50 metres from the other. One of the tanks received a direct hit from a Romanian 105mm artillery gun, damaging the commander's tank. Another Tiger gun fired, sending the crew of the 105mm and the weapon to oblivion. The Tigers continued to manoeuvre and the fog provided cover, however, some Tigers had been hit 24 times before pulling back into a safer position. Russian troops were amazed. The Tigers continued but now split, some moving towards Törökszent-Miklós. The 2nd Company/503 Battalion had also finally arrived. The Germans continued to move northwards, with the 24th Panzer Division elements and the 4th SS PG Division meeting some six km from Törökszent-Miklós. By some accounts, the area had 22 AT guns and four artillery guns. During the day, the Russians did infiltrate into the towns of Mezotur and Turkeve.

The beleaguered German 3rd Panzer Corps continued to struggle. Its 13th Panzer and FHH Divisions had fallen back from Balmazújváros, Hajdúböszörmény by some six km and three km north of Hajdúhadháztó. In hot pursuit was the Romanian 3rd Division and Russian 337th Cavalry Division. The Romanian 1st Cavalry Corps and the 1st Cavalry Division advanced towards the northwest. To their left, were the Russian 110th Guards, 1st Guards Airborne Divisions, and the 228th and 375th Divisions of the 3rd Army. None of them had realized that the Germans had retreated, even though the Romanian attack had been repelled.

Lt. General Pliyev continued to direct his units northwards. The 5th Guards Cavalry Corps managed to seize Nyírtétet, Demecser and Kemecsét. The 23rd Tank Corps took the towns of Ibrány, Vencsello and Rakamaz. The 4th Guards Cavalry Corps continued to defend the Western and southwestern flanks around Nyíregyházá. While the Russians were quite elated with regards to their lightning advance that seemed to have cut off the German 8th Army, there was a downside. The downside was that this advance had created a very long front to defend and there were gaps. The 27th Army was still in the south at Nagykálló, some 25 km away. Pliyev did not possess enough infantry to plug the gaps.

German units of the 1st Panzer Division were scattered like seeds having been blown around by the wind. Its 37th Panzer Artillery battalion was near Hajdúnánás, its Panzer Reconnaissance battalion at Hajdúdorog, its 113th PG Regiment near Újfehértó. The 1st PG Regiment was defending near Téglást. These German units all defended against numerous attacks conducted by the Russian 7th Mechanized Corps. The Panzer division then conducted a small counter-attack towards Balkany, making only modest gains.

The 23rd Panzer Division was also around Újfehértó and 15 km northeast of Nagykálló. Its *Kampfgruppe* Fischer contained three PzKpfw V, four PzKpfw IV, three StuG III. Hardly a force to scare the Red Army! The group also contained the divisional reconnaissance battalion. Both of the divisional Panzer Grenadier regiments and its Panzerjäger battalion (JgPz IV) combined in an attack towards Nagykallo. Russian resistance was quite stiff and the attack stopped after a few kilometres. The ground was muddy, making manoeuvre difficult. Another attempt was conducted and by mid-morning, the town's railway station had been surrounded. It was around noon that the panzer grenadiers began their assault. The Russian defences were very strong and the Germans suffered losses to their already very weak Panzer division. However, the Russians suffered more and by 1600 the town belonged to the 23rd Panzer Division.

North of the town, the Division's 51st Panzer Pioneer Battalion and three StuG IIIs secured the area. *Kampfgruppe* Fischer had also intervened despite heavy Russian artillery and air attacks upon it. The 128th Artillery Regiment moved from the Ujfeherto area towards Nagykallo. The Russian armour in the northwest and north began to conduct weak attacks upon the Germans in the Nyíregyházá area. However, by 1800 hours, the German 29th Corps of 8th Army had succeeded in its own attack towards Kiskallo, taking it and thereby linked up with some units from the 23rd Panzer Division. Thus, both the Russian 5th Guards Cavalry and 4th Guards Cavalry Corps had been cut-off by the moves of the 23rd Panzer Division.

Like most days during the operation, Monday, the 23rd, was sunny and dry. The Russians had cut into the flank of the German 24th Panzer Division/4th Panzer Corps creating a 3 km gap supported by armour. This further stalled any advance by the Division until it was dealt with. German reconnaissance moved south of Törökszentmiklós and around Mezotur. The reports filtering in were all ominous. The Russians were massing 2,000 men and 60 tanks northwest of Mezotur. The 24th Panzer Division decided to pull back a few kilometres.

Both the Russian 6th Guards Tank Army (by this time, however, it had nowhere near the strength of an army) and the 18th Tank Corps attacked in the morning with infantry towards Kenderes. The units pierced the lines of the 4th SS PG Division's 8th PG Regiment. Russian infantry rode on the T–34s and attacked the positions held by the divisional artillery near Szapárfalut. German artillery fired repeatedly, some lowered their barrels in direct fire fashion.

It was the arrival of the 1st and 3rd companies from the 503rd Tiger Battalion that saved the German position. The Tiger tanks managed to disperse the Russians in bitter fighting. The Russians had indeed encircled the SS troops and were firing from all sides. They would have been utterly destroyed had not the Tigers arrived. The remaining SS troops joined the Tigers in a counter-attack, which restored the defences. The Russians lost 12 tanks.

The two Tiger companies now merged temporarily. Since their arrival on the 19th, four days previously, they had destroyed 120 Russian tanks and 19 guns. The Tigers had travelled 250 km without a major engine breakdown. It was not unusual for all of the Tigers to have at least 20 hits upon their armour. According to German sources, between 12th and 23rd October, the 4th Panzer Corps had caused the Romanians the following losses: 18 tanks, 280 various artillery guns, 17 AA guns, 58 cars, 235 MG, 45 AT guns, 112 LMG, 424 rifles, 4,521 POWs and 2,400 KIA.

The Hungarian 2nd Armoured Division on the right flank of the 3rd Panzer Corps fought but was forced to retreat a few kilometres towards Polgar, the main crossing over the Tisza. Also in the area were the Hungarian 59th Infantry Battalion and a battalion of German artillery. On the west bank of the river the Hungarian 25th Division defended along with German AA units.

The 13th Panzer Division successfully attacked towards Balmazújváros, despite its threadbare condition. It beat off numerous Russian attacks and the unit arrived west of Hajdúböszörmény.

The FHH and 46th Division were able to repulse all of the Russian assaults, as well.

The Russians were in an awkward position. What had been a success had now turned into a real concern since all of the Russian reserves had been sent to oppose the 4th Panzer Corps threat from Szolnok. The Germans now had a thin line stretching from Hajdúdorog-Ujfehértó –Nagykálló. This cut off Russian units around Nyireghaza. The 27th Russian Army between Hajdúböszörmény—Hajdúdorog was ordered to breach the line and merge with Pliyev's units.

Pliyev's five corps had lost some 200 tanks and self-propelled guns. The 7th Mechanized Corps was south of Újfehértó and battled with the 1st Panzer Division along the highway and railways around Gesztered. A stalemate between them ensued.

The 23rd Panzer Division's positions around Nagykallo were also continually contested by the enemy. By some accounts it had only 20 tanks and StuGs. The 2nd PG Battalion/126th PG Regiment attacked southwards towards Biri against the Russian 13th Guards Cavalry Division from 6th Guards Cavalry Corps. This was in an effort to meet the German 29th Corps attacking westwards.

This German attack fell apart when ambushed by the tanks of the Russian 250th Tank Regiment. The Russians attempted to outflank the Germans, however, this also failed. The German assault did gain a few kilometres, and they were able to take Biri and Balkany.

Arriving nearby was the artillery of the German 3rd Mountain Division. The 23rd Panzer Division was being approached from the north, northeast, and northwest, by Russian units. Elements of the Russian units were able to take Nagykáliót and Dombrad. Arriving at Nagykaroly and at Kocsord was the Hungarian 27th Division from Hungarian 9th Corps. Its 9th Reserve Division also had reached Nyírbaktáná.

Most of the German 29th Corps advance was northeast of Nagykallo or at Kisleta and Nyirboga.

The weather finally began to change, with rain falling on the 24th. The 4th Panzer Corps began its withdrawal back to Szolnok. Enough was enough. The German attack had served a purpose, even though Debrecen was never reached: it had drawn off the Russian reserves westward. By 1800 hours, the 24th Panzer Division had succeeded in pulling back to their start positions.

Meanwhile, by noon, the 4th SS PG Division had withdrawn into a small bridgehead north of Vezseny and Szajol. The Germans had relinquished Torokszentmiklos, the SS troops fighting various small rearguard actions during the withdrawal. However, the Russian 36th Guards Division did cross the Tisza, which created a whole new dilemma for the division. From the northwest area, elements of the 503rd Tiger Battalion acted as a rear screen keeping the Russian T–34s at a safe distance. Yet again, small groups of Russian units were able to move west to Tiszabot. The German 72nd Corps countered the Russain 53rd Army's attempt to cross the river and at the Tiszafuredi bridgehead.

The Hungarian 1st National Defence Company/36th Battalion (83 men), and the 2nd Company/20th Assault Gun Battalion withdrew but had arrived too late along the Tisza. The Germans had already blown a key bridge. Luckily, a nearby pontoon bridge had been laid. As troops raced to cross, many trucks with supplies were abandoned, artillery or AT guns left behind. The Russians were only a few kilometres away. These units evaded the Russians stretching from Nagyvarad-Berettyoujfalun-Poscaj-Debrecen-Tiszafured. The company had lost 154 men. The 20th Assault Gun Battalion contained eight Hungarian Zrinyi assault guns and three Turan tanks and moved in a southeast direction. During their retreat westward the Germans came under air attack from the roving Russian aircraft. In one case, 43 75mm AT guns and four 88mm, all being towed, fell into the Russian sights. Many were lost. The air defences around the Hungarian-German bridgehead were weak and defended with only four 20mm AA guns – hardly effective. The swampy area was also a major hindrance for wheeled vehicles. Many got stuck and left behind. This forced vehicles to remain on the roads or use a partially-destroyed railroad bridge.

Meanwhile, the Russian 13th Guards Airborne Regiment from the 1st Guards Airborne Division had already infiltrated around the 1st Company/36th Battalion and crossed the Tisza River. The Hungarian 2nd Battalion/38th Regiment attacked east of Tiszabábolna encountering a Russian cavalry company. Little was gained. The Hungarian 2nd Armoured Division also soon arrived, seeking the protection of the Tisza River. The unit had acquired a few PzKpfw Vs and its assorted tank company moved southwards from Polgar towards Kuntanya where it met six Russian AT guns. The unit was also approached from another direction by Russian T–34s. On its right, were elements from the German 13th Panzer Division (a tank company). The tank company had destroyed 16 Russian tanks within 10 days.

Many of the remaining elements of the 13th Panzer Division were in the Balmazújváros area. Both it and the Hungarian 2nd Armoured Division fended off various attacks conducted by the Russian 53rd Army towards Polgar. The 66th PG Regiment conducted their attack from northwest of Hajdúböszörmény towards the west. During this attack, it had destroyed 21 Russian artillery guns and 37 AT guns, plus a number of American-made vehicles. Likewise, the German FHH PG Division and 46th Division all repulsed successive raids made by the Russians.

The Romanian 2nd Division attacked Teglas, defended by elements of the 1st Panzer Division – this failed. Several attempts continued until some of the Romanians penetrated through the Lions. The same scenario occurred between the same units at Gesztered; this time, the Germans retreated.

The 23rd Panzer Division and the 3rd Mountain Division met near Nagykallo. The first elements of the 3rd Mountain, including 1st Battalion/138th Mountain Jager Regiment and the 112th Mountain Artillery Regiment, had arrived, followed by the 144th Mountain Jager Regiment. The 3rd Mountain units now attacked into the suburbs of Nyiregyhaza loosely held by the Russian 9th Guards Cavalry Division. The 23rd Panzer Division moved to the Hajdúdorog area and was detected by Russian reconnaissance units as it neared the Nyíregyháza area.

The Russian 30th Cavalry Division from the 4th Guards Cavalry Corps and the 3rd Tank Brigade (20–30 tanks) from the 23rd Tank Corps near Nyíregyháza, attacked towards the southwest, towards Hajdúnánás, in an effort to cut off retreating elements of the German 8th Army, which were moving westwards. However, this effort totally failed. In the attack, the Russians encircled Hajdúdorog, defended by elements of the 128th PG Regiment. Several T–34s penetrated into the town and battled the German Jagdpanzer IVs. The Russians pulled back after several tanks were lost. The 126th and 128th PG Regiments counter-attacked the weakly defended Hajdúdorog area. These units continued to advance for several more kilometres. The Russian battalion holding the town was ripped apart – it lost two 76.2mm AT guns, eight HMG, 10 trucks. Many of the German attacks were only successful due to the air support provided by Luftwaffe ground-attack units, which was quite active during the day. The 3rd and 4th companies from the Panzer Reconnaissance Battalion and 23rd Panzer Regiment combined and successfully attacked towards Kálmánháza where only weak Russian defences existed and were crushed. This group succeeded in taking Hajdúdorog and connected with the 128th PG Regiment at Hajdúnánásra. The 126th PG Regiment soon followed in a more northerly direction. The main thing was the 23rd Panzer Division had succeeded in collecting most of its units within a small area once again!

The Division had destroyed another 13 tanks, 64 artillery guns, 24 AT guns, 11 rocket artillery launchers, two AA guns, and seven MG belonging to the opposing Russian forces.

During the day, German-Hungarian aircraft flew over 90 missions and found a very lucrative target: the Russian 30th Cavalry Division. Out in the open and with no enemy fighters around, the Axis air units ravaged it. In the end, the division lost 100 horses, two tanks, 11 trucks, and 80 artillery and AT guns.

The commander of the Russian 27th Army was not aware that the Pliyev Group had been cut off. The German mobile defences had proven too difficult for the Russians to predict. It was hoped that elements of the 27th Army could combine with some of the Pliyev units in the Nagykallo area.

North of Hajdúdorog, much of the German 6th Army deployed. Amazingly, it had been the 23rd Panzer Division that had, indeed, prevented the Russians from further progress. The Division's attacks southwards seriously delayed the advance. The German 8th Army was in the area near Kistégláson, and continued its own attacks north of Nyíregyházát and along the Tisza. Attacks from the Tokay area had also pushed back the Russians towards the southeast of Tiszanagyfalu. The Hungarian 9th Corps stood near Napkor, while the German 29th Corps was northeast of Nagykallo and 10 km from Nyíregyházá. In the area of Nyirte, the Russian 43rd Cossack Regiment from the 5th Guards Cavalry Corps held. It was ordered to occupy Nyírturáig. The Russians battled the 8th SS AA Battalion and elements from the Hungarian 9th Corps.

The German 29th Corps fought against stiff Russian resistance south of Nagykálló. The 15th Division assaulted enemy positions south and southwest of Nyírbogáttói.

October 25 Wednesday – weather: cloudy, 13°C

The Russians continued to make gains against the 4th SS PG Division, which was forced to retreat from Szajolna towards the southeast. They also attempted to cross the Tisza at Tiszapüspökin and Nagykörun, with some success. Both the 4th SS PG Division and all of the 503rd Tiger Battalion had withdrawn to the west bank of the Tisza River, after which the main Szolnok highway bridge was blown up.

The Hungarian 1st Cavalry and 20th Infantry Division attacked the 2nd Romanian Division, forcing them to the right bank of the Tisza. The Hungarians, bolstered by this success, then launched another attack using the 3rd and 8th Infantry Divisions plus the remnants of the 1st Armoured Division to eradicate the growing Alpar bridgehead created by the Romanian 19th Division. This time, the Romanians won and inflicted heavy losses on already weak Hungarian units.

The Russian 13th Guards Airborne Regiment from the 1st Guards Airborne Division was able to secure a small bridgehead over the Tisza with one of its battalions. The Hungarian 48th Regiment from the 12th Hungarian Division was unable to prevail despite several counter-attacks. The 20th Hungarian Division was ordered to defend south of Sznolnok. The German 72nd Corps and Hungarian 12th Reserve Division were ordered towards the Dunaföldvári bridgehead. The 2nd Hungarian Army was ordered to move along the Tisza. The Russians used their 228th Division in yet another attempt to cross the Tisza near Tiszafüredi. The division attempted three times, each time it was repulsed. Southeast of Tiszabábolnát, a small Russian bridgehead was created and kept at bay by the Hungarian 38th Regiment from the Hungarian 12th Division.

The German 3rd Panzer Corps meanwhile halted six kilometres northwest of Polgar. Its units came under a Russian attack during the night near Hajdúböszörménytol, but it was repulsed.

Its 13th Panzer Division elements joined elements from the Hungarian 2nd Armoured Division some 15 km south of Polgar when the Russians attacked towards. The Russian attack was able to create a 3 km gap, which could not be sealed. Thus, Russian units ripped through, capturing a key highway bridge.

Because of this incursion, both the 23rd and 13th Panzer Divisions' avenue to the Tisza was in jeopardy. Near Nyiregyhaza, the Russians pulled back as more and more enemy units arrived to the south and north.

However, Russian troops continued in their attacks and eventually seized Téglás and moved northwards towards Ujfeherto. This was accomplished by noon. The German-Hungarian 1st Air Corps appeared overhead with 50 aircraft in this area and destroyed six tanks.

By now, the 23rd Panzer Division sent the 2nd Battalion/128 PG Regiment towards Hajdúdorog and Hajdúnánás with three PzKpfw V. The 37th Panzerjäger Battalion was joined by 2 PzKpfw V and one Marder and also sent there. The Hungarian 2nd Armoured Division had only 700 men, eight 75mm AT guns and 18 artillery guns.

The Germans counter-attacked towards Ujfeherto and were able to advance two kilometres south of it. Due to nightfall, three tanks from the attack force were pulled back into Hajdúnánásra, while the 128th PG Regiment held Ujfeherto for the night. Its 1st PG Battalion moved and occupied the town of Nagymicskepusztá, The 126th PG Regiment departed at 1530 for Nagykálló and was able to link up with elements of the German 3rd Mountain

Divison (8th Army) and the 8th SS Reconnaissance Battalion. Later, the 106th Regiment of 15th Division arrived near Hajdúdorog.

During the day, the German 29th Corps supported by a few tanks managed to repel all of the Russian attacks upon it originating from the northeast, northwest and the south. Much of 8th Army continued towards Dombrádo and Beszterece. The Hungarian 9th and German 29th Corps' own attack upon Nyíregyháza stalled. Russian resistance remained quite strong. The Hungarian 9th Division controlled Nyírturát after a bitter fight with the Russian 43rd Guards Cavalry Regiment.

By the end of the day, German forces were northeast of Napkor, northwest of Kiskálló. Southwest of Kiskallo, the 91st Brigade from the 4th Mountain Division joined the 23rd Panzer Divisional elements in attacking Nagykálió.

By the 26th, both the German 4th Panzer Corps and 72nd Corps came under attack at dawn from the Romanian 1st Army and Russian 53rd Army. Many of these units had attacked or crossed the Tisza during the early morning hours. The bulk of the heavy attacks were focused towards Tószegtol, while minor attacks were directed at Tiszapüspök. Fighting the Russian 36th Guards Cavalry Division proved to be a bloody affair. The Russian unit had attacked Tószegre three times but was repulsed each time by Hungarian and German units along the west river bank. The 4th SS PG Division had suffered heavy losses during this fighting.

The Russian 7th Guards Army also attacked the German 4th Panzer Corps after crossing the Tisza. Elements of their 233rd and 81st Guards Divisions were able to create a small bridgehead near Tiszapüspökitol. To combat this, the Germans sent in 10 Tiger tanks from the 503rd Tiger Battalion, which were unable to destroy the bridgehead. Russian sources claimed two Tigers had been lost.

Likewise, the German 72nd Corps sent what troops it had to seal the bridgehead, which was only partially successful. Also arriving was the 13th Regiment of the 1st Guards Airborne Division which came under attack from a variety of Hungarian units. Russian units also attempted to advance towards Árokton.

Elsewhere, the German 13th Panzer Division attacked towards Hajdúböszörmény, the Russians counterattacked and stalemate set in. Along the Tiszacsege-Polgár railway, the Russians had managed to bust through the defensive line towards the northeast on a broad front. The German 13th Panzer, 46th and FHH Divisions all conducted well-executed counter-attacks in a vain effort to seal the gap. The appearance of Romanian troops elsewhere complicated this and eventually the Germans were repulsed.

Throughout the day, both the 128th Panzer Artillery Regiment and 1st Battalion/128th PG Regiment from the 23rd Panzer Division battled with various Russian units from the 27th Army southeast of Ujfeherto. The Russian penetrated several times but were repulsed as they tried to save the cut off corps. The 1st Panzer Division held its positions north of the city. The 23rd Panzer elements were forced to pull back in the Ujfeherto-Nagykallo area when the Russian attacked from south of Nyíregyháza.

During the battle, the German 128th PG Regiment had become quite fragmented and gaps in its lines began to appear. The 1st Panzer Reconnaissance Battalion had struck into the flank of the Russians and destroyed six AT guns and over 20 trucks and other vehicles. A tenuous connection had also developed between it and the 23rd Panzer Divison. Lt. General Pliyev was ordered to breakout using his 23rd Tank Corps and units from the 4th and 6th Guards Cavalry Corps towards Nagykallo and merge with units of the Russian 27th Army. These orders arrived directly from the 2nd Ukrainian Front. The basic plan called for the 3rd Guards Airborne Division and the 3rd Tank Brigade of 23rd Tank Corps, which had held much of the Nyíregyházá area, to depart at 1800 hrs and advance towards Nagykallo.

However, the 23rd Panzer Division struck long before (0900 hours) the plan was activated attacking towards Nyíregyháza. From the southwest, German troops also broke through 5 km northwest of Hajdúdorogtól and were advancing towards Nyíregyháza, as well. A weak connection had also been created with the German 3rd Mountain Division moving westward towards the Tisza.

Kampfgruppe Fischer (consisting of 3 PzKpfw V, 1 PzKpfw IV, 4 StuGs from 23rd Panzer Regiment, 23rd Panzer Reconnaissance Battalion, a Panzer Grenadier Battalion, and 1st Battalion/128th Panzer Artillery Regiment – all from 23rd Panzer Division) led the attack and followed later by the 126th PG Regiment in various trucks loaded with infantry.

When the German group reached to within a few kilometres of Nyíregyházá, the group separated, with all of the 126th PG Regiment assaulting the city. The others continued northwards and then turned eastwards, assaulting the city from the northwest. The northern group quickly cleared pockets of resistance in the western suburbs of the city The 126th PG also managed to clear the city from the southern approaches and reached the city's centre by noon. Russian resistance was sporadic and disorganized. The sudden surprise attack had done its job on the Russian forces. However, it was in the centre of the city that caused the German 126th PG Regiment the most problems. This is where they experienced the heaviest resistance. The German force had also managed to rescue over 1,000 Hungarian and German soldiers held in captivity. Some of the Russian troops had been displaced towards the southeast and north. These small pockets were finally dealt with by 1600 hrs. The attack had been a total success. The 3rd Mountain Division was able to withdraw and moved to the safety of the Tisza River. The 23rd Panzer Division, despite its own mauled condition, seemed to have performed a miracle. It had destroyed 13 tanks, 100 AT guns, 17 artillery guns, 19 rocket launchers, 7 AA guns, 19 MG, 88 trucks, 11 cars, 8 motorcycles, and 332 other vehicles. The Germans lost 92 men to the Russian 650, and 1,014 POWs.

During this urban combat, the Russians appeared confused as to what was happening. Their soldiers were confused and frightened as German tanks seemed to have appeared out of nowhere. Huge explosions instantly shattered buildings and reduced them to rubble. The local population was elated at the German's arrival! Despite the danger, they were greeted along the roadsides once word had spread of their advance. Women ran up and kissed soldiers. Men saluted with admiration. Eyes watered. When the shooting began, the population went into hiding, seeking safety. Of course, not all were safe, explosions and combat did kill many civilians. Bodies dotted the avenues. Following the fall of the city to the Germans horrific stories which appalled even hardened German soldiers, began to emerge. The Cossack division that had held the city had taken its vengeance upon the Hungarians. Hungarian women were routinely selected and raped by Russian soldiers in vacant buildings. Some groups numbered as many as 20 men. Key public figures were simply beheaded or had their throats slit. One 17-year-old was raped over 20 times by a group of men, one after another. Some of the POWs were also tortured. Some Hungarians attempted to escape by wearing Russian uniforms. Those who were caught were shot in the head.

The German 8th Army's 29th Corps continued to move. Its 4th Mountain Division had reached Kiskállótól and held the Kiskálló-Kállósemjén line. The corps' eastern flank moved westwards as did the 9th Hungarian Corps. It had reached Rohodon. Elements of the army approached the northwest near *Kampfgruppe* Fischer. Another German *Kampfgruppe*, Scholze, had seized Demecsert and Nyírbogdány. By afternoon, much of the Russian resistance had ceased in the area Buj-Kotaj-Nyírpazony. The Hungarian 9th Division fought a stiff battle at Mészáros Béla. Units from the 28th Regiment assaulted the Russian positions and hand-to-hand combat ensued. Strong Russian resistance had halted the Hungarian 9th Corps at Nyírpazonyná, who were assisted by elements of the 23rd Panzer Division.

The 144th and 138th Mountain Jäger Regiments of the German 3rd Mountain Division continued to move from Nyíregyháza – its reconnaissance units fanned out in all directions attempting to detect the location of the Russian pockets. It then ran into elements of the Russian 5th Guards Cavalry Corps, which had been totally startled and was unprepared for the coming combat. Russian confusion was obvious. These units simply dropped their weapons and fled. The German division continued advancing northwest of Kiskálló.

Much of the defiant Russian resistance came from the 11th Guards Cavalry Division of the 5th Guards Cavalry Corps in the Kiskálló- Nyíregyházár area, where it fought a tenacious battle with the 3rd Mountain Divison as it attempted to retreat. The battle with this division last for over five hours and required the support of the 23rd Panzer Division before the mountain troops could occupy Nyíregyházá. The battle had caused both sides serious losses.

South of Nagykálióná stood the bulk of the 8th Army – the 91st Mountain Jäger Regiment from 4th Mountain Division, 94th Mountain Artillery Regiment, 15th Infantry Division, 15th SS Cavalry Regiment from the 8th SS Cavalry Division, the 8th SS Reconnaissance Battalion driving Volkswagens, the 1st Battalion/138th Mountain Jäger Regiment and the 112th Mountain Artillery Regiment from 3rd Mountain Division.

Meanwhile, the Russian 27th Army attempted two attacks with heavy artillery fire against the German lines to no avail—both failed. By noon, some of the German 8th Army began to filter through from Nagykallo to Ujfeherto, along the roads in a southeasterly direction. The first units to arrive were the artillery of the 4th Mountain Division and its 91st Regiment, and the Panzerjäger Battalion from the 15th Infantry Division consisting of seven Jagdpanzer 38 tanks.

The Russians continued to try to breakout of the trap west and southwest of Nagykallo. The Russians immediately encountered the German 4th Mountain Division and elements of the 8th SS Cavalry Division, who counterattacked. The 152nd Guards Tank Regiment from the 4th Guards Cavalry Corps also attempted to burst through five times, failing each time. The Russian 4th and 6th Guards Cavalry Corps, along with the 23rd Tank Corps, had nearly been dismantled. Large quantities of abandoned and destroyed equipment and tanks lined the countryside and roads. Eventually, the 23rd Panzer Division relocated near Nyíregyházá.

In the air, much of the Russian 5th Air Army focus was on attacking the German 6th Army and their 4th Panzer Corps. Some 180 missions were flown. The Hungarian 102nd Squadron, flying Me 210 aircraft, bombed west of Debrecen.

On the 27th October, the 4th SS PG and 24th Panzer Divisions (4th Panzer Corps) attacked towards the Tiszavarkonyi railway station. Russian units had crossed the river and established a small bridgehead with a few battalions. This was removed after a brief battle.

All of the German divisions that had fought in this battle were now threadbare, and it is a testament to their training and abilities that they had managed to do what they had. It had been very costly:

The 24th Panzer Division had 11 PzKpfw IV and seven StuGs. Its combat strength was 1,600 men, 13 75mm AT guns.

The 4th SS PG Division had a combat strength of 1,100 men, 41 artillery guns, 18 AT guns, and eight StuGs.

The 503rd Tiger Battalion remained the strongest unit with 30 Tiger II tanks.

The 76th Infantry Division had 1,900 combatants, two 75mm AT Guns, and 13 artillery guns.

The 1176 StuG Battalion had two operational Jagdpanzer 38s.

The 72nd Corps held a thin line along the Tisza River except for a 3 km Russian bridgehead and a smaller one at Tiszadorogmán. Russians had also crossed near Tiszafured in very small groups. These were not threatening. Russian units also attacked the Germans at Tiszafured with heavy artillery. The attack failed.

In the early morning, Russian units also attacked the German-Hungarian forces in the Tiszafüred area. The main defending unit was the Hungarian 12th Reserve Division and five German StuGs. The Hungarian 57th and 38th Regiments fought well and repulsed yet another Russian attempt to cross the Tisza. The Russians made another attempt near Aroktot, and once again, failed.

The remnants of the 13th Panzer Division stood in the Hajdúböszörmény-Polgár area. Its artillery stood between Tiszacsege-Balmazújváros. Its operational tank strength was a mere six PzKpfw V, one PzKpfw III, one Pz IV L/70. The total number of Panzer Grenadiers came to 1,100 men, and 14 artillery guns. It, like the others, had performed many miracles since October 6.

At 0800, the German FHH PG Division repulsed another Russian attack. The division was battered and it was suggested that the unit should withdraw through Polgarhoz to the other side of the Tisza River. This could not be accomplished because of the daring attack stemming from the Russian 6th Guards Tank Army. A need for refitting was definitely there,as the FHH Division had 10 StuGs, seven 75mm guns, and only 900 effective combatants. The Russians also attempted another incursion against the German 46th Division, which was only repulsed after bitter battles.

The 1st Panzer Division fought similar battles with the Russian 3rd Guards Airborne Division and a number of T-34s south of the Ujfeherto. Here, the Russians were able to create several breaks in the German line after fierce fighting. The Russian units then advanced in a northerly direction towards Szomjúhá. The Germans counter-attacked, halting any further advance. In the area between Ujfeherto and Nagykallo, the German 23rd Panzer Division beat off several small Russian attacks. By afternoon, the Division had relocated near Hajdúdorog and Hajdúnánás.

By now, the 1st Panzer Division contained nine PzKpfw IV, two StuGs, and eight PzKpfw V operational tanks. It had a total of 1,000 Panzer Grenadiers. It had 11 75mm AT guns and its artillery regiment contained 30 guns.

The 23rd Panzer Division had two PzKpfw IV and PzKpfw V tanks, 28 StuGs, 850 combatants, nine 75mm AT guns, and 30 artillery guns.

The Hungarian 2nd Reserve Division of the 9th Hungarian Corps spent much of the day in the Nyíregyházá area, while the German 3rd Mountain Division (29th Corps) was nearby to the southeast. The 9th Corps then marched westward towards the Tiszalök-Büdszentmihály line.

It was in this area that heavy fighting continued throughout the day, as trapped Russian units attempted in vain to break through the German lines to unite with other isolated groups. Near Nagykallo, an isolated Russian battalion attempted an attack towards the south, if failed.

Much of the German 29th Corps marched southwest of Nagykálló. The 3rd Mountain and 8th SS Cavalry Divisions attacked the isolated Russian units southeast of Nyíregyháza. The 4th Mountain Division advanced towards Ujfeherto using the Ujfeherto-Nagykálló roads. These marches were not without fighting. Much of the advance encountered various groups of enemy soldiers or units, resulting in some heavy combat. The 8th SS Cavalry Division lost 16 KIA and 78 WIA. The German 88th Regiment/15th Division attempted an attack from the north against Russian units, which failed. Much of the 3rd Panzer Corps itself was being extracted from the Nyíregyháza area. Battling the Russian 5th Guards Cavalry Corps was the German 3rd Mountain Division at Nyíregyháza, resulting in several sporadic and intense periods of combat. When the battle was over, some 852 Russians were dead and 34 POWs. The Russian unit had also lost 14 tanks, 49 AT Guns, 79 LMG, 69 MG, 58 anti-tank rifles, 15 German 20mm AA guns, 28 82mm mortars, two 120mm mortars, 11 artillery guns, 384 vehicles, 554 horses, 34 trucks.

The 3rd Mountain Division possessed 2,000 combatants, 10 StuGs, five 75mm AT Guns. Its artillery came to 35 guns.

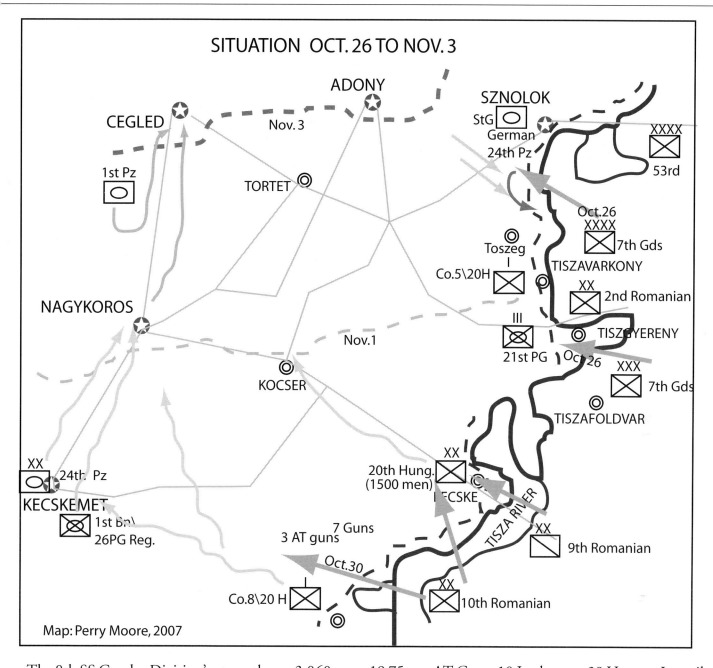

SITUATION OCT. 26 TO NOV. 3

Map: Perry Moore, 2007

The 8th SS Cavalry Division's strength was 3,060 men, 19 75mm AT Guns, 10 Jagdpanzer 38 Hetzers. Its artillery came to 37 guns.

The 15th Infantry Division had 900 combatants, 14 75mm AT Guns, and three artillery guns.

The 1015 StuG Battalion had six Hetzers.

The 4th Mountain Division contained 3,350 combatants, 12 75 AT Guns, 35 artillery guns, 17 StuGs.

By noon, the 9th Hungarian Corps had reached Tiszától, the 3rd Mountain and 8th SS Divisions were in the Hajdúdorog-Hajdúnánás area, the 4th Mountain Division had moved close to the Tisza, behind the 1st Panzer Division near Ujfeherto.

Between October 21st and 28th, the Russian 5th Air Army had flown over 1,500 missions, only about 250 of these were flown in the Nyíregyháza area. The remainder were against the 3rd and 4th Panzer Corps. The German 4th Air Army flew 130, missions mostly over the Tiszafüred and Debrecen-Nyíregyháza districts. Some of the German airfields had been captured, and in one case 20 aircraft fell into enemy hands. According to German records, the Russians lost 25–30 aircraft.

It was decided to have the German 4th Panzer Corps hold the Jászberény area. One armoured group from the 3rd Panzer Corps would cross the Tisza and deploy between this river and the Danube, conducting an attack southwards to destroy the Russian units in this area. Thus, the 3rd Panzer Corps, without the 1st Panzer Division, moved across the Tisza. The 3rd Hungarian Army was also unable to deal with the Russian units near the Budapest area, and who had begun to seriously threaten that city. Much of the 8th Army had reached the safety of the Tisza River.

The state of the Russian 6th Guards Tank Army was severely reduced, it had only 36 operational tanks! The 5th Guards Cavalry Corps had 21 tanks and the 9th Guards Mechanized Corps, 15 AFVs. The 9th was withdrawn away from the fighting and placed in the 2nd Ukrainian Front reserve near Püspökladány. Like its foe, it too, had been reduced to a threadbare unit.

Saturday October 28th – weather: cloudy, rainy, 12°C

On the last day of this twenty-three day offensive, the usual Russian attempts across the Tisza continued with the normal outcome of the Germans repelling them. Serious battles continued in the Tiszavárkony and Tiszabo districts with German artillery causing grave losses to the Russians. According to German plans, the 72nd Corps evacuated the Tiszafuredi bridgehead. These troops had been retreating and fighting for eight days with much of the movement being conducted at night. In some cases, the soldiers crossed the Tisza in boats or across pontoon bridges leaving heavy weapons behind. The losses to the corps had also been heavy.

Heavy fighting occurred around Polgar between the 13th Panzer Division, Hungarian 2nd Reserve Division and Russian units. Heavy artillery fire from both sides announced another Russian attempt to break through, successful in some areas. But in the end, all of the breakthroughs were contained and resealed.

The 3rd Panzer Corps stood about 5 km northeast of Polgar. Like all of the units involved in the battle, it too, was amazingly threadbare:

The 325 StuG Battalion had eight StuGs.
The 228 StuG Battalion had 13 StuGs.
The 1172 StuG Battalion had two StuGs.
The 1335 StuG Battalion had one Jagdpanzer 38.
The 1257 StuG Battalion had no vehicles.

The FHH PG Division was now ordered to move towards Tiszántúl, as the 13th Panzer Division screened to the east checking for any Russian advances. Both the 1st and 23rd Panzer Divisions were in a fragmented state between Hajdúdorog and Hajdúnánás, some of the units were also on the west back of the Tisza. The last of the 1st Panzer units would not cross the river until the 29th.

During the day, numerous Russian attacks from the 27th Army were conducted northwards along and 8 km front. These attacks were supported with heavy artillery and directed towards Kállósemjén. The penetrations were all sealed. Elements of the German 8th Jager Division, with seven tanks and little artillery struggled its way into safety from the east of Nyíregyházá. Meanwhile, the German 29th Corps with the 3rd Mountain and 8th SS Cavalry Divisions moved from the Hajdúnánás area and towards Hajdúdorog. The Hungarian 9th Corps with its 9th Division marched westwards moving within 25 km of Büdszentmihálytó. By 1800, the Hungarians had surrounded the Tiszaluci bridge. The 27th Division moved towards Taktaharkány. By this time, 29th Corps StuG unit, the 286th, contained only six operational AFVs.

Much of the Russian resistance in and around Nyíregyházá ended as the battle wore on. The Germans had destroyed three Russian corps, loss data varies depending on the source used.

In the Nyíregyházá area alone, the Russians had suffered losses amounting to 552 POWs, 3,434 men KIA, 78 tanks destroyed, six SP AFVs, 76 artillery guns, 151 AT guns, 30 AA guns, 86 rocket launchers, 325 rifles and machine guns, 600 horses and many anti-tank rifles.

With Budapest now being threatened by the Russian 46th Army, attention now began to turn away from this area. The 13th Panzer and the Hungarian 2nd Division together attacked nearby Russian forces in the Polgar area, again, acting as a shield allowing for the remains of the 8th Army to escape. These two divisions finally crossed the Tisza on the 31st. The city of Nyíregyházá had finally been vacated by the Germans, which was promptly occupied by the Russians once again.

By the 29th, the FHH Division had been reduced to only six StuGs. The German 3rd Mountain Division arrived in the Polgar area on November 1, and the 4th Mountain Division continued to act as a rearguard, withdrawing towards the Tiszadobi bridgehead. Also in the same area was the 46th Infantry Division.

Both sides had been decimated. Both had delivered near knock-out blows but like a fierce warrior each rose again. Neither had the strength to go on, especially the Germans, whose divisions had been ripped to shreds. Yet, somehow they had pulled off a defensive miracle. They had reduced a once very strong foe into a much weaker one, but they too, had been metaphorically 'sent to the dogs'. Much of Hungary had now been lost. As November dawned, Budapest was threatened. Yet, both foes had won. For the Germans had saved their 8th Army from certain destruction. For the Russians, it was one more step closer to Berlin. Right until the end of the Third Reich. Hitler refused to let Hungary turn Red!

The chaos of the battles on the Hungarian Plains had used up valuable armour and men – hundreds of twisted tank wrecks were strewn about the land. Well over 30,000 men lost their lives. Their body parts painted the soil red and polluted the Tisza River. Many lives lost from one stray bullet, in one flashing second, a precious life vanished forever, for eternity. Such is war.

German AFVs

PzKpfw VI Ausf B Tiger II, from the 3rd Company, schwere Heeres Panzer Abteilung 503

PzKpfw IV SdKfz 161/1 Ausf H of unidentified unit

German AFVs

PzKpfw IV SdKfz 161/2 Ausf J tank from 1st Panzer Regiment, 1st Panzer Division

PzKpfw V SdKfz 171 Ausf G Panther, 1st Panzer Rgt, 1st Panzer Division

German AFVs

PzKpfw V SdKfz 171 Ausf G Panther from the 1st Abteilung 24th Panzer Regiment, 24th Panzer Division

Sturmgeschütz IV SdKfz 167 assault gun from the 4th SS StuG Abteilung, 4th SS Polizei Panzer Grenadier Division

German AFVs

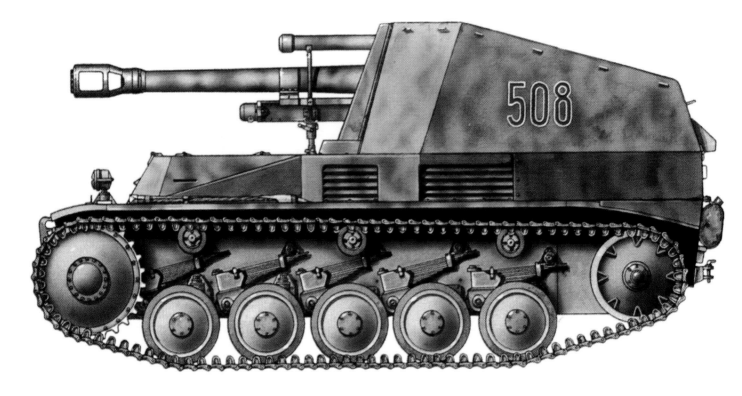

SdKfz 124 Wespe self-propelled gun, 73rd Panzer Artillery Regiment, 1st Panzer Division

Marder III SdKfz 138 SP gun, unidentified Panzer Division

Hungarian AFVs

43M Turan II tank from 2nd Armoured Division

Zrinyi II assault gun, 2nd Armoured Division

Soviet AFVs

T-34/85 tank from the 147th Armoured Brigade

IS-2 tank from unidentified unit

Soviet AFVs

Infantry Tank Mark III Valentine Mark IX from the 10th Armoured Brigade 6th Guards Tank Army

T-70 tank from unidentified unit

Soviet AFVs

SU-76M SP gun, unidentified unit

SU-85M SP gun from 6th Guards Tank Army

APPENDIX I

Orders of Battle / Strengths

I.1 Order of Battle of Axis ground troops

31 August 1944
OKH theatre of war

Army Group 'South Ukraine'

8th Army:

XVII Corps: 8th Jaeger Division, 3rd Mountain Division
LVII Panzer Corps: 4th Mountain Division, 46th Infantry Division (remnants), battle group of 20th Panzer Division (remnants), 76th Infantry Division (remnants)

6th Army:

Army reserves: command of LXXII Corps
XXIX Corps: 306th Infantry Division (remnants), 153rd Field Training Division (remnants), 10th Panzer-Grenadier Division (remnants), 13th Panzer Division (remnants)

OKW theatre of war

Commander of the German troops in Hungary:

8th SS Cavalry Division 'Florian Geyer' (rebuilding), 22nd SS Cavalry Division 'Maria Theresia' (forming), 23rd SS Mountain Division 'Kama' (Croatian Nr 2) (forming), SS Mountain Brigade (Tatar Nr 1) (forming), Panzer Brigade 109 + Panzer Brigade 110 (forming)

16 September 1944
OKH theatre of war

Army Group 'South Ukraine':

Army Group reserves: command of III Panzer Corps, 23rd Panzer Division, battle group of 22nd SS Cavalry Division, command of LXXII Corps

8th Army:

Army reserves: command of IX Corps (Hung.), 27th Light Division (Hung.)
XVII Corps: Group 'Walker', 8th Jaeger Division, 3rd Mountain Division
Group 'General Abraham': 2nd Reserve Division (Hung.), part of the battle group of 20th Panzer Division, 46th Infantry Division

Army Grouping 'Fretter-Pico' [6th Army and 2nd Army (Hung.)]:

6th Army:

LVII Panzer Corps: Group 'General Breith' (4th Mountain Division, remnants of 76th Infantry Division, part of 20th Panzer Division), Group 'General Winkler'
Group 'Transylvania': 8th SS Cavalry Division 'Florian Geyer'

2nd Army (Hung.):

II Corps (Hung.): 9th Reserve Division (Hung.), 7th Reserve Division (Hung.), 2nd Armoured Division (Hung.), 25th Infantry Division (Hung.), blocking formation 'von Kessel' (part of 20th Panzer Division), 2nd Mountain Reserve Brigade (Hung.), 1st Mountain Reserve Brigade (Hung.)

Corps Group XXIX (command of XXIX Corps):

VII Corps (Hung.): Brigade 'Catatos', 12th Reserve Division (Hung.), 4th Reserve Division (Hung.)
IV Corps (Hung.): 8th Reserve Division (Hung.), 1st Armoured Division (Hung.), 20th Infantry Division (Hung.), 6th Reserve Division (Hung.)
4th SS Police Panzer-Grenadier Division

OKW theatre of war

Commander of the German troops in Hungary:

18th SS Panzer-Grenadier Division 'Horst Wessel' (forming), part of 22nd SS Cavalry Division 'Maria Theresia' (forming), 23rd SS Mountain Division 'Kama' (Croatian Nr 2) (forming), SS Mountain Brigade (Tatar Nr 1) (forming), Panzer Brigade 109 and Panzer Brigade 110 (forming), 247th Volks-Grenadier Division and 326th Volks-Grenadier Division (forming)

28 September 1944
OKH theatre of war

Army Group 'South':

Army Group reserves: command of LXXII Corps, Group 'Transylvania', 76th Infantry Division (rebuilding)

8th Army:

Army reserves: command of IX Corps (Hung.)
XVII Corps: 9th Border Guard Brigade (Hung.), 8th Jaeger Division, Group 'Rath', 3rd Mountain Division
Group 'General Schopper': 2nd Reserve Division (Hung.), 46th Infantry Division
XXIX Corps: 4th Mountain Division, Group 'General Winkler', 8th SS Cavalry Division 'Florian Geyer'

Army Grouping 'Fretter-Pico' [6th Army and 2nd Army (Hung.)]:

2nd Army (Hung.):

II Corps (Hung.): blocking formation 'von Kessel' [1st Mountain Reserve Brigade (Hung.), 2nd Mountain Reserve Brigade (Hung.), 7th Reserve Division (Hung.)], 9th Reserve Division (Hung.), 25th Infantry Division (Hung.), 2nd Armoured Division (Hung.)

6th Army:

VII Corps (Hung.): 12th Reserve Division (Hung.), 4th Reserve Division (Hung.)
Group 'General Breith' (III Panzer Corps): 27th Light Division (Hung.), 23rd Panzer Division

3rd Army (Hung.):

II Reserve Corps (Hung.): 6th Reserve Division (Hung.), 20th Infantry Division (Hung.), 8th Reserve Division (Hung.), 23rd Reserve Division (Hung.)
LVII Panzer Corps: 1st Armoured Division (Hung.) + battle group of 22nd SS Cavalry Division, 4th SS Police Panzer-Grenadier Division

OKH reserves:

Panzer Corps Kleemann: 13th Panzer Division (rebuilding), 10th Panzer-Grenadier Division (rebuilding), Panzer-Grenadier Division 'Feldherrnhalle' (rebuilding)

OKW theatre of war

Army Group 'F' (Commander-in-Chief Southeast):

Commander of the German troops in Hungary:

18th SS Panzer-Grenadier Division 'Horst Wessel' (forming), part of 22nd SS Cavalry Division 'Maria Theresia' (forming), 23rd SS Mountain Division 'Kama' (Croatian Nr 2) (forming), SS Mountain Brigade (Tatar Nr 1) (forming), Panzer Brigade 109 (forming), 247th Volks-Grenadier Division and 326th Volks-Grenadier Division (forming)

13 October 1944
OKH theatre of war

Army Group 'South':

Army Grouping 'Wöhler' [8th Army and 2nd Army (Hung.)]:

8th Army:

XVII Corps: 9th Border Guard Brigade (Hung.), 8th Jaeger Division, 27th Light Division (Hung.)
IX Corps (Hung.): 3rd Mountain Division, 2nd Reserve Division (Hung.)
XXIX Corps: 4th Mountain Division, 8th SS Cavalry Division 'Florian Geyer', 9th Reserve Division (Hung.)

2nd Army (Hung.):

II Corps (Hung.): 2nd Armoured Division (Hung.), 25th Infantry Division (Hung.) (remnants), 7th Reserve Division (Hung.), 15th Infantry Division, 2nd Mountain Reserve Brigade (Hung.)

6th Army:

Army reserves: 24th Panzer Division (arriving), command of IV Panzer Corps
LXXII Corps: command of VII Corps (Hung.), 76th Infantry Division, 12th Reserve Division (Hung.), 4th Reserve Division (Hung.)
III Panzer Corps: 46th Infantry Division, battle group of Panzer-Grenadier Division 'Feldherrnhalle', battle group of 22nd SS Cavalry Division 'Maria Theresia', 23rd Panzer Division, 1st Panzer Division, 13th Panzer Division

3rd Army (Hung.):

VIII Corps (Hung.): 8th Reserve Division (Hung.), 23rd Reserve Division (Hung.), 1st Armoured Division (Hung.)
LVII Panzer Corps: 4th SS Police Panzer-Grenadier Division, 20th Infantry Division (Hung.), 1st Cavalry Division (Hung.)

Commander of the German troops in Hungary:

18th SS Panzer-Grenadier Division 'Horst Wessel' (forming), 22nd SS Cavalry Division 'Maria Theresia' (less one battle group) (forming), 23rd SS Mountain Division 'Kama' (Croatian Nr 2) (forming), SS Mountain Brigade (Tatar Nr 1) (forming), 153rd Field Training Division, 31st SS Volunteer Grenadier Division (forming), 277th Volks-Grenadier Division (forming), 326th Volks-Grenadier Division (forming)

Information in the above section courtesy of Kamen Nevenkin.

I.2 Order of battle of Army Group 'South', October 2 1944

Army Group 'South' assets: Plenipotentiary General of the German Armed Forces in Hungary; Commander of the rear area in Hungary.
Engineers: Engineer Bridge-Building Battalions 624 and 699; Light Assault Boat Company 906; Engineer Bridge-Building Staff's Section 939; Bridge Columns 'B' (mot.) 13, 16, 138, 2./408 and 667; Heavy Tank

Bridge Column (mot.) 842; Light Tank Bridge Column (mot.) 4; Bridge Column 94; Engineer Depot Battalion 571.
Armor: Anti-Tank Battalion 93 (*Hornisse*).

LXXII Army Corps: 76.Infantry Division (rebuilding).
Assets:
Engineers: Engineer Bridge-Building Staff's Section 921.

8.Army

XVII Army Corps: 9.Border-Guard Brigade (Hung.), Group *'Rath'*, 8.Jaeger Division, 3.Mountain Division, 2.Resereve Division (Hung.), Group *'Scholze'*, 27.Light Division (Hung.).
Assets:
Artillery: Arko 7.
Engineers: Engineer-Regiment-Staff 700; Engineer Battalion (mount.) 74.

IX Army Corps (Hung.): 46.Infantry Division.
Assets:
Artillery: Artillery-Regiment-Staff (mot.) 959; Artillery Observation Battalion (mot.) 32.
Engineers: Engineer Brigade (mot.) 52; Engineer Battalion (mot.) 666; Engineer Battalion (part. mot.) 635.
Armor: 1.Company/Anti-Tank Battalion (mot.) 662 (*8.8 cm sPak*).

XXIX Army Corps: 8.SS-Cavalry Division, 4.Mountain Division.
Assets:
Artillery: Arko 124; Artillery-Regiment-Staff (mot.) 781; Assault Artillery Brigade 239; Artillery Battalion III./140 (*le.F.H./RSO*); Artillery Battalion 607 (*s.F.H./mot.*); Artillery Observation Battalions (bicycle-mobile) 25 and 40; Anti-Aircraft Artillery Battalion (static) 1054 (*7.5 cm Flak*).
Engineers: Engineer-Regiment-Staff 681.
Armor: Anti-Tank Battalion 721 (*sPak, mot Z.*); Anti-Tank Company 1257 (*Hetzer*).

8.Army assets: Korück 558.
Artillery: Harko 310; Assault Gun Brigade 228; Anti-Aircraft Artillery Battalion (static) 289; Reinforced Weather Platoon 13.
Engineers: Engineer Bridge-Building Battalions 531 and 577; Engineer Bridge-Building Staff's Section 923; Bridge Columns 'B' (mot.) 1, 54, 297 and 603; Engineer Depot Battalion 591.

Army Grouping *'Fretter-Pico'* (the command of 6.Army)

2.Army (Hung.)

Blocking Formation 'von Kessel' (the command of 20.Panzer-Division)*:* Blocking Formation *'Ludwig'*, 1.Mountain Reserve Brigade (Hung.), part of 76.Infantry Division, part of 7.Reserve Division (Hung.).
Assets:
Artillery: Arko 114; Artillery-Regiment-Staff 511; Assault Gun Brigade 286; Artillery Battalion II./818 (*le.F.H./RSO*); Artillery Battalion II./52 (*s.F.H./mot.*); Artillery Battalion 736 (*21 cm Mörser*); Artillery Observation Battalion (mot.) 32.
Engineers: Engineer Brigade (mot.) 127; Engineer-Regiment-Staff 617; Engineer Battalions (mot.) 52, 127 and 651.
Armor: Anti-Tank Battalions 661 and 663 (*sPak, mot Z.*); Anti-Tank Companies 1179 and 1335 (*Hetzer*).

II Army Corps (Hung.): 2.Armoured Division (Hung.), 25.Infantry Division (Hung.), remnants of 9.Reserve Division (Hung.).
Assets:
Artillery: Arko 102; Artillery Battalion III./818 (*le.F.H./RSO*); Artillery Battalion I./127 (*s.F.H./mot.*).
2.Army (Hung.) reserves: 7.Reserve Division (Hung.), 2.Mountain Reserve Brigade (Hung.).

6.Army

Group *'Breith'* (command of the III Panzer Corps):

III Panzer Corps: 23.Panzer-Division, 1.Panzer-Division (arriving).

Assets:
Artillery: Arko 3; Artillery Battery 800 (*17 cm K/mot.*); Artillery Battalion 809 (*21 cm Mörser*); Artillery Observation Battalions (mot.) 36 and 43.
Engineers: Engineer-Regiment-Staff 518.
Armor: Anti-Tank Battalion 662 (*Hornisse + 8.8 cm sPak/mot.*).

VII Army Corps (Hung.): 4.Reserve Division (Hung.), 12.Reserve Division (Hung.).
6.Army assets: Korück 593.
Artillery: Harko 306; Assault Gun Brigade 325; Artillery Battalion I./77 (*le.F.H./RSO*); Artillery Observation Battalion (mot.) 29.
Engineers: Engineer-Regiment-Staff 685; Engineer Battalions (part. mot.) 255 and 741; Engineer Bridge-Building Battalions (mot.) 21 and 552; Engineer Bridge-Building Staff's Section 927; Bridge Columns 'B' (mot.) 7, 8, 37, 50, 85, 110, 129 and 651; Engineer Depot Battalion 541.

3.Army (Hung.)

LVII Panzer Corps: battle group of 22.SS-Cavalry Division, 1.Armoured Division (Hung.), 4.SS-Police-Panzer-Grenadier Division.
Assets:
Artillery: Arko 121; Artillery Battalion 844 (*s.F.H./mot.*).
Engineers: Engineer-Regiment-Staff 678; Engineer Battalion (part. mot.) 207; Engineer Bridge-Building Battalion 646; Engineer Bridge-Building Staff's Section 925; Bridge Columns 'B' (mot.) 59 and 663.
VIII Army Corps (Hung.): 23.Reserve Division (Hung.), 8.Reserve Division (Hung.), 6.Reserve Division (Hung.), 20.Infantry Division (Hung.).

Information in the above section courtesy of Kamen Nevenkin.

I.3 Order of battle of Army Group 'South', October 16 1944

Army Group 'South' assets: Plenipotentiary General of the German Armed Forces in Hungary; Commander of the rear area in Hungary (with subordinated 153.Field-Training Division).
Artillery: Light Topographic Detachment 650.
Engineers: Engineer Bridge-Building Battalion 699; Light Assault Boat Companies 906 and 912; Engineer Bridge-Building Staff's Section 939; Bridge Columns 'B' (mot.) 13, 16, 138, 2./408 and 667; Heavy Tank Bridge Column (mot.) 842 (parts); Light Tank Bridge Column (mot.) 4; Bridge Column 94; Engineer Depot Battalion 571.
Army Group 'South' reserves: 24.Panzer-Division (arriving), Heavy Panzer Battalion 503 (*Tiger*) (arriving).
Air Force: Air Fleet 4; 15.Anti-Aircraft Artillery Division.

Army Grouping 'Wöhler' (the command of 8.Army)

8.Army + 2.Army (Hung.)

XVII Army Corps: 9.Border-Guard Brigade (Hung.), 8.Jaeger Division, 27.Light Division (Hung.).
Assets:
Artillery: Arko 7.
Engineers: Engineer-Regiment-Staff 700; Engineer Battalion (mot.) 635.

IX Army Corps (Hung.): 3.Mountain Division, 2.Reserve Division (Hung.), 4.Mountain Division.
Assets:
Artillery: Artillery Observation Battalion (mot.) 32.
Engineers: Engineer Brigade (mot.) 52, Engineer Battalion (mot.) 666.

II Army Corps (Hung.): 25.Infantry Division (Hung.), 9.Reserve Division (Hung.).
Assets:
Engineers: Engineer Brigade (mot.) 127, Engineer Battalions (mot.) 52 (less 1.Company) and 127; Engineer Battalion (mount.) 74; Engineer Battalions 651 and 207.

XXIX Army Corps: 8.SS-Cavalry Division, 15.Infantry Division, 7.Resereve Division (Hung.), 2.Mountain Reserve Brigade (Hung.) + the remnants of 1.Mountain Reserve Brigade (Hung.)

Assets:
Artillery: Arko 124; Assault Artillery Brigade 239; Artillery Observation Battalions (bicycle-mobile) 25 and 40.
Engineers: Engineer-Regiment-Staff 681; 1.Company/Engineer Battalion (mot.) 52.

8.Army assets: Korück 558.
Artillery: Harko 310; Arko 102; Artillery-Regiment-Staff (mot.) 781; Assault Gun Brigade 286; Artillery Battalion II./818 (*le.F.H./RSO*); Artillery Battalion I./127 (*s.F.H./mot.*); Anti-Aircraft Artillery Battalion (static) 289 (*8.8 cm Flak*); Artillery Observation Battalion (mot.) 13.
Engineers: Engineer-Regiment-Staff 617; Engineer Bridge-Building Battalions 531, 577 and 624; Engineer Bridge-Building Staff's Section 923; Bridge Columns 'B' (mot.) 1, 54, 297 and 603; Engineer Depot Battalion 591.

6.Army

LXXII Army Corps: Blocking Formation *'Ludwig'*, part of 76.Infantry Division.
Assets:
Artillery: Arko 114; Artillery-Brigade-Staffs 511 and 959; Assault Gun Brigade 325; Artillery Battalions I./77 and III./818 (*le.F.H./RSO*); Artillery Battalion III./140 (*s.F.H./mot.*) (less 7.Battery) and 3.Battery/Artillery Battalion 844 (*s.F.H./mot.*); Artillery Battalions 607, 736 and 809 (less 3.Battery) (*21 cm Mörser*), Anti-Aircraft Artillery Battalion (static) 1054 (*7.5 cm Flak*).

Group 'Breith' (command of the III Panzer Corps):
III Panzer Corps: 46.Infantry Division, 23.Panzer-Division, battle group of 22.SS-Cavalry Division, 1.Panzer-Division, Panzer-Grenadier Division *'Feldherrnhalle'*, 13.Panzer-Division, 2.Armoured Division (Hung.).
Assets:
Artillery: Arko 3; Assault Gun Brigade 228; Artillery Battery 800 and 3.Battery/Artillery Battalion 809 (*17 cm K/mot.*); Artillery Battalion I./52 (*s.F.H./mot.*); Artillery Observation Battalion (mot.) 43; Artillery Observation Battalion (bicycle-mobile) 36.
Engineers: Engineer-Regiment-Staff 518; Bridge Columns 'B' (mot.) 7 and 50.

VII Army Corps (Hung.): 4.Reserve Division (Hung.), 12.Reserve Division (Hung.).

IV Panzer Corps: 4.SS-Police-Panzer-Grenadier Division.

6.Army assets: Korück 593.
Artillery: Harko 306; Artillery Observation Battalion (mot.) 25; Light Topographic Detachment 638.
Engineers: Engineer-Regiment-Staff 685; Engineer Battalions (part. mot.) 255 and 741; Engineer Bridge-Building Battalions 21 and 552; Engineer Bridge-Building Staff's Sections 921 and 927; Bridge Columns 'B' (mot.) 8, 37, 85, 129 and 651; Heavy Tank Bridge Column (mot.) 842 (parts); Engineer Depot Battalion 541.
Armor: Anti-Tank Battalions 661, 663 and 721 (*sPak, mot Z.*); Anti-Tank Companies (*Hetzer*) 1179, 1257 and 1335; Anti-Tank Battalion 662 (*Hornisse + 8.8 cm sPak/mot.*).

3.Army (Hung.)

LVII Panzer Corps: Remnants of 20.Infantry Division (Hung.), 1.Huszar Division (Hung.), Anti-Aircraft Artillery Group *'Hortian'*.
Assets:
Artillery: Arko 121; Artillery Battalion 844 (less 3.Battery) and 7.Battery/Artillery Battalion 140 (*s.F.H./mot.*), Artillery Observation Battalion (mot.) 43.
Engineers: Engineer-Regiment-Staff 678; Engineer Bridge-Building Battalion 646; Engineer Bridge-Building Staff's Section 925; Bridge Columns 'B' (mot.) 59, 110 and 663.
VIII Army Corps (Hung.): 23.Reserve Division (Hung.), 8.Reserve Division (Hung.), remnants of 2. Armoured Division (Hung.).

Information in the above section courtesy of Kamen Nevenkin.

I.4 Hungarian 1st Army

1. Hungarian Army (Lt. Gen. dálnoki Miklós Béla)
   HQ
      III. Corps (Maj. Gen. Aggteleky Béla)

HQ
2. Mountain Brigade
    HQ
        3. Mountain Artillery Battalion
           1. Mountain Artillery Battery
           6. Mountain Artillery Battery
           11. Mountain Artillery Battery
        4. Mountain Artillery Battalion
           10. Mountain Artillery Battery
           13. Mountain Artillery Battery
           25. Mountain Artillery Battery
        2. Mountain AT Company
        2. Mountain AA Company
        2. Mountain Combat Engineer Company
        2. Signal Company
      1. Mountain Infantry Battalion
      10. Mountain Infantry Battalion
      11. Mountain Infantry Battalion
      13. Mountain Infantry Battalion
      25. Mountain Infantry Battalion
6. Infantry Division
    HQ
        4. Artillery Battalion
        5. Artillery Battalion
        6. Artillery Battalion
        72. Artillery Battalion
        6. Reconnaissance Battalion
        6. AA Company
        52. Combat Engineer Battalion
        6. Signal Battalion
      3. Infantry Regiment
      16. Infantry Regiment
      22. Infantry Regiment

V. Corps (Maj. Gen. Algya-Papp Zoltán)
    HQ
13. Infantry Division
    HQ
        13. Artillery Battalion
        14. Artillery Battalion
        15. Artillery Battalion
        76. Artillery Battalion
        13. Reconnaissance Battalion
        13. AA Company
        55. Combat Engineer Battalion
        13. Signal Battalion
      7. Infantry Regiment
      9. Infantry Regiment
      20. Infantry Regiment
1. Mountain Brigade
    HQ
        1. Mountain Artillery Battalion
           3. Mountain Artillery Battery
           4. Mountain Artillery Battery
           12. Mountain Artillery Battery
        2. Mountain Artillery Battalion

2. Mountain Artillery Battery
5. Mountain Artillery Battery
33. Mountain Artillery Battery
1. Mountain AT Company
1. Mountain Cavalry Company
1. Mountain AA Company
1. Mountain Combat Engineer Company
1. Signal Company
2. Mountain Infantry Battalion
3. Mountain Infantry Battalion
4. Mountain Infantry Battalion 12. Mountain Infantry Battalion 33. Mountain Infantry Battalion

VI. Corps (Maj. Gen. Farkas Ferenc)
HQ
16. Infantry Division
HQ
16. Artillery Battalion
17. Artillery Battalion
18?. Artillery Battalion
?. Artillery Battalion
15. Reconnaissance Battalion
15. AA Company
56. Combat Engineer Battalion
16. Signal Battalion
10. Infantry Regiment
11. Infantry Regiment
19. Infantry Regiment
10. Infantry Division
HQ
10. Artillery Battalion
11. Artillery Battalion
12. Artillery Battalion
74. Artillery Battalion
10. Reconnaissance Battalion
10. AA Company
54. Combat Engineer Battalion
10. Signal Battalion
6. Infantry Regiment
8. Infantry Regiment
18. Infantry Regiment
24. Infantry Division
HQ
22. Artillery Battalion
23. Artillery Battalion
24. Artillery Battalion
78. Artillery Battalion
24. Reconnaissance Battalion
24. AA Company
58. Combat Engineer Battalion
24. Signal Battalion
12. Infantry Regiment
21. Infantry Regiment
24. Infantry Regiment

I.5 Hungarian 2nd Army

2. Hungarian Army (Lt. Gen. dálnoki Veress Lajos)
  II. Corps (Maj. Gen. Kiss István)
    HQ
    7. Field Replacement Division
      HQ
        ?. Replacement Artillery Battalion
        ?. Replacement Engineer Company
        ?. Replacement Mixed Signal Company
      13. Replacement Infantry Regiment
      14.Replacement Infantry Regiment
      23.Replacement Infantry Regiment
      20th Reconnaissance Bn
      VII Antiaircraft
      57th Gun Company
  9. Field Replacement Division
    HQ
      Replacement Artillery Battalion
      Replacement Engineer Company
      Replacement Mixed Signal Company
    25th Replacement Infantry Regiment
    26th Replacement Infantry Regiment
    25th Reconnaissance Bn
    9th Gun (3 batteries)
    89th Gun Company
  25. Infantry Division (50% of the required manpower)
    HQ
      2. Artillery Battalion
      25. Artillery Battalion
      26. Artillery Battalion
      ?. Artillery Battalion
      25. Reconnaissance Battalion
      25. AA Company
      59. Combat Engineer Battalion
      25. Signal Battalion
    1st Infantry Regiment
    25th Infantry Regiment
    26th Infantry Regiment
    79th Gun Company
  2. Armoured Division
    HQ
    3rd Tank Regiment (2 Tank Bns)
    3rd Motorized Infantry Regiment
    4. Motorized Battalion
    5. Motorized Battalion
    6. Motorized Battalion
    2nd Armoured Reconnaissance Battalion
    2nd Motorized Artillery Battalion
    6th. Motorized Artillery Battalion
    52nd AA Battalion
    52nd AA Battalion
    2nd Combat Engineer Company
    3nd Combat Engineer Company
  1. Mountain Replacement Brigade

HQ
    1. Replacement Mountain Artillery Battery
    ?. Replacement Mountain Artillery Battery
    ?. Replacement Mountain Engineer Company
    1. Replacement Mountain Mixed Signal Company
  2. Replacement Mountain Infantry Battalion
  3. Replacement Mountain Infantry Battalion
  4. Replacement Mountain Infantry Battalion
  ?12. Replacement Mountain Infantry Battalion (conflicting sources)
  ?20. Replacement Border Guard Battalion (conflicting sources)
  33. Replacement Mountain Infantry Battalion
2. Mountain Replacement Brigade
  HQ
    3rd Replacement Mountain Artillery Battery
    4th Replacement Mountain Artillery Battery
    2nd Replacement Mountain Engineer Company
    ?. Replacement Mountain Mixed Signal Company
  1. Replacement Mountain Infantry Battalion
  10. Replacement Mountain Infantry Battalion
  11. Replacement Mountain Infantry Battalion
  13. Replacement Mountain Infantry Battalion
  ?25. Replacement Mountain Infantry Battalion (conflicting sources)
  ?16. Replacement Border Guard Battalion (conflicting sources)
  ?31. Replacement Border Guard Battalion (conflicting sources)

IX. Corps (Maj. Gen. Kovács Gyula)
  HQ
  2nd Field Replacement Division
    HQ
      ?. Replacement Artillery Battalion
      ?. Replacement Engineer Company
      ?. Replacement Mixed Signal Company
    3rd Replacement Infantry Regiment
    16th Replacement Infantry Regiment
    22nd Replacement Infantry Regiment
  9th Border Guard Brigade
    HQ
      ?. Border Guard AA Company
      ?. Mountain Combat Engineer Company
      ?. Signal Company
    ?. Mountain Border Guard Battalion
    ?. Mountain Border Guard Battalion
    ?. Mountain Border Guard Battalion
    ?. Mountain Border Guard Battalion
    ?. Mountain Border Guard Battalion
  27th Light Division (Székely)
    HQ
      27. Artillery Battalion
    27. Infantry Regiment
    57. Infantry Regiment

I.6 Hungarian 3rd Army

3. Hungarian Army
  VIII. Corps (Maj. Gen. Lengyel Béla)
    HQ

8. Field Replacement Division
    HQ
        ?. Replacement Artillery Battalion
        ?. Replacement Engineer Company
        ?. Replacement Mixed Signal Company
    12th Replacement Infantry Regiment
    21st Replacement Infantry Regiment
    24th Replacement Infantry Regiment
6. Field Replacement Division
    HQ
        4–6. Replacement Artillery Battalion
        52nd Replacement Engineer Company
        ?. Replacement Mixed Signal Company
    3rd. Replacement Infantry Regiment
    16th Replacement Infantry Regiment
    22nd Replacement Infantry Regiment
20. Infantry Division
    HQ
        19. Artillery Battalion
        20. Artillery Battalion
        21. Artillery Battalion
        77. Artillery Battalion
        20. Reconnaissance Battalion
        20. AA Company
        57. Combat Engineer Battalion
        20. Signal Battalion
    13. Infantry Regiment
    14. Infantry Regiment
    23. Infantry Regiment
1st Armoured Division
    HQ
    1. Tank Regiment
    1. Motorized Infantry Regiment
        4. Motorized Battalion
        5. Motorized Battalion
        6. Motorized Battalion
    1. Armoured Reconnaissance Battalion
    1. Motorized Artillery Battalion
    5. Motorized Artillery Battalion
    51. AA Battalion
    51. AA Battalion
    1 Combat Engineer Company
23. Reserve Division
    HQ
        23. Cavalry Company
        23. AA Company
        ?. Combat Engineer Company
        23. Signal Company
    42. Infantry Regiment
    51. Infantry Regiment
    54. Infantry Regiment
VII. Corps (Maj. Gen. Vörös Géza)
    HQ
    4. Field Replacement Division
        HQ
            ?. Replacement Artillery Battalion

       ?. Replacement Engineer Company
       ?. Replacement Mixed Signal Company
     6.? Replacement Infantry Regiment
     8.? Replacement Infantry Regiment
   17.? Replacement Infantry Regiment
12. Reserve Division
   HQ
      12. Cavalry Company
      12. AA Company
      ?. Combat Engineer Company
      12. Signal Company
   36. Infantry Regiment
   38. Infantry Regiment
   48. Infantry Regiment

I.7 Hungarian troops outside Hungary

1. Cavalry Division
   HQ
      1. Cavalry Tank Battalion
      15. Bicycle Battalion
      1. Cavalry Artillery Battalion
      2. Cavalry Artillery Battalion
      3. Cavalry Artillery Battalion
      55. AA Battalion
      4. Combat Engineer Company
      1. Cavalry Signal Company
   2. Cavalry Regiment
   3. Cavalry Regiment
   4. Cavalry Regiment
5. Field Replacement Division
      HQ
      ?. Replacement Artillery Battalion
      ?. Replacement Engineer Company
      ?. Replacement Mixed Signal Company
     7.? Replacement Infantry Regiment
     9.? Replacement Infantry Regiment
   20.? Replacement Infantry Regiment

I.8 Summary of Hungarian OOB

1. Hungarian Army (Lt. Gen. Dálnoki Miklós Béla)
   III. Corps (Maj. Gen. Aggteleky Béla)
      2. Mountain Brigade
      6. Infantry Division
   V. Corps (Maj. Gen. Algya-Papp Zoltán)
      13. Infantry Division
      1. Mountain Brigade
   VI.Corps (Maj. Gen. Farkas Ferenc)
      16. Infantry Division
      10. Infantry Division
      24. Infantry Division
2. Hungarian Army (Lt. Gen. dálnoki Veress Lajos)
   II. Corps (Maj. Gen. Kiss István)
      7. Field Replacement Division
      9. Field Replacement Division
      25. Infantry Division (50% of the required manpower)

      2. Armoured Division (in very wrong shape)
      1. Mountain Replacement Brigade
      2. Mountain Replacement Brigade
    IX. Corps (Maj. Gen. Kovács Gyula)
      2. Field Replacement Division
      9. Border Guard Brigade
      27. Light Division (Székely)
3. Hungarian Army
    VIII. Corps (Maj. Gen. Lengyel Béla)
      8. Field Replacement Division
      6. Field Replacement Division
      20. Infantry Division
      1. Armoured Division
      23. Reserve Division
    VII. Corps (Maj. Gen. Vörös Géza)
      4. Field Replacement Division
      12. Reserve Division
Outside of Hungary
    1. Cavalry Division
    5. Field Replacement Division

I.9 Order of Battle of the Hungarian 12th Reserve Division September 1944

2nd Battalion/36th Regiment with three 75mm AT guns
2nd Battalion/38th Regiment
3rd Battalion/48th Regiment
53rd Battalion (one bicycle company)
57th Frontier Battalion
2nd Motorized Battalion and one anti-aircraft unit
12th Cavalry Company
61st Engineer Company
VIII Corps Engineer Company
Battery 1, 12th Artillery (three 105mm guns)
Battery 2, 12th Artillery (three 105mm guns)
Battery 1, Independent Artillery (obsolete guns)
VIII Corps (two 150mm howitzer guns)
Five 40mm AA guns
3rd Battery/10th Assault Gun Battalion (three Zrínyi II)
Each battalion in the infantry regiments contained 300–400 combat soldiers

I.10 German Armour Strengths September 25–October 5 1944

Unit	Tanks	Assault Guns	Panzerjäger
1 Pz Div	66	7	12
13 Pz Div	42	—	11
23 Pz Div	64	13	10
FHH PG Div	—	31	—
109 Pz Brig	40	—	11
4 SS PG Div	2	34	—
228 StuG Brig	—	34	—
239 StuG Brig	3	8	—
286 StuG Brig	—	21	—

325 StuG Brig	—	19	—
905 StuG Bn	—	5	—
1257 StuG Bn	—	—	9
8 SS Cav Div	—	7	—
1179, 1015, 1176 StuG Bns	—	7 ea.	—
1335 StuG Bn	—	3	—
1008 StuG Bn	—	5	—
662 PzJag Bn	—	—	5

I.11 German Armour Strengths October 10 1944

1 Pz Div	24 AFV
13 Pz Div	20 AFV
23 Pz Div	21 AFV
FHH PG Div & 109 Pz Brig	61 AFV
325 StuG Brigade	26 AFV

German strengths by October 19th:

1 Pz Div	36 AFV
13 Pz Div	3 AFV
23 Pz Div	10 AFV
24 Pz Div	36 AFV (17 were Pz IVL/70)
FHH PG Div & 109 Pz Brig	74 AFV
4 SS PG Div	12 AFV
228 StuG Brigade	30 AFV
325 StuG Brigade	12 AFV
503 Tiger Btn	11 AFV
1179, 1257 StuG Bns	1 each
1176 StuG Bn	4 AFV
1335 StuG Bn	7 AFV

German strengths on Oct 28th:

1 Pz Div	19 AFV
13 Pz Div	8 AFV
23 Pz Div	32 AFV
24 Pz Div	18 AFV
FHH PG Div & 10 9Pz Brig	10 AFV
228 StuG Brigade	13 AFV
325 StuG Brigade & 4 SS PG Div	8 AFV
503 Tiger Bn	30 AFV
1176 StuG Bn	2 AFV

I.12 Order of Battle of the Axis Air Force, September 5 1944

4th Air Fleet:
 I Air Corps:
– *Fighter Wing 77:* Staff/Fighter Wing 77, Fighter Group II./51, Fighter Group II./52, Fighter Group I./53, Fighter Group III./77
– *Bomber Group I./4*
– *Ground Attack Wing:* Staff/Ground Attack Wing 2, Ground Attack Group I./2, Ground Attack Group II./2, Ground Attack Group III./2, Ground Attack Squadron (Anti-tank) 10./2, Ground Attack Squadron (Anti-tank) 14./9, Ground Attack Group III./10
– *Night Harassment Group 5*
– *Close Reconnaissance Group 14:* Staff/Close Reconnaissance Group 14, Close Reconnaissance Squadron 1./14, Close Reconnaissance Squadron 2./14, Close Reconnaissance Squadron 2./16
– *Close Reconnaissance Squadron 2./12*
– *Hungarian units:* Fighter Squadron 1, Fighter Squadron 2, Night Fighter Squadron 2, Ground Attack Squadron 1, Ground Attack Squadron 2
 V Anti-Aircraft Artillery Corps:
– *15th Anti-Aircraft Artillery Division*

Information in the above section courtesy of Kamen Nevenkin.

I.13 German 4th Luftwaffe Air Fleet strengths on October 1, 1944

I/JG 53	24 Bf 109
II/JG 51	34 Bf 109
III/JG 52	15 Bf 109
IV/NJG 6	31 Bf 109, 2 Ju 88
I/SG2	25 FW 190
II/SG2	27 FW 190
III/SG2	23 Ju 87 D5
10/SG2	5 Ju 87 D5, 17 Ju 87 G2
14/SG 9	16 Hs 129 B2
I/SG 10	36 FW 190
II/SG 10	25 FW 190
III/SG 10	26 FW 190
II/ KG4	37 H16, H20
III/KG4	37 H16, H20
III/TG2+3	58 Ju 52
3/f/121	6 Ju 188

I.14 Hungarian 102nd Fighter Unit

50 Me 210
4 FW 189
26 Bf 109
7 Ju 88
16 FW 190 F8

I.15 Order of Battle of Soviet ground troops, September 1 1944

Formations	Rifle, Airborne, Cavalry troops	Artillery troops	Tank and Mechanized troops	Engineer troops	Flame-thrower troops
2nd Ukrainian Front					
40.Army	**50.RC** (133.RD, 240.RD), **51.RC** (42.GRD, 38.RD, 232.RD), 54.FRn, 159.FRn	139.CnABr, AR(no number), 680.ATR, 10.MR(mb), 800. AAR, 981.AAR	34.ArTr	4.EBr	21.FtBn, 176. BkFtCo
7.G.Army	**24.GRC** (72.GRD, 81.GRD, 6.RD), **25.GRC** (6.GAbD, 36.GRD, 53.RD), 227.RD	41.GCnABr, 114.GATR, 115.GATR, 263.MR, 290. MR, 5.AAD, 162.GAAR	38.ArTr	60.EBr	4.FtBn
27.Army	**35.GRC** (3.GAbD, 93.GRD, 180.RD), **33.RC** (78.RD, 202.RD, 337.RD), **104.RC** (4.GAbD, 163.RD, 206.RD)	11.AD, 16.BAD, 27.CnABr, 30.ATBr, 34.ATBr, 881. ATR, 1669.ATR, 480.MR (mb), 492.MR, 9.AAD, 225. GAAR, 249.AAR, 459.AAR	27.GTBr	14.AEBr, 43.EBr	3.FtBn, 27. FtBn
53.Army	**49.RC** (1.GAbD, 110.GRD, 375.RD), **57.RC** (203.RD, 228.RD, 243.RD), **75.RC** (74.RD, 299.RD), 25.GRD, 233.RD	152.CnABr, 31.ATBr, 1316. ATR, 461.MR		54.EBr	
6.Tank Army			5.GTK, 5.MC, 18.TC, 6.SPABr, 49.GTR, 156.TR, 364.GHSPAR, 4.McR	22.MEBr	
Front assets	**27.GRC** (214.RD, 297.RD, 409.RD), 303.RD, **4.GCvC** (9.GCvD, 10.GCvD, 30. CvD), **5.GCvC** (11.GCvD, 12.GCvD, 63.CvD), **6.GCvC** (8.GCvD, 13.GCvD, 8.CvD), 1.ID (Rum.), 1.IBr (Yug.)	5.GBAD, 98.HHABr, 12. ATBr, 22.ATBr, 24.ATBr, 6.GMD, 11.AAD, 26.AAD, 27.AAD, 30.AAD, 272. GAAR, 257.AAR, 622.AAR	23.TC, 10.ArTr, 25.ArTr, 61. ArTr	5.MnEBr, 27. MEBr, 1.BgBBr, 2.BgBBr, 8. HBgBR, 61.EBn, 72.EBn	

Information in the above section courtesy of Kamen Nevenkin.

I.16 Order of Battle of Soviet ground troops, October 1 1944

Formations	Rifle, Airborne, Cavalry troops	Artillery troops	Tank and Mechanized troops	Engineer troops	Flame-thrower troops
2nd Ukrainian Front					
40.Army	**50.RC** (240.RD), **51.RC** (38. RD, 133.RD, 232.RD), 42. GRD, 54.FRn, 159.FRn	153.CnABr, AR(no number), 680.ATR, 10.MR(mb)	34.ArTr	4.EBr	21.FtBn, 176. BkFtCo
7.G.Army	**24.GRC** (72.GRD, 81.GRD, 6.RD), **25.GRC** (6.GAbD, 36.GRD, 53.RD), 227.RD	41.GCnABr, 114.GATR, 115.GATR, 263.MR, 290. MR, 493.MR, 5.AAD	38.ArTr	60.EBr	4.FtBn
27.Army	**35.GRC** (3.GAbD, 93.GRD, 180.RD, 202.RD), **33.RC** (78.RD, 337.RD), **104.RC** (4.GAbD, 163.RD, 206.RD)	11.AD, 16.BAD, 27.CnABr, 30.ATBr, 315.GATR, 480. MR(mb), 492.MR, 9.AAD, 249.AAR, 459.AAR	27.GTBr, 25.TR, 697.SPAR, 1458.SPAR	43.EBr	3.FtBn, 27. FtBn
53.Army	**27.GRC** (297.RD, 409.RD), **49.RC** (1.GAbD, 110.GRD, 375.RD), **57.RC** (203.RD, 228.RD, 243.RD)	5.GBAD, 152.CnABr, 11. ATBr, 31.ATBr, 1316.ATR, 461.MR, 27.AAD	18.TC	54.EBr	
46.Army	**10.GRC** (49.GRD, 59.GRD, 86.GRD, 109.GRD), **31. GRC** (4.GRD, 34.GRD, 40. GRD), **37.RC** (108.GRD, 320.RD)	7.BAD, 45.GCnABr, 92. GCAR, 437.ATR, 462.MR, 38.AAD		51.EBr	
6.G.Tank Army		301.ATR	5.GTK, 9.GMC, 6.SPABr, 49. GTR, 364.GHSPA R, 4.GMcR	22.MEBr	
Front assets	25.GRD, 303.RD, **4.GCvC** (9.GCvD, 10.GCvD, 30. CvD), **5.GCvC** (11.GCvD, 12.GCvD, 63.CvD), **6.GCvC** (8.GCvD, 13.GCvD, 8.CvD), 1.ID (Rum.), 1.IBr (Yug.)	202.LABr, 2.ATBr, 12. ATBr, 22.ATBr, 24.ATBr, 34.ATBr, 17.GMR, 47. GMR, 48.GMR, 57.GMR, 66.GMR, 80.GMR, 97.GMR, 302.GMR, 309.GMR, 324. GMR, 328.GMR, 11.AAD, 26.AAD, 30.AAD, 225. GAAR, 272.GAAR, 622. AAR, 800.AAR, 981.AAR, 1651.AAR,	23.TC, 2.GMC, 7.MC, 10.ArTr, 10.ArTr, 25.ArTr, 61.ArTr	5.MnEBr, 14. AEBr, 27.MEBr, 1.BgBBr, 2.BgBBr, 8.HBgBR, 61.EBn, 72.EBn	

Abbreviations key to I.15 & I.16:

AABn – Anti-aircraft Artillery Battalion
AAD – Anti-aircraft Artillery Division
AAR – Anti-aircraft Artillery Regiment
AD – Artillery Division
AR – Artillery Regiment
AbBr – Airborne Brigade
AEBr – Assault Engineer Brigade
ArTr – Armored Train
ATBn – Anti-Tank Battalion
ATBr – Anti-Tank Brigade
ATR – Anti-Tank Regiment
BAC – Breakthrough Artillery Corps
BAD – Breakthrough Artillery Division
BgBBn – Bridge-Building Battalion
BgBBr – Bridge-Building Brigade
BgBR – Bridge-Building Regiment
BkFtCo – Backpack Flamethrower Company
CnABr – Canon Artillery Brigade
CvD – Cavalry Division
CzAC – Czechoslovakian Army Corps
EBn – Engineer Battalion
EBr – Engineer Brigade
FRn – Fortified Region
FtBn – Flamethrower Battalion
GAAR – Guards Anti-aircraft Artillery Regiment
GAbD – Guards Airborne Division
GATBr – Guards Anti-Tank Brigade
GATR – Guards Anti-Tank Regiment
GBAD – Guards Breakthrough Artillery Division
GCAR – Guards Corps Artillery Regiment
GCnABr – Guards Canon Artillery Brigade
GCvC – Cavalry Corps
GCvD – Cavalry Division
GFRn – Guards Fortified Region
GHSPAR – Guards Heavy Self-propelled Artillery Regiment
GMBn – Guards Mortar Battalion
GMhBr – Guards Mechanized Battalion
GMC – Guards Mechanized Corps
GMnRD – Guards Mountain Rifle Division
GMcR – Guards Motorcycle Regiment
GMD – Guards Mortar Division
GMR – Guards Mortar Regiment
GARcBn – Guards Reconnaissance Artillery Battalion
GRC – Guards Rifle Corps
GRD – Guards Rifle Division
GSHHABr – Guards Super-Heavy Howitzer Artillery Brigade
GSPABr – Guards Self-propelled Artillery Brigade
GTBr – Guards Tank Brigade
GTC – Guards Tank Corps
GTR – Guards Tank Regiment
HAR – Howitzer Artillery Regiment
HHABr – Heavy Howitzer Artillery Brigade
HBgBR – Heavy Bridge-Building Regiment
IBr – Infantry Brigade

ID – Infantry Division
LABr – Light Artillery Brigade
(mb) – (mule-borne)
MBgBBn – Mechanized Bridge-Building Battalion
MBgBR – Mechanized Bridge-Building Regiment
MBr – Mortar Brigade
MC – Mechanized Corps
McBn – Motorcycle Battalion
McR – Motorcycle Regiment
MEBr – Mechanized Engineer Brigade
MnEBr – Mountain Engineer Brigade
MnRC – Mountain Rifle Corps
MnRD – Mountain Rifle Division
MR – Mortar Regiment
MrIBr – Marine Infantry Brigade
RC – Rifle Corps
RD – Rifle Division
SmBn – Sub-machinegun Battalion
SPABr – Self-propelled Artillery Brigade
SPAR – Self-propelled Artillery Regiment
SpMBn – Special Motorized Battalion
TBn – Tank Battalion
TBr – Tank Brigade
TC – Tank Corps
TR – Tank Regiment

Information in the above section courtesy of Kamen Nevenkin.

I.17 Order of Battle of the Soviet Air Force

5th Air Army:

2nd Assault Air Corps (renamed **3rd Guards Assault Air Corps** on 27.10.1944): 7th Guards Assault Air Division, 231st Assault Air Division (renamed 12th Guards Assault Air Division on 27.10.1944)
5th Assault Air Corps (added in September 1944): 4th Guards Assault Air Division, 264th Assault Air Division, 331st Fighter Air Division
3rd Guards Fighter Air Corps: 13th Guards Fighter Air Division, 14th Guards Fighter Air Division
279th Fighter Air Division
6th Guards Assault Air Division (added in September 1944)
10th Guards Assault Air Division (detached in September 1944)
218th Bomber Air Division
312th Night Bomber Air Division
Other air units: 511th Reconnaissance Air Regiment, 207th Correction-Reconnaissance Air Regiment, 95th Transport Air Regiment, 714th Air Signals Regiment (till December 1944), 5th Air Signals Regiment (from the spring of 1945), 18th Air Regiment of the Civil Air Fleet (till October 1944), 44th Air Regiment of the Civil Air Fleet (from November 1944)
1st Air Corps (Romanian): Fighter Wing, Bomber Wing
Anti-Aircraft Artillery: 1254th Anti-Aircraft Artillery Regiment, 1562nd Anti-Aircraft Artillery Regiment, 1662nd Anti-Aircraft Artillery Regiment (from the spring of 1945), 1673rd Anti-Aircraft Artillery Regiment (from the spring of 1945), 1681st Anti-Aircraft Artillery Regiment, 1975th Anti-Aircraft Artillery Regiment (till November 1944)

2nd Ukrainian Front's Air Units:

Front assets: 85th Ambulance Air Regiment, 1001st Ambulance Air Regiment, 714th Air Signals Regiment (from December 1944)

6th Guards Tank Army:

207th Guards Signal Air Regiment (from December 1944)

Information in the above section courtesy of Kamen Nevenkin.

APPENDIX II

General Officer Listings

A gallery of German commanders

Colonel-General Johannes Friessner, Army Group South. (Bundesarchiv 146–1984–018–27A)

General der Panzertruppe Hermann Breith, III Panzer Corps. (Bundesarchiv 183–J16804)

General der Gebirgstruppe Hans Kreysing, XVII Corps.
(Bundesarchiv 146–2008–0013)

General der Panzertruppe Friedrich Kirchner, LXVII
Panzer Corps. (Bundesarchiv 146–1997–018–33)

Lieutenant-General August Schmidt, LXXII Corps.
(Bundesarchiv 146–2008–0014)

Major-General Eberhard Thunert, 1st Panzer Division.
(Bundesarchiv 146–1992–049–28A)

Major-General Gerhard Schmidhuber, 13th Panzer Division. (Bundesarchiv 101I–088–3743–15A)

Major-General Josef von Radowitz, 23rd Panzer Division. A post-war image from 1956. (Bundesarchiv 183–43539–0006)

Colonel Günther Pape, Panzer Grenadier Division 'Feldherrnhalle'. (Bundesarchiv 183–B16918)

Lieutenant-General Erich Reuter, 46th Infantry Division. (Bundesarchiv 183–B22619)

167

Lieutenant-General Siegfried von Rekowski, 76th Infantry Division. (Bundesarchiv 101I–024–3548–

Lieutenant-General Christian Philipp, 8th Jaeger Division. (Bundesarchiv 101I–100–0779–26)

Lieutenant-General Paul Klatt, 3rd Mountain Division. (Bundesarchiv 146–1997–021–20)

Lieutenant-General Friedrich Breith, 4th Mountain Division. (Bundesarchiv 146–1989–053–20)

SS-Brigadeführer Fritz Schmedes, 4th SS Police
Panzer Grenadier Division. (Phil Nix)

SS-Brigadeführer Joachim Rumohr, 8th SS Cavalry
Division 'Florian Geyer'. (Bundesarchiv 183–S73622)

SS-Brigadeführer August Zehender, 22nd SS Cavalry
Division 'Maria Theresia'. (Bundesarchiv 146–1993–
066–28A)

II.1 German troops

Army Group 'South': Colonel-General Johannes Friessner

6th Army: General der Artillerie Maximilian Fretter-Pico
8th Army: General der Infanterie Otto Wöhler
4th Air Fleet: Colonel-General Otto Dessloch

III Panzer Corps: General der Panzertruppe Hermann Breith
IV Panzer Corps/ Panzer Corps 'Feldherrnhalle': General der Panzertruppe Ulrich Kleemann
XVII Corps: General der Gebirgstruppe Hans Kreysing
XXIX Corps: Lieutenant-General (from 15 October 1944 – General der Infanterie) Kurt Röpke
LVII Panzer Corps: General der Panzertruppe Friedrich Kirchner
LXXII Corps: Lieutenant-General August Schmidt
Plenipotentiary General of the German Wehramcht in Hungary: General der Infanterie Hans von Greiffenberg
I Air Corps: Lieutenant-General Paul Deichmann
Commanding General of Luftwaffe in Hungary: Lieutenant-General Kuno Heribert Fütterer
V Anti-Aircraft Artillery Corps: General der Flakartillerie Otto-Wilhelm von Renz

8th Jaeger Division: Lieutenant-General Christian Philipp
15th Infantry Division: Major-General Hans Längenfelder
46th Infantry Division: Lieutenant-General Erich Reuter
76th Infantry Division: Lieutenant-General Siegfried von Rekowski
3rd Mountain Division: Lieutenant-General Paul Klatt
4th Mountain Division: Lieutenant-General Friedrich Breith
1st Panzer Division: Major-General Eberhard Thunert
13th Panzer Division: Major-General Gerhard Schmidhuber
23rd Panzer Division: Major-General Josef von Radowitz
24th Panzer Division: Colonel Gustav-Adolf von Nostitz-Wallwitz
Panzer-Grenadier Division 'Feldherrnhalle': Colonel Günther Pape
4th SS Police Panzer-Grenadier Division: SS-Brigadenführer Fritz Schmedes
8th SS Cavalry Division 'Florian Geyer': SS-Brigadenführer Joachim Rumohr
22nd SS Cavalry Division 'Maria Theresia': SS-Brigadenführer August Zehender
15th Anti-Aircraft Artillery Division: Major-General Theodor Herbert (until 18 January 1945); Colonel Johann-Wilhelm Doering-Manteuffel

II.2 Hungarian troops

1st Army: Lieutenant-General Béla Miklós (until 16 October 1944); Lieutenant-General Dezsö Lászlo
2nd Army: Lieutenant-General Lajoss Veress (until 16 October 1944); Lieutenant-General Jenö Major
3rd Army: Lieutenant-General József Heszlényi

I Corps: Major-General Szilárd Bakay (until 8 October 1944); Major-General Béla Aggteleky (until 15 October 1944); Lieutenant-General Iván Hindy
II Corps: Major-General István Kiss
III Corps: Major-General Béla Aggteleky (until 8 October 1944); Major-General László Hollósy-Kuthy
IV Corps: Major-General József Heszlényi (until 10 September 1944)
V Corps: Major-General Zoltán Algya-Pap
VI Corps: Major-General Ferenc Farkas (until 16 October 1944); Brigadier-General Miklós Nagyöszy
VII Corps: Major-General Géza Vörös (until 17 October 1944); Lieutenant-General Janós Markóczy
VIII Corps/ II Reserve Corps: Major-General Belá Lengyel
IX Corps: Brigadier-General Gyula Kovács

6th Infantry Division: Brigadier-General László Karátsony
10th Infantry Division: Brigadier-General Kornél Oszlányi
12th Reserve Division/ 12th Infantry Division: Brigadier-General Ference Mikófalvy
13th Infantry Division: Brigadier-General Gyula Hankovszky (until 16 October 1944); Brigadier-General Jénö Sövényházi

16th Infantry Division: Brigadier-General József Vasváry
20th Infantry Division: Brigadier-General Frigyes Vasváry (until 26 October 1944); Brigadier-General Jenö Tömöry
23rd Reserve Division/ 23rd Infantry Division: Brigadier-General Gustáv Deseö (until October 1944); Brigadier-General Ferenc Osztovies (until 20 October 1944); Brigadier-General Géza Fehér
24th Infantry Division: Brigadier-General János Markóczy (until 15 October 1944); Colonel Ferenc Karlóczy
25th Infantry Division: Brigadier-General Antal Benda (until ? September 1944); Brigadier-General László Hollósy-Kuthy (until 10 October 1944); Major-General Ferenc Horváth
27th Light Division: Colonel András Zákó (until 16 October 1944); Brigadier-General Gyözö Horváth
2nd Reserve Division: Colonel Imre Czlenner (until 13 October 1944); Colonel Dénes Dobák
4th Reserve Division: Brigadier-General Árpád Tarnaváry (until 23 September 1944); Colonel Jenö Tömöry (until 28 September 1944); Colonel Ferenc Mikófalvy
5th Reserve Division: Major-General Imre Kálmán
6th Reserve Division: Brigadier-General György Vukováry
7th Reserve Division: Brigadier-General József Finta (until 16 October 1944); Brigadier-General József Kisfaludy
8th Reserve Division: Brigadier-General Bela Temesy
9th Reserve Division: Brigadier-General Janós Mindszenty (until October 1944); Colonel Janós Fónagy
1st Armoured Division: Colonel Ferenc Koszorus (until 23 September 1944); Colonel Ferenc Deák (until 10 October 1944); Colonel Béla Tiszay (until 21 October 1944); Colonel Zoltán Schell
2nd Armoured Division: Brigadier-General Zoltán Zsedényi
1st Cavalry Division: Major-General Mihály Ibrányi

II.3 Soviet troops

2nd Ukrainian Front: Army General (from 10 September 1944 – Marshal) Rodion Malinovskii

27th Army: Lieutenant-General (from 13 September 1944 – Colonel-General) Sergei Trofimenko
40th Army: Lieutenant-General Philip Zhmachenko
46th Army: Lieutenant-General Ivan Shlemin
53rd Army: Lieutenant-General Ivan Managarov
7th Guards Army: Colonel-General Mikhail Shumilov
6th Tank Army/ 6th Guards Tank Army: Lieutenant-General (from 13 September 1944 – Colonel-General) Andrei Kravchenko
Cavalry-Mechanized Group/ 1st Guards Cavalry-Mechanized Group: Lieutenant-General Issa Pliev
5th Air Army: Colonel-General Sergei Goriunov

33rd Rifle Corps: Major-General Alexei Semenov
37th Rifle Corps: Major-General Feodor Kolchuk
49th Rifle Corps: Major-General Gurii Terentiev
50th Rifle Corps: Major-General Serafim Merkulov
51st Rifle Corps: Major-General Ilia Liubovtsev (until 28 August 1944); Major-General Sergei Timoshkov (until 21 September1944); Major-General Alexander Rumiantsev
57th Rifle Corps: Major-General Feodor Ostashenko
75th Rifle Corps: Major-General Andrian Akimenko
104th Rifle Corps: Lieutenant-General Alexander Petrushevskii
10th Guards Rifle Corps: Major-General (from 13 September 1944 – Lieutenant-General) Ivan Rubaniuk
24th Guards Rifle Corps: Major-General Peter Avdeenko
25th Guards Rifle Corps: Major-General Ganii Safiulin
27th Guards Rifle Corps: Major-General Evgenii Alekhin
31st Guards Rifle Corps: Major-General Sergei Bobruk
35th Guards Rifle Corps: Lieutenant-General Sergei Goriachev
4th Guards Cavalry Corps: Lieutenant-General Issa Pliev (until 12 November 1944); Major-General Vasilii Golovskii
5th Guards Cavalry Corps: Major-General (from 13 September 1944 – Lieutenant-General) Sergei I. Gorshkov

A gallery of Soviet commanders

Marshal Rodion Yakovlevich Malinovsky, commander of the 2nd Ukrainian Front 1944–45. (Military History Museum Budapest)

Lt Gen Issa Alexandrovich Pliyev, commander of the Pliyev (later 1st Guard) Cavalry-Mechanized Group 1944–45. (Military History Museum Budapest)

Gen Katkov, commander of the Soviet 7 Mechanized Corps. (Photo archive of the Bulgarian Ministry of Defence)

6th Guards Cavalry Corps: Lieutenant-General Sergei Sokolov
18th Tank Corps: Major-General Vasilii Polozkov (until 29 August 1944); Colonel Ivan Kolesnikov (until 24 September 1944); Major-General Peter Govorunenko
23rd Tank Corps: Major-General (from 13 September 1944 – Lieutenant-General) Aleksei Akhmanov
5th Guards Tank Corps: Lieutenant-General Vasilii Alekseev (until 26 August 1944); Major-General Mikhail Saveliev
5th Mechanized Corps/ 9th Guards Mechanized Corps: Lieutenant-General Mikhail Volkov
7th Mechanized Corps: Major-General Fedor Katkov
3rd Guards Fighter Air Corps: Major-General (from 13 September 1944 – Lieutenant-General) Ivan Podgornyi
2nd Assault Air Corps/ 3rd Guards Assault Air Corps: Lieutenant-General Vasilii Stepichev
5th Assault Air Corps: Major-General Nikolai Kamanin

6th Rifle Division: Colonel (from 13 September 1944 – Major-General) Ivan Obushenko
38th Rifle Division: Major-General Sergei Timoshkov (until 5 September 1944); Colonel Mikhail Sazhin (until 22 September 1944); Major-General Sergei Timoshkov (until 9 October 1944); Colonel Mikhail Sazhin
53rd Rifle Division: Colonel David Vasilevsky
74th Rifle Division: Colonel Kutub Gizatulin (until 5 October 1944); Colonel Konstantin Sychev
78th Rifle Division: Major-General Nikolai Mikhailov
133rd Rifle Division: Colonel Vladimir Beloded (until 9 October 1944); Colonel I. Dubrovin
163rd Rifle Division: Colonel (from 13 September 1944 – Major-General) Fedor Karlov
180th Rifle Division: Major-General Vasilii Kindiukhin
202nd Rifle Division: Colonel Ivan Hohlov
203rd Rifle Division: Major-General Gavril Zdanovich
206th Rifle Division: Colonel M. Abramov (until 29 September 1944); Colonel F. Dremenkov
214th Rifle Division: Lieutenant-Colonel I. Elin (until 29 September 1944); Colonel Georgii Tomilovskii
227th Rifle Division: Major-General Georgii Preobrazhensky
228th Rifle Division: Colonel Ivan Esin
232nd Rifle Division: Major-General Maxim Kozyr
233rd Rifle Division: Colonel Timofei Sidorenko
240th Rifle Division: Colonel (from 13 September 1944 – Major-General) Terentii Umanskii
243rd Rifle Division: Colonel M. Tkachev (until 21 September 1944); Colonel N. Parfentiev
297th Rifle Division: Colonel Andrei Kovtun-Stankevich
299th Rifle Division: Major-General Nikolai Travnikov
303rd Rifle Division: Major-General Konstantin Fedorovsky
320th Rifle Division: Colonel Josif Burik
337th Rifle Division: Colonel Taras Gorobets
375th Rifle Division: Major-General Vasilii Karnuhin
409th Rifle Division: Major-General Evstafii Grechanyi
4th Guards Rifle Division: Colonel Kuzma Parfenov
25th Guards Rifle Division: Major-General Grigorii Krivolapov
34th Guards Rifle Division: Colonel (from 13 September 1944 – Major-General) Josif Maksimovich (until 14 October 1944); Colonel Gerasim Kuks
36th Guards Rifle Division: Major-General Georgii Lilenkov
40th Guards Rifle Division: Major-General Grigorii Panchenko (until 23 September 1944); Colonel Lev Bransburg
42nd Guards Rifle Division: Major-General Fedor Bobrov (until 9 October 1944); Major-General Sergei Timoshkov
49th Guards Rifle Division: Colonel (from 13 September 1944 – Major-General) Vasilii Margelov
59th Guards Rifle Division: Major-General Georgii Karamyshev
72nd Guards Rifle Division: Major-General Anatolii Losev
81st Guards Rifle Division: Major-General Ivan Morozov
86th Guards Rifle Division: Colonel (from 13 September 1944 – Major-General) Vasilii Sokolovskii
93rd Guards Rifle Division: Major-General Nikolai Zolotuhin
108th Guards Rifle Division: Major-General Sergei Dunaev
109th Guards Rifle Division: Colonel Ilya Baldynov

110th Guards Rifle Division: Major-General Mikhail Ogorodov
1st Guards Airborne Division: Colonel Dmitrii Sobolev
3rd Guards Airborne Division: Colonel (from 13 September 1944 – Major-General) Ivan N. Konev
4th Guards Airborne Division: Major-General Alexander Rumyantsev (until 21 September 1944); Colonel A.Kostrykin
6th Guards Airborne Division: Major-General Mikhail Smirnov
8th Cavalry Division: Colonel Peter Hrustalev
30th Cavalry Division: Major-General Vasilii Golovskoi
63rd Cavalry Division: Major-General Pavel Krutovskih
8th Guards Cavalry Division: Major-General Dmitrii Pavlov
9th Guards Cavalry Division: Colonel David Demchuk
10th Guards Cavalry Division: Colonel Grigorii Reva (until 2 October 1944); Colonel V. Nikiforov
11th Guards Cavalry Division: Colonel Leonid Slanov
12th Guards Cavalry Division: Major-General V. Grigorovich
13th Guards Cavalry Division: Major-General Grigorii Belousov
11th Artillery Division: Major-General Andrei Popovich
7th Breakthrough Artillery Division: Major-General Alexander Pavlov (until 22 September 1944); Major-General Ivan Bobrovnikov
16th Breakthrough Artillery Division: Major-General Nikolai Gusarov (until 22 September 1944); Colonel P. Yurko
5th Guards Breakthrough Artillery Division: Colonel Vladimir Ivanov
5th Anti-Aircraft Artillery Division: Colonel M. Kudryashov (until 18 September 1944); Colonel V. Okorkov
9th Anti-Aircraft Artillery Division: Colonel Nikolai Raschitskii
11th Anti-Aircraft Artillery Division: Colonel K. Pavlov
26th Anti-Aircraft Artillery Division: Colonel G. Desnitsky
27th Anti-Aircraft Artillery Division: Colonel A. Nekrasov
30th Anti-Aircraft Artillery Division: Colonel V. Zenkov
38th Anti-Aircraft Artillery Division: Colonel F. Rodin
6th Guards Mortar Division: Colonel A. Makarov
279th Fighter Air Division: Colonel Vsevolod Blagoveschenskii
331st Fighter Air Division: Colonel Ivan Semenenko
13th Guards Fighter Air Division: Colonel Ivan Taranenko
14th Guards Fighter Air Division: Colonel Alexei Yudakov
231st Assault Air Division/ 12th Guards Assault Air Division: Colonel Leonid Chizhikov
264th Assault Air Division: Colonel Evgenii Klobukov
4th Guards Assault Air Division: Colonel Valentin Saprykin
7th Guards Assault Air Division: Lieutenant-Colonel G. Shuteev
10th Guards Assault Air Division: Major-General Andrei Vitruk
218th Bomber Air Division: Lieutenant-Colonel (from 26 October 1944 – Colonel) Nikolai Romanov
312th Night Bomber Air Division: Colonel Vasilii Chanpalov

II. 4 Romanian troops

1st Army: Corps-General Nicolae Macici
4th Army: Corps-General Gheorghe Avramescu

II Corps: Corps-General Nicolae Dăscălescu
IV Corps: Divisional-General Nicolae Stoenescu (until 12 September 1944); Brigadier-General Dumitru Tudosie (until 29 September 1944); Divisional-General Nicolae Stoenescu (until 3 December 1944); Corps-General Ion Boiþeanu
VI Corps: ??????? Nicolae Tătăranu (until 28 September 1944); ??????? Agricola Filip (until 12 October 1944); Corps-General Emanoil Leoveanu (until 27 October 1944); Divisional-General Gheorghe Gheorghiu
VII Corps: Corps-General Nicolae Sova
Cavalry Corps: ???? Gheorghe Cialâk
Mountain Corps: ????? Ion Dumitrache
Mechanized Corps: Lieutenant-General Gheorghe Rozin

1st Air Corps: ????? Emanoil Ionescu

1st Volunteer Infantry Division 'Tudor Vladimirescu': Colonel Nicolas Cambrea (until 1 October 1944); Colonel Mircea Haupt

2nd Infantry Division: Brigadier-General Dumitru Tudosie (until 16 October 1944); Brigadier-General Romulus Stănescu (until 23 October 1944); Brigadier-General Mihail Voicu

3rd Infantry Division: ?????? Corneliu Calotescu (until 12 October 1944); Brigadier-General Ioan Dumitriu (until 4 November 1944); Brigadier-General Ioan D. Popescu

4th Infantry Division: ?????? Dumitru Petrescu (until 30 September 1944); ?????? Platon Chirnoagă (until 20 October 1944); ?????? Mihail Voicu (until 23 October 1944); Lieutenant-Colonel Ilie Ionescu

5th Infantry Division: ?????? Grigore Nicolau

6th Infantry Division: Major-General R. Gheorghe Gheorghiu (until 27 October 1944); Brigadier-General Ion Spirea (until 8 November 1944); Brigadier-General Mihail Corbuleanu (until 10 December 1944); Brigadier-General Gheorghe Marinescu

9th Infantry Division: Major-General Costin Ionaºcu (until 4 December 1944); Colonel Ion Iucăl

11th Infantry Division: ?????? Edgar Rădulescu

18th Infantry Division: Brigadier-General Vasile Pascu (until 14 October 1944); ?????? Petre Camenita

19th Infantry Division: ?????? Mihail Lăcătuºu

21st Infantry Division: ?????? Polihron Dumitrescu (until 28 November 1944); Colonel Ion Constantinescu

1st Cavalry Division: Colonel Vladimir Constantinescu (until 20 October 1944); Colonel Constantin Talpeº (until 30 November 1944); ?????? Dumitru Popescu

8th Cavalry Division: Brigadier-General Corneliu Todorini (until 3 November 1944); Colonel Ioan Crăciunescu (until 25 November 1944); ?????? Hercule Fortunescu

9th Cavalry Division: ?????? Dumitru Popescu (until 31 October 1944); Colonel Dumitru Neferu (until 2 December 1944); ?????? Vasile Botezatu (until 17 December 1944); ?????? Ilie Antonescu

1st Mountain Division: ?????? Grigore Bălan (until 5 September 1944); Brigadier-General Ioan Beldiceanu

2nd Mountain Division: Colonel Gheorghe Bartolomeu (until 15 September 1944); ?????? Constantin Iordăchescu

3rd Mountain Division: ?????? Leonard Mociulschi

103rd Mountain Division: ?????? Ilie Creþulescu

Information in this Appendix courtesy of Kamen Nevenkin.

A gallery of Romanian commanders

Corps-General Nicolae Dăscălescu, II Corps. (Photo archive of the Bulgarian Ministry of Defence)

Colonel Nicolas Cambrea, 1 Volunteer Infantry Division 'Tudor Vladimirescu'. (Photo archive of the Bulgarian Ministry of Defence)

Major-General Costin Ionaºcu, 9th Infantry Division. (Photo archive of the Bulgarian Ministry of Defence)

APPENDIX III

Hungarian TOEs and AFVs

III.1 TO&E of Hungarian forces in 1944

Mountain Brigade
  HQ
  5 Infantry Battalions, each
    HQ
        1 Pioneer Platoon (3 LMG)
        1 Field Telephone Platoon
        1 Scout Platoon
        1 AT Platoon (4 ATG (37mm))
        1 Heavy Mortar Platoon (4 mortars (120mm))
      3 Infantry Companies (each: 12 LMG + 6 HMG)
      1 Machine Gun Company (12 HMG + 8 mortars (81mm))
  2 Mountain Artillery Battalions, each
      3 Light Artillery Batteries (each: 4 mountain guns (75mm))
  1 Motorized Artillery Battery (4 towed field howitzers (149mm))
  1 Mountain Cavalry Company (9 LMG + 3 HMG + 6mortars (50mm))
  1 AT Company (6 ATG (37mm))
  1 Motorized AT Company (9 ATG (75mm) + 9 LMG)
  1 Mountain Combat Engineer Company (4 LMG + 2 HMG)
  1 Mountain Signal Company (5 LMG)
  1 AA Battery (6 motorized AAG (80mm))
  1 AA Battery (6 motorized AAG (40mm))
  1 Mountain Engineer Company (3 LMG + 2 HMG +2 flamethrowers)

Infantry Division
  HQ
  3 Infantry Regiments
    HQ
        1 Bicycle Pioneer Platoon (3 LMG)
        1 Field Telephone Platoon
        1 Cavalry Scout Platoon (3 LMG + 2 mortars (50mm))
        1 Bicycle Scout Platoon (3 LMG +2 mortars (50mm))
        1 Mortar Company (12 mortars (120mm))
        1 Motorized AT Company (9 ATG (75mm) + 9 LMG)
      3 Infantry Battalions, each
        1 Field Telephone Platoon
        1 AT Platoon (4 ATG (40mm))
        3 Infantry Companies (each: 12 LMG + 6 HMG)
        1 Machine Gun Company (12 HMG + 8 mortars (81mm))
  1 Reconnaissance Battalion
    HQ
        1 Armoured Car Platoon (4 Csaba armoured cars)
        1 Bicycle Pioneer Platoon (3 LMG)
        1 Bicycle Telephone Platoon
        1 Motorized Maintenance Platoon

1 Motorized AT Platoon (3 ATG (75mm) + 3 LMG)
1 Mortar Company (8 mortars (81mm)+ 4 mortars (120mm))
1 Bicycle Infantry Company (9 LMG + 3 HMG + 6 mortars (50mm))
1 Cavalry Company (9 LMG + 3 HMG + 6 mortars (50mm))
1 Combat Engineer Battalion
   3 Combat Engineer Companies (each: 4 LMG + 2 HMG)
   1 Heavy Combat Bridge Column
1 Signal Battalion
   1 Telephone Company (5 LMG)
   1 Radio Company (4 LMG)
1 Assault Gun Battalion
   2 Assault Gun Batteries (each: 10 Zrinyi (75mm) assault guns)
   1 Assault Gun Battery (10 Zrinyi (105mm) assault guns)
3 Artillery Battalions, each
   2 Light Artillery Batteries (each: 4 horse-drawn field howitzers (100mm))
   1 Heavy Artillery Battalion (4 horse-drawn field howitzers (149mm))
1 Motorized Heavy Artillery Battalion
   2 Motorized Artillery Batteries (each: 4 towed field howitzers (149mm))
1 Artillery Observation Battery
1 AA Battery (12 motorized AAG (40mm))
1 Military Labour Battalion
   3 Military Labour Companies

Reserve Division
  HQ
  3 Infantry Regiments
    HQ
      1 Bicycle Pioneer Platoon (3 LMG)
      1 Field Telephone Platoon
      1 Cavalry Scout Platoon (3 LMG)
      1 Mortar Company (8 mortars (81mm))
      1 AT Company (8 ATG (40mm))
    3 Infantry Battalions, each
      1 Field Telephone Platoon
      1 AT Platoon (4 ATG (40mm))
      3 Infantry Companies (each: 12 LMG + 2HMG)
      1 Machine Gun Company (12 HMG + 4 mortars (81mm))
  1 Reconnaissance Battalion
    HQ
      1 Armoured Car Platoon (4 Csaba armoured cars)
      1 Bicycle Pioneer Platoon (3 LMG)
      1 Bicycle Telephone Platoon
      1 Motorized AT Platoon (4 ATG (40mm))
      1 Mortar Platoon (4 mortars (81mm))
      1 Bicycle Infantry Company (12 LMG + 2 mortars (50mm))
      1 Cavalry Company (9LMG + 2 mortars (50mm) + 2ATR(20mm))
  1 Combat Engineer Battalion
    3 Combat Engineer Companies (each: 4 LMG + 2 HMG)
    1 Heavy Combat Bridge Column
  1 Signal Battalion
    1 Telephone Company (5 LMG)
    1 Radio Company (4 LMG)
  3 Artillery Battalions, each
    2 Light Artillery Batteries (each: 4 horse-drawn field howitzers (100mm))
    1 Heavy Artillery Battalion (4 horse-drawn field howitzers (149mm))
  1 Artillery Observation Battery

1 AA Battery (12 motorized AAG (40mm))

Light Division
  HQ
  2 Infantry Regiments
    HQ
        1 Bicycle Pioneer Platoon (3 LMG)
        1 Field Telephone Platoon
        1 Cavalry Scout Platoon (3 LMG)
        1 Mortar Company (8 mortars (81mm))
        1 AT Company (8 ATG (40mm))
      3 Infantry Battalions, each
        1 Field Telephone Platoon
        1 AT Platoon (4 ATG (40mm))
        3 Infantry Companies (each: 12 LMG + 6HMG)
        1 Machine Gun Company (12 HMG + 8 mortars (81mm))
  1 Reconnaissance Battalion
    HQ
        1 Armoured Car Platoon (4 Csaba armoured cars)
        1 Bicycle Pioneer Platoon (3 LMG)
        1 Bicycle Telephone Platoon
        1 Motorized AT Platoon (3 ATG (75mm) + 3LMG)
        1 Mortar Platoon (4 mortars (81mm))
        1 Bicycle Infantry Company (12LMG + 2 mortars (50mm))
        1 Cavalry Company (9 LMG + 2 mortars (50mm))
  1 Combat Engineer Company (4 LMG + 2 HMG)
  1 Signal Company (5 LMG)
  2 Artillery Battalions, each
      2 Light Artillery Batteries (each: 4 horse-drawn field howitzers (100mm))
      1 Heavy Artillery Battalion (4 horse-drawn field howitzers (149mm))
  1 AA Battery (6 motorized AAG (80mm))
  1 AA Battery (12 motorized AAG (40mm))

Armoured Division
  HQ
  1 Tank Regiment
    HQ
        1 Motorized Pioneer Platoon (3LMG)
        1 Motorized Traffic Control Platoon
        1 Signal Platoon (2 Turán (40mm) command tanks + 1 Turán (40mm) tank)
        1 Light Tank Platoon (5 Toldi (20mm) tanks)
        1 AA Company (3 Toldi(20mm) command tanks + 12 Nimród (40mm) self-propelled AA guns)
        1 Motorized Maintenance Company
    1 Tank Battalion
      HQ
          1 Motorized Pioneer Platoon (3 LMG)
          1 Motorized Traffic Control Platoon
          1 Signal Platoon (2 Turán (40mm) command tanks + 1 Turán (40mm) tank)
          1 Light Tank Platoon (5 Toldi (20mm) tanks)
          Motorized Supply Company
        2 Heavy Tank Companies (each: 2 Turán (40mm) command tanks + 9 Turán (75mm) tanks)
        2 Medium Tank Companies (2 Turán (40mm) command tanks +16 Turán (40mm) tanks)
  1 Motorized Infantry Regiment
    HQ
        1 Motorized Pioneer Platoon (3 LMG)
        1 Motorized Telephone Platoon
        1 Motorized Traffic Control Platoon

        1 Motorcycle Reconnaissance Platoon (3 LMG + 2 HMG)
        1 AA Company (3 Toldi (20mm) command tanks + 12 Nimród (40mm) self-propelled AA guns)
        1 Motorized Maintenance Company
     3 Motorized Infantry Battalions, each
        HQ
           1 Motorized Pioneer Platoon (3 LMG)
           1 Motorized Telephone Platoon
           1 Motorcycle Reconnaissance Platoon (3 LMG + 2 HMG)
           1 Motorized Maintenance Platoon
           1 Motorized Heavy AT Platoon (3 ATG(75mm) + 3LMG)
        3 Motorized Infantry Companies (each: 12 LMG + 6HMG)
        1 Motorized Heavy Company (12 HMG + 8 mortars(81mm))
     1 Motorized Combat Engineer Battalion
        2 Combat Engineer Companies (each: 4 LMG + 2 HMG)
        2 Motorized Heavy Combat Bridge Columns
   1 Armoured Reconnaissance Battalion
     HQ
           1 Motorized Pioneer Platoon (3 LMG)
           1 Motorized Field Telephone Platoon
           1 Motorized Maintenance Platoon
           1 Motorized Heavy AT Platoon (3 ATG(75mm) + 3LMG)
           1 Motorized Mortar Company (8mortars (81mm) + 4 mortars(120mm))
           1 Light Tank Company (18 Toldi (20mm) tanks
           2 Motorcycle Infantry Companies (each: 12 LMG + 6 HMG)
           1 Motorized Infanry Company (12 LMG + 6HMG)
   2 Motorized Light Artillery Battalions, each
        3 Motorized Light Artillery Batteries (each: 4 towed field howitzers (105mm))
   1 Motorized Heavy Artillery Battalion
        2 Motorized Heavy Artillery Batteries (each: 4 towed field howitzers (149mm))
   1 Motorized AA Battalion
        2 Motorized AA Batteries (4 AAG(80mm))
        2 Motorized AA Batteries (6 AAG(40mm))
   1 Self-Propelled AA Platoon
        1 Motorized Maintenance Platoon
        3 AA Companies (each: 1 Toldi (20mm) command tank + 6 Nimród (40mm) self-propelled AA guns)
   1 Motorized Signal Battalion
        1 Motorized Telephone Company (5LMG)
        1 Motorized Heavy Telephone Company (5 LMG)
        1 Motorized Radio Company (4 LMG)

Cavalry Division
   HQ
   3 Hussar Regiments, each
     HQ
        1 Mounted Pioneer Platoon
        1 Mounted Field Telephone Platoon
        1 Mounted Heavy Mortar Company (12 mortars(120mm))
        1 Motorized AT Company (9 ATG (75mm) + 9LMG)
     2 Cavalry Battalions, each
        HQ
           1 Mounted Field Telephone Platoon
           1 Mounted Assault Platoon (3 LMG)
        3 Cavalry Companies (each: 9 LMG + 2HMG + 2 mortars (50mm) + 2 ATR)
        1 Heavy Company
           1 Mounted Heavy Machine Gun Platoon (12 HMG)
           1 Mounted Medium Mortar Platoon (8 mortars (81mm))

Motorized Heavy AT Platoon (3 ATG (75mm) + 3LMG)

1 Armoured Reconnaissance Battalion
    HQ
        1 Motorized Pioneer Platoon
        1 Motorized Field Telephone Platoon
        1 Motorized Heavy AT Platoon (3ATG (75mm) + 3 LMG)
        1 Motorized Maintenance Platoon
        1 Motorized Mortar Company (8 mortars (81mm) + 4 mortars (120mm))
        2 Armoured Car Companies (each: 13 Csaba armoured cars)
        1 Light Tank Company (18 Toldi (20mm) light tanks)
        2 Motorcycle Infantry Companies (each: 12 LMG + 6 HMG)
        1 Motorized Infantry Company (12 LMG + 6 HMG)
1 Cavalry Tank Battalion
    HQ
        1 Motorized Pioneer Platoon (3 LMG)
        1 Motorized Traffic Control Platoon
        1 Signal Platoon (3 Turán (40mm) command tanks)
        1 Light Tank Platoon (5 Toldi (20mm) tanks)
        1 Motorized Suply Company
        1 Motorized Maintenance Platoon
      1 Heavy Tank Company (2 Turán (75mm) command tanks + 15 Turán (75mm) tanks)
      3 Medium Tank Companies (each: 2 Turán (40mm) command tanks + 25 Turán (40mm) tanks)
1 Motorized Signal Battalion
    1 Motorized Telephone Company (5 LMG)
    1 Motorized Radio Company (4 LMG)
2 Horse Artillery Battalions, each
    3 Horse Artillery Batteries (each: 4 horse-drawn cavalry guns (76.5mm))
1 Motorized Artillery Battalion
    3 Motorized Light Artillery Batteries (each: 4 towed field howitzers (105mm))
1 AA Battalion
    1 Motorized AA Battery (4 AAG(80mm))
    2 Motorized AA Batteries (each: 6 AAG (40mm))
1 Bicycle Infantry Battalion
    HQ
        1 Bicycle Pioneer Platoon
        1 Bicycle Field Telephone Platoon
        1 Motorized AT Platoon (3 ATG (75mm) + 3 LMG)
        1 Motorcycle Platoon (3 LMG + 2 HMG)
        1 Motorized Artileery Battery (4 field howitzers (105mm))
      2 Bicycle Infantry Companies (each: 12 LMG + 6 HMG)
      1 Motorcycle Infantry Company (12 LMG + 6 HMG)
      1 Motorized Heavy Company (6 HMG + 8 mortars (81mm))
1 Motorized Combat Engineer Company (4 LMG + 2HMG)

Field Replacement Division (estimated)
    HQ
    3 Infantry Regiments, each
        HQ
            1 Bicycle Pioneer Platoon (3 LMG)
            1 Field Telephone Platoon
            1 Cavalry Scout Platoon (3 LMG)
            1 Mortar Company (8 mortars (81mm))
        2 Infantry Battalions, each
            2 Infantry Companies (each: 6 LMG)
    1 Signal Company (5 LMG)
    1 Engineer Battalion

3 Engineer Companies (each: 4 LMG)
1 Artillery Battalion
  2 Light Artillery Batteries (each: 4 horse-drawn field howitzers (smaller than 100mm))
  1 Heavy Artillery Battalion (4 horse-drawn field howitzers (smaller than 149mm))

Mountain Replacement Brigade (estimated)
  HQ
  4 or 5 Infantry Battalions, each
    HQ
      1 Pioneer Platoon (3 LMG)
      1 Scout Platoon
    3 Infantry Companies (each: 12 LMG + 6 HMG)
    1 Machine Gun Company (12 HMG + 8 mortars (81mm))
  2 Light Artillery Batteries (each: 4 mountain guns (75mm))
  1 Mountain Signal Company (5 LMG)
  1 Mountain Engineer Company (3 LMG + 2HMG + 2 flamethrowers)

Border Guard Brigade
  HQ
  5 Infantry Battalions, each
    HQ
      1 Pioneer Platoon (3 LMG)
      1 Field Telephone Platoon
      1 Scout Platoon
      1 AT Platoon (4 ATG (37mm))
      1 Heavy Mortar Platoon (4 mortars (120mm))
    3 Infantry Companies (each: 12 LMG + 6 HMG)
    1 Machine Gun Company (12 HMG + 8 mortars (81mm))
  2 Mountain Artillery Battalions, each
    3 Light Artillery Batteries (each: 4 mountain guns (75mm))
  1 Motorized Artillery Battery (4 towed field howitzers (149mm))
  1 Mountain Cavalry Company (9 LMG + 3 HMG + 6mortars (50mm))
  1 AT Company (6ATG (37mm))
  1 motorized AT Company (9 ATG (75mm) + 9 LMG)
  1 Mountain Combat Engineer Company (4 LMG +2 HMG)
  1 Mountain Signal Company (5 LMG)
  1 AA Battery (6 motorized AAG (80mm))
  1 AA Battery (6 motorized AAG (40mm))
  1 Mountain Engineer Company (3 LMG + 2HMG + 2 flamethrowers)

III.2 Hungarian AFV Specifications

AFV Type	Gun	Armour	Crew
39 M Csaba Armoured Car	20mm + 8mm MG	9mm	4
38M Toldi Light Tank	20mm	F: 33mm S/T: 13mm	3
38M Toldi IIA	40mm + 8mm MG	Same as above	3
40M Nimrod	40mm AA	T: 13mm	6
40M Turan Medium Tank	40mm + 2 8mm MG	F:50mm S: 25mm T: 50mm	5
41M Turan II Medium Tank	75mmL25 + 2 8mm	Same as above	5
Zriny Assault Gun	105mmL20	F: 75mm S: 25mm	4
44M Zyriny Assault Gun	75mm	Same as above	4

APPENDIX IV

Losses

IV.1 Soviet & Romanian Losses

2nd Ukrainian Front Losses from October 6–28
20,019 KIA, 71,364 WIA

1st Romanian Army
347 KIA, 8,720 WIA

4th Romanian Army
861 KIA, 630 WIA

According to German sources, the Russian losses at Szolnok and Nyíregyháza came to:
   10,596 KIA (Szolnok), 14,400 (Nyiregyhaza), 5,973 POWs, 3,965 Romanians deserted. A total of 25,095 men. For all of the Russian 2nd Ukrainian Front, losses came to 35,000 men.
   The average Russian division in this battle contained 6,000–7,500 men at the start, by the end, it contained 4,000–5,500 men. Thus, on an average, each division lost around 2,000 men during the battle period.
   As to armour, the losses sustained by the 2nd Ukrainian Front and armies (not Corps) during the Debrecen Operation were as follows, per Russian sources:
   6th Guards Tank Army with 5th Guards Tank Corps and 9th Guards Mechanized Corps = 91.
   Plijev and Gorskov: 4th Guards Cavalry Corps, 6th Guards Cavalry Corps, 7th Mechanized Corps, 5th Guards Cavalry Corps and the 23rd Tank Corps = 353.
   53rd Army = 65.
   Total: 509 AFVs lost.

According to German data, the Russian lost 629 battle tanks and 22–29 SP Guns.
   On October 3rd the 2nd Ukrainian Front possessed (according to Russian data) a total of 825 tanks and SP or Assault Guns. At the end of October, this figure was 525 battle tanks and 181 Assault Guns (altogether 706 AFVs). This includes the newly-arrived 2nd and 4th Guards Mechanized Corps, which had a combined total of 400 AFVs. So, the real strength remaining after the battle for the whole front was around 300 AFVs. German accounts as to Russian AFV losses refer to all armoured vehicles, not just tanks. Thus, the Russian lost around 525 AFVs during this time.
   The 6th Guards Tank Army began with 166 AFVs and ended up with 56! Pliyev and Gorskov Corps' started with 525 AFVs combined and had only 200, at most, remaining. The 18th Tank Corps started with 72 AFVs, and ended with 30. All combined, the Russians had only 286 AFVs left.

Russian Army AFV Strengths

Army	Corps Attached	AFVs on Oct 6 1944	AFV Strength on Oct 28
6th Guards Tank Army	5th Guards Tank, 9th Mechanized Corps	130	91
Plijev and Gorskov Groups	4th Guards,6th Guards Cavalry Corps, 7th Mechanized Corps, 5th Guards Tank Corps, 23rd Tank Corps	535	353
53rd Army	18th Tank Corps	72	46
Total	(8 Corps)	737	490

In the air, records seem to suggest that the Russian 5th Air Army lost 291 aircraft between October 3 and November 1. At the start of October, the 5th Air Army possessed 1,216 aircraft, on November 1, it had 925. However, in this time period there were four days when the Red Air Army flew over Budapest during the Russian attack towards that city. German records note that over Budapest, the Russians lost 29–30 aircraft.

Romanian Losses between September 21 to October 25

2. Ukrainin Front	Date	Total Combat Strength	KIA and MIA	MIA	Total	Percentage Lost
Romanian 1st Army	Sept 21–Oct 25	67,347	?	?	8,720	13%
Romanian 4th Army	Sept 21–Oct 25	120, 861	?	?	24,630	20%

Specific Losses at Two Battle Areas: Szolnok (west) and Nyiregyhaza(North) for Russian\Romanian forces:

	Szolnok Oct. 12–23	Nyíregyháza Oct. 21–28
KIA	2,400	3,434
POWs	4,521	552
Tanks	18	78
SP Guns	—	6
Artillery Guns		76
Infantry Support Guns	} 280	—
Anti-Tank Guns		151
Anti-Aircraft Guns	17	30
Anti-Tank Infantry Weapons	45	136
Machine Guns	235	325
Vehicles	266	359

IV.2 German Losses

The German losses between October 1st and 31st, came to 2,338 KIA, 10,103 WIA, and 2,724 MIA, for a total of 15,165.

Unit	KIA Officers	WIA Officers	MIA Officers	KIA Enlisted Men	WIA Enlisted Men	MIA Enlisted Men	Total
1st Pz Div.	4	29	—	176	729	126	1,064
3rd Mtn. Div	5	12	—	93	319	10	439
4th Mtn. Div.	9	24	—	195	817	75	1,120
4th SS PG Div.	6	9	1	256	1,038	94	1,404
8th SS Cav. Div.	3	7	4	238	764	89	1,105
8th Jag. Div	5	19	1	93	353	36	507
13th Pz Div	3	11	1	78	466	133	692
FHH PG Div	2	21	1	169	768	159	1,120
15th Inf. Div.	12	42	1	243	1,366	209	1,873
23rd Pz Div.	4	24	—	225	1,065	60	1,378
24th Pz Div.	3	10	—	74	357	12	456
46th Inf. Div.	2	25	—	114	572	47	760
76th Inf. Div.	7	31	1	139	569	438	1,185
6th Army Command	2	3	13	9	52	20	99
8th Army Command	6	22	6	135	539	104	812
Misc.	9	3	84	19	37	999	1,151
Total	82	292	113	2,256	9,811	2,611	15,165

AFV totals for the 1st, 23rd Panzer Divisions and FFH PG Division October 1–31, 1944
Numbers in each cell = total strength/operational

Unit	Pz V	Pz IV	Assault Guns	SP Artillery	Total/ Operational	Operational Percent	Armour received
1st Pz Div.	44/16	22/19	7/3	12/3	85/41	48%	17 Panzer IV
23rd Pz Div.	49/15	13/4	13/5	5/2	80/26	32%	21 SP Arty
FHH PG Div.	36/24	11/5 (L/70)	31/12	—	78/41	52%	—
Total	129/55	46/28	51/20	17/5	243/108	44%	38

Between September 1 and October 23, the German army groups operated 69 PzKpfw V, 100 PzKpfw IV and StuGs, and 29 88mm guns, according to German sources. This number does not include any AFVs then in repair.

According to Russian data the German-Hungarian losses between October 6 and October 20 came to 248 AFVs, 122 SP/Assault Guns. The 4th Luftwaffe contained 177 aircraft in early October.

Battle losses are always tricky to calculate. For instance, with AFVs, are these actual tanks with turrets, or assault guns? Are self-propelled guns included and counted as an assault gun (no turret)? Exactly when is either considered to be destroyed? Is a tank that is able to fire yet unable to move counted as destroyed or not? Then there is a question of the AFVs in repair shops, are these counted by either side? At best, any cited combat strengths or losses are only a rough estimate.

Bibliography

US National Archives, AGS microfilm roll 625, 631, 639, 626

Bayer, Hanns, *Die Kavallerie der Waffen SS*, Heidelburg, 1980

Bishop, Chris, *Luftwaffe Squadrons 1939–45*, Staplehurst, 2006

Bonhardt-Sárhidai-Winkler, *A Magyar Királyi Honvédség fegyverzete*, Budapest, 1992
   A book about the equipment used by the Hungarian Royal Army (mostly tanks and aeroplanes).

Ciobanu, Nicolae, *The Defensive Operation of the 1st Romanian Army in WW2*, Bucharest, 1997

Csima, János, *Adalékok a Horthy-hadsereg szervezetének és háborús tevékenységének tanulmányozásához*, Budapest, 1961
   It was a closed book (only registered researchers could use it), it has the most detailed information based on the Hungarian sources available at that time.

Dálnoki, Veress Lajos, *Magyarország honvédelme a II. VH előtt és alatt 1920–1944*, n.p., n.d.
   He was the Hungarian 2nd Army commander, and he produced a very good collection of maps based on the Hungarian High Command's maps.

Dombrády, Lóránd-Tóth Sándor, *A magyar királyi honvédség 1919–1945*, Budapest, 1987
   Includes good maps.

Fey, Will, *Armor Battles of the Waffen SS 1943–45*, Winnipeg, 1990

Fleischer, Wolfgang, *Das letzte Jahr des Deutschen Heeres 1944–1945*, Friedberg, 1997

Adonyi-Naredy, F. Von, *Ungarns Armee im Zweiten weltkrieg*, Neckargemünd, 1971

Friessner, Hans, *Verratene Schlachten. Die Tragödie der deutschen Wehrmacht in Rumänien und Ungarn*, Hamburg, 1956
   He was the commander of the Army Group South, a very German point of view.

Gosztonyi, Péter, *A magyar honvédség a második világháborúban*, Budapest, 1992
   Written by a well-known Hungarian historian, who lives in Western Europe.

Haupt, Werner, *Die Schlachten der Heersgruppe Sud*, Friedberg, 1985

Hoffman, Dieter, *Zur Geschichte der 13th Infanterie und 13th Panzer Division*, n.p., 1999

Illésfalvi, Péter, *Emlékezés a hegyicsapatokra*, Budapest, 1999
   A good (but thin) book about the mountain brigades (and new information about the mountain replacement brigades).

Jainek, Erich, *Soldaten der Feldherrnhalle*, n.p., 1977

Jentz, Thomas, *Die DeutschePanzertruppe 1943–45*, Friedberg,1999

Kissel, Hans, *Panzerschlacten in der Puszta*, Neckargemünd, 1960

Lasd, Szabo, *A 2 Ukran front budapesti hadmuveletenek*, Budapest, 1969

Löser, Jochen, *Bittere Pflicht. Kampf und Untergang der 76. Berlin-Brandenburgischen Infanterie-Division*, Osnabrück,1986

Madeja, W. Victor, *Russo-German War Autumn 1944*, n.p., 1987

Mehner, K. (ed.). *Die geheimen Tagesberichte der Deutschen Wehrmachtsführung im Zweiten Weltkrieg: 1939 – 1945; die gegenseitige Lageunterrichtung der Wehrmacht-, Heeres- und Luftwaffenführung über alle Haupt- und Nebenkriegsschauplätze …; aus den Akten im Bundesarchiv/Militärarchiv, Freiburg i.Br.; im Anhang: Kriegsgliederungen, Stellenbesetzungen, Formations- und Ortsregister, dokumentarische Nachweise und Lageskizzen Band 11, Sept–Dec 1944*, Osnabrück, 1984

Mujzer, Peter, *The Royal Hungarian Army Vol 2 Mobile Forces*, Bayside NY, 2000

Niehorster, Leo W.G. *The Royal Hungarian Army 1920–1945 Vol. 1*, Bayside NY, 1998
   This is the more detailed information source for OOB and TO&E, but basically it is based on western information sources. I used it in the process as a starting book.

Olvedi, Ignac, *Harccselekmenyek a debreceni … Oct. 13–20, 1944*, Budapest, 1965

Olvedi, Ignac, *A Budai Var es a debreceni csata*, Budapest, 1974

Olvedi, Ignac, *1. Maygar Hadsereg tortenete, Jan. 1944 – Oct. 1944*, Budapest, 1989

Petrescu, Alexandru Maj.Gen., *Detasamentul Paulis*, Bucharest, 1965

Poirer, Robert, *The Red Army Order of Battle*, Novato CA, 1985

Rebentisch, Ernst, *Zum kaukasus und zu den Tauren: Geschichte der 23. Panzer Division*, Stuttgart, 1982

Ravasz, István, *Erdély újra hadszíntér*, Budapest, n.d.
> This is a very detailed (and good) book about the Transylvanian operations in 1944 (mostly the 2 Hungarian Army), and about the Torda (Turda) operation.

Rosado, Jorge, *Wehrmacht Panzer Divisions 1939–45*, Staplehurst, 2005

Sanchez, Alfonso, *Feldherrnhalle: Forgotten elite,* Bradford, 1996

Sewell, Stephen, *Tanks-Lend Lease to Russia 1941–45,* Moscow, 2000

Stoves, Rolf, *1. Panzer-Division 1935–1945. Chronik einer der drei Stamm-Divisionen der deutschen Panzerwaffe*, Bad Nauheim, 1961

Stoves, Rolf, *Die gepanzerten und motorisierten deutschen Grossverbande 1935–45,* Friedberg, 1994

Sipos, Péter: *Magyarország a második világháborúban*, Budapest, n.d.
> This is a lexicon about Hungarian forces in the WWII, and it is based all the available sources (western, russian, and Hungarian). I used it to correct Niehorster information.

Szabo Balazs, *A hadmuveszet tortenete,* Budapest, 1980

Szabo, Peter et.al., *Erdely A Hadak Utjan 1940–1944,* Budapest, 2005

Szamveber, Norbert, *Nehezpancelosk: Tiger 503,* Budapest, 2000

Szamveber, Norbert, *Pancelosok a Tiszantulon,* Budapest, 2002

Száva, Péter, *Magyarország felszabadítása,* Budapest, 1980 This book is based on mostly the Russian sources.

Tesin, Georg, *Verbande und Truppen der deutschen Wehrmacht und Waffen SS im WW2, 1941–45,* Osnabrück, 1972

Ungváry, Krisztián, *A Vörös Hadsereg offenzívája,* n.p., n.d.
> This is an essay, and it has new information about TO&E, and about the field replacement divisions. These divisions existed only months (sometimes weeks), not a much documentation survived about them.

Varakin, P. *6th Guards Tank Army in Operation Debrecen,* n.p., 1975

Also available from Helion & Company

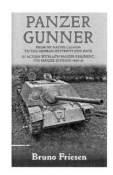

Panzer Gunner
From my Native Canada to the German Ostfront and Back.
In Action with 25th Panzer Regiment, 7th Panzer Division 1944–45
B. Friesen
264pp., 50 photos, ills, maps
Hardback   ISBN 978–1–906033–11–8

From Retreat to Defeat
The Last Years of the German Army on the Eastern Front
1943–45: A Photographic History
Ian Baxter
160pp., 190 photos, maps
Hardback   ISBN 978–1–906033–01–9

Panzer Lehr Division 1944–45
Fred Steinhardt (ed.)
304pp., 25 photos, 85 maps plus tables & diagrams
Hardback   ISBN 978–1–874622–28–4

A SELECTION OF FORTHCOMING TITLES

Under Himmler's Command: The Personal Recollections of Oberst Hans-Georg Eismann,
Operations Officer, Army Group Vistula, Eastern Front 1945
edited by Fred Steinhardt   ISBN 978–1–874622–43–7

After Stalingrad: The Red Army's Winter Offensive, 1942–1943
D.M. Glantz   ISBN 978–1–906033–26–2

Road to Destruction: Operation Blue & The Battle of Stalingrad 1942–43, A Photographic History
Ian Baxter   ISBN 978–1–906033–15–6

HELION & COMPANY
26 Willow Road, Solihull, West Midlands, B91 1UE, England
Tel 0121 705 3393   Fax 0121 711 4075
Email: publishing@helion.co.uk Website: http://www.helion.co.uk